# Studying and Designing Technology for Domestic Life:

# Lessons from Home

# Studying and Designing Technology for Domestic Life:

# Lessons from Home

**Tejinder K. Judge**

**Carman Neustaedter**

AMSTERDAM • BOSTON • HEIDELBERG • LONDON
NEW YORK • OXFORD • PARIS • SAN DIEGO
SAN FRANCISCO • SINGAPORE • SYDNEY • TOKYO

Morgan Kaufmann is an imprint of Elsevier

Acquiring Editor: Meg Dunkerley
Editorial Project Manager: Lindsay Lawrence
Project Manager: Priya Kumaraguruparan
Cover designer: Serena Hillman
Cover Photo Credit: Image Source/Getty Images

Morgan Kaufmann is an imprint of Elsevier
225 Wyman Street, Waltham, MA, 02451, USA

**Library of Congress Cataloging-in-Publication Data**
Tejinder K. Judge.
    Studying and Designing Technology for Domestic Life: Lessons from Home / [Edited by] Tejinder K.
Judge, Carman Neustaedter.
        pages cm
    Includes bibliographical references and index.
1. Environmental psychology–Data processing. 2. Domestic relations. 3. Assistive computer technology.
I. Neustaedter, Carman. II. Title.
    BF353.J83 2014
    640.285–dc23

                                    2014027623

**British Library Cataloguing-in-Publication Data**
A catalogue record for this book is available from the British Library.

ISBN: 978-0-12-800555-2

For information on all MK publications
visit our website at www.mkp.com

Working together
to grow libraries in
developing countries

www.elsevier.com • www.bookaid.org

*As a lesson from home, we have always been taught to be thankful for everything we have. We are extremely thankful for our families, their love, and support.*

*We dedicate this book to Charanjeet and Rajindar Judge and the Four Ks of the Neustaedter family. Thank you for being with us from start to finish.*

# Contents

## PART 2  TECHNOLOGY DESIGN AND EVALUATION

# Acknowledgments

No effort is successful without the support of many people.

We would like to acknowledge those who first discussed the idea of a book on methods to study domestic life. The very first thoughts of such a book occurred during a workshop we helped organize at the ACM CSCW Conference 2008. The theme was also brought forward by attendees at a Special Interest Group (SIG) session at the ACM CHI Conference 2009, a workshop at the ACM GROUP Conference 2010, and a workshop at the ACM CHI Conference 2013. As such, we are grateful to those who organized these workshops and sessions with us, including A.J. Brush, David McDonald, Lana Yarosh, Abigail Sellen, Steve Harrison, Erick Oduor, and Gina Venolia. We also acknowledge the help and support of those who attended these workshops. They laid the intellectual foundations for the book with their thought-provoking discussions during each workshop.

We humbly thank our amazing colleagues and collaborators who contributed to this book. Thank you for believing in us and this book. Thank you also for sharing your knowledge, expertise, and untold stories. This book would not be possible without you.

Thank you to Saul Greenberg, John Tang, Abigail Sellen, Steve Whittaker, and Tony Tang for feedback on our early ideas for this book. Your support was much appreciated in helping us get this project off the ground.

We also received help with editing certain chapters. For this, we are thankful to Steve Whittaker and John Tang.

A special thanks to Christian Bohland for being an invaluable design partner and for creating the concept for the book cover. We also thank Munish Dabas for his design expertise and help in getting the cover ready for print.

We would like to thank and acknowledge the many individuals who helped and supported us throughout this process. Pardha Pyla and Kathy Baxter, thanks for sharing the knowledge you gained from working on your respective books. Mike Brzozowski, Laura Granka, and Ed Chi, thank you for being valuable partners at Google and for encouraging this effort.

Thank you to members of the Connections Lab at Simon Fraser University for your feedback, support, and encouragement. Thank you, Serena Hillman, for your countless hours and design talents as we iterated through cover options. We are grateful for your timeliness and patience.

The studies in this book hinged on the many participants who opened up their homes and lives to the chapter authors. We thank these families for their participation, time and openness.

On a personal level, we are extremely grateful for the support of our family and friends. Thank you for being patient with us during the long work hours it took to put this book together. We could not have completed it without your encouragement and support.

# Foreword

In the past, technology was deployed in rather limited contexts such as the workplace. Today technology pervades all areas of our lives. One of the most significant trends in human computer interaction (HCI) over the last few years has been the move to studying the design, deployment, and effects of technology use in complex contexts such as the home. A great strength of past HCI research was the development of reliable scientific methods for evaluating and redesigning technology in contexts that were relatively well understood. While there is some disagreement about the details, researchers and practitioners effectively deployed techniques such as task-based evaluation, heuristic evaluation, cognitive walkthroughs, and contextual design. However, these tried and trusted methods fare less well in domestic contexts. Designing and deploying technology in new contexts, such as the home, has given rise to many new and pressing questions, which this book tackles head on.

Domestic technology design is challenging in many unique ways. First, adoption is *voluntary*: unlike in the workplace, no one legislates that specific technologies must be used by a family. As with many other consumer applications, this means that good design is a requirement. Users are volunteers and must be motivated to use the technology; they will rapidly abandon annoying applications that lack obvious benefits. Second, domestic spaces are *private*, which means that researchers hoping to study them must be sensitive about disclosure, both when studying families and when orienting to issues of privacy in their designs. Third, domestic spaces are *personal* and *inhabited*. Family practices are well developed and nuanced, and family spaces generally must be comfortable to live in. From a design perspective, domestic technologies therefore need to mesh well with existing family practices and fit into the aesthetic and sensibility of the home. Another important characteristic is that family spaces are highly *differentiated*: practices and design requirements are very different in shared public areas, such as the kitchen or family room, compared to private spaces, such as the bedroom or study. As several chapters observe, families are now complex in their configurations, with family members not necessarily living under one roof, or having complex arrangements that arise from divorce and separation. Finally, domestic technologies may be *social:* they need to match the practices of diverse users with differing interest in and expertise with technologies. The experienced researcher of domestic technology must deal with a range of users, from tech-savvy teens who are anxious to adopt new technologies to very young children and older adults, who may be fearful and skeptical of what technology might do for them.

The chapters speak to all of these issues. The advocated approach is iterative, user-centric design. The book does an excellent job of leading the reader through each stage of the iterative design method with refreshing honesty about what works and what doesn't. This honesty is critical for researchers and designers who are seeking to apply these ideas, and what we learn from the information in this book is very different from textbook descriptions of these techniques.

The first part of the book discusses techniques we can use to understand what is going on when families interact with each other and with technology in the home. Most of the chapters advocate the use of interviews, guiding the reader through complex issues around recruiting and scheduling, especially where busy families with young children are concerned. They also discuss triangulating various reactions from family members. Several chapters add to these basic interview methods by addressing the use of additional information derived from design probes and observations. Other critical points are made, in particular, that requirements analysis doesn't stop at the design stage. Privacy concerns are addressed directly, with one chapter discussing how to engender trust and gather reliable information for topics where participants are wary about disclosure. The book does an admirable job of including a wide span of user types and situations, covering in-care elderly, young children, and families that are separated and divorced.

In the second part of the book, the reader is presented with fascinating descriptions of how to evaluate several potential designs. The above considerations mean that it is extremely difficult to design effective new domestic technologies and have them succeed the first time. One strong theme of the book is its focus on deployment, along with other approaches such as autobiographical and community-focused design. Deploying working prototypes is a highly effective way to gather concrete user feedback about new design ideas in context. Observing whether and how uptake occurs and gathering reactions to actual use make feedback much more useful than simply asking users about hypothetical scenarios or gathering reactions in short-term, structured task settings. Of course, the deployment approach has its limitations: there is tremendous effort involved in designing and deploying working technologies in contexts where domestic practices are well established, technological infrastructure may be missing, and users may be apathetic or, occasionally, hostile. However, the reader is left convinced that, despite these challenges, this is a compelling approach. The book provides a wealth of practical detail and advice gleaned from these deployments, including the need for permanent, remote system monitoring, the ability to respond to and troubleshoot unforeseen problems, and how to deploy technologies across multiple distanced households with differing participant skills and infrastructures. Various techniques are discussed that address this array of complex challenges, including using autobiographical design, embedding researchers into the participant setting, gathering remote logfile usage data, and providing online support. The case study approach is invaluable to both practitioners and academics.

This is an important book from methodological and research perspectives. As HCI research moves from the lab into people's homes and domestic lives, the shortage of information about the practical details of how to execute informative but sensitive research in complex, real-life settings is apparent. This book fills that gap. In particular, it provides very specific information about how to design and evaluate new technologies that are actually deployed in real-life contexts. Anyone venturing into the design of new domestic technologies needs to read it.

**Steve Whittaker**
(University of California at Santa Cruz)

# An Introduction to Studying and Designing Technology for Domestic Life

1

**Tejinder K. Judge\*, Carman Neustaedter**[§]

*Google Inc., Mountain View, CA, USA\*; School of Interactive Arts and Technology, Simon Fraser University, Surrey, BC, Canada*[§]

## THE CHANGING LANDSCAPE OF COMPUTING

As we all know and have experienced, computational technology is now deeply engrained in our lives, from the way we listen to music and watch television to the ways in which we stay connected to people, places, and information. Whether we think about it or not, most people carry and use multiple computational devices throughout their day, including smartphones, laptops, computers, and tablets. There are also hidden or "invisible," computational devices embedded in the everyday things we use, from our cars to our kitchen appliances to our entertainment systems. Thus, we are continually faced with technology usage in our homes, vehicles, workplaces, shopping malls, and virtually every other location we inhabit.

This changing landscape of computing and the ubiquity of technology has caused a shift in how we as a society aim to design new technologies and understand their usage. No longer are we concerned just with how one might use a computer at work. Instead, we are interested much more broadly in how technology affects our everyday lives. One important aspect of this is how technology is designed for and used as a part of domestic life within and outside the home for the fulfillment of connection, communication, coordination, social play, and the everyday accomplishment of seemingly mundane domestic activities. With more technology being designed for homes and families comes an increasing need for research in this domain to uncover insights about families' routines and needs for technology design. It is also increasingly important to gain a deep understanding of how technology has changed family relationships and routines and in what ways it will continue to do so. With these shifts comes an increasing challenge for researchers and designers to design new technologies for domestic life, and study and evaluate them to understand how they affect people's routines, activities, and, even more broadly, culture.

## THE CHALLENGE OF STUDYING AND DESIGNING FOR DOMESTIC LIFE

Performing research and technology design for domestic life is by no means easy. Family life is increasingly rich and complex. Communication, awareness, and interaction routines are highly nuanced, and family members have different roles and dynamics. These may change from situation to situation or day to day, or vary based on location. Using existing research methods such as a laboratory study may be excruciatingly challenging if not impossible to do in this context. Many domestic activities occur within the context of the home or other private locations that are considered to be sacred places for only family and friends. By this we mean that many of the behaviors and rituals conducted at home are not privy to non-family members or those who do not live there. This makes it increasingly difficult to gather information from families about their actual routines and needs for technology. Domestic life also involves situations and activities that occur outside of the home, often interwoven with work, play, and other events. The notion of getting permission to study a family's activities as the family members move through them in various locations and contexts is, again, increasingly challenging.

There is a plethora of books that cover design and research methods in the field of Human-Computer Interaction (HCI). They cover topics such as conducting contextual inquiry in workplaces, performing controlled laboratory studies, deploying and studying technologies in the field, conducting interface inspections through formalized processes, and performing usability evaluation studies (Beyer and Holtzblatt 1998; Nielsen 1993; Rosson and Carroll 2002; Dix et al. 1998; Lazar et al. 2010; Hartson et al. 2012). While beneficial, these design and research methods are limited in that their use is not described for any one specific context. This makes it challenging to understand how these methods might be applied to present-day technology research within specific domains. When applied to families and domestic life, the methods may easily require alterations, or new methods may be needed altogether to overcome the complexities of studying domestic environments. Thus, there is a need for documentation on more specialized methods for conducting research in the area of domestic technology design and evaluation.

This idea comes from other researchers besides just us. Over the past five years, along with our collaborators, we have organized a series of workshops and special interest group (SIG) sessions at various HCI conferences. These include workshops at the ACM Conference on Computer-Supported Cooperative Work (CSCW) (Neustaedter et al. 2008), the ACM Conference on Computer-Human Interaction (CHI) (Neustaedter et al. 2009; Oduor et al. 2013), and the ACM Conference on Supporting Group Work (GROUP) (Neustaedter et al. 2010). One common theme that emerged during discussions in each and every workshop was a need for focused documentation on *research methods for studying families, domestic life, and domestic technology design.* In all cases, workshop attendees had many questions about conducting research with families and in people's homes. They had all experienced challenges in studying families and had explored their own variations on research methods or sought new ways to better study family practices and technology design. As a result of discussions like these, academics, researchers, and designers attending our workshops pointed out that a strong need exists for a collected book on methods for studying and evaluating technologies for families. *This book is just that.*

## THE PURPOSE OF THIS BOOK

This book documents the ways in which researchers are studying and researching technology design and evaluation in the context of the home and domestic life. However, it is not a typical research methods book. Instead, you can think of this book as the "inside scoop" for people learning how to perform research in the area of domestic life and home technology design. Each chapter is a candid discussion about one or more methods that were successfully used for research studies with a focus on the challenges that the researchers faced while using the methods and the best practices they learned. Chapters document and reveal the challenges and lessons learned by experienced researchers when studying or evaluating domestic technology, the application of existing research and design methods in new situations that require alterations to the methods, and new methods for studying and designing technology for domestic life. The authors of the chapters are established academics or researchers in the field of domestic computing. They have successfully used the methods they describe in the chapters, and most have published the results from their studies using these methods.

Of course, one could turn to journal articles or conference papers to learn about the research methods that others are employing when designing technology for domestic life or studying its usage, and we welcome readers to do so. However, such method descriptions will be vastly different than what you will find in this book. Journal articles and conference papers are limited in space, and the focus is often on the results of one's research and not the finer details about the methods employed. Researchers also often utilize tips or tricks they have learned throughout their experiences in conducting research but do not typically discuss these in journal articles or conference papers. This is the focus of our book: *the untold stories of how research methods were applied in real research projects,* including the ways in which a study might have gone wrong and the steps taken by researchers to fix the problems. It also includes specifics of the research methods used, rather than the typical high-level overview that we often see in journal and conference publications. There is also an underlying theme throughout the book that explores the *ethical considerations* when studying domestic routines and technology usage practices.

## HOW TO USE THIS BOOK

With the increasing interest in designing and evaluating technologies for domestic life, this book can serve as a resource for academics, researchers, designers, and students wanting to learn about methods for conducting research on domestic life. First, it could be used as a textbook or a supplementary resource for university courses focused on studying domestic routines, technology usage, or designing and evaluating technology for families. The entire book or specific chapters could be used to teach and learn about particular methods and their applications in domestic settings. Second, this book can be used as a resource for students or new researchers wanting to learn about conducting studies of domestic life or domestic technology design. The information in the collection of chapters should enable them to learn about methods that have been successfully used and how to apply them. The chapters are also a resource in and of themselves, as each chapter includes a literature review and references related work. And finally, this book can be used as a reference for choosing an appropriate method for a research problem being worked on. Our companion website, lessonsfromhome.org, also contains additional materials from the studies described throughout the book.

Given the interdisciplinary nature of HCI research, this book can also act as a resource for researchers in various fields including design, computer science, engineering, sociology, psychology, and anthropology.

## TOPICS AND ORGANIZATIONAL OVERVIEW

Throughout this book a range of topics is covered, with a focus on studying everyday practices and technology usage as well as the design and evaluation of new and innovative technologies. We have organized these topics into two sections—"Understanding Domestic Life" and "Technology Design and Evaluation"—with several chapters in each. Each chapter describes a research problem, choosing a research method, recruiting strategies, developing a study protocol, and collecting and analyzing data from the field.

### SECTION 1: UNDERSTANDING DOMESTIC LIFE

The book begins with a collection of foundational chapters that focus on ways to *understand domestic life*. These chapters shed light on tried and tested methods that have been used to learn about the home and domestic life *before* designing and evaluating new technology or *during* the design process and creation of new technologies.

**Chapter 2: Remote participants, interview, video chat.** The first section begins with Hillman, Forghani, Pang, Neustaedter, and Judge's chapter that discusses ways to conduct interviews with remote participants. Often the focus of a research project is on studying certain demographics that are not easily found within close proximity to the researchers. Also, families are no longer defined only as those who live together but include those separated by divorce or split between two locations due to job restrictions or other complex living situations. To study families like these as well as families in other regions and countries, video communication technologies now play a pivotal role in user studies. This chapter discusses the challenges and lessons learned from conducting user studies with remote participants in three domains: family communication between grandparents and grandchildren, family communication during cases of chronic illness, and people's shopping behaviors on mobile devices while at home and when outside the home.

**Chapter 3: In-home interviews, large families, children.** Building on interviewing techniques, we move to Leshed and Håkansson chapter, which discusses best practices for conducting interviews with different types of families. This chapter starts off by discussing how the researchers interviewed and collected data from a fairly unique population: families who live and work on small organic farms. Although farm families may seem like a very specific type of family, Leshed and Håkansson draw lessons that extend beyond this population to studying families in various situations. For example, they share ways to deal with dynamic interviews, where family members may come and go during the interview, and also share strategies and considerations when recruiting families in unique situations.

**Chapter 4: Children, adolescents, in-home interviews.** Next, we shift the focus from interviewing families, to studying the behaviors and activities of children. Foss, Guha, and Druin draw from their rich experience in conducting studies of children and adolescents' search behaviors on the Internet. As one might expect, conducting studies with children is significantly different from doing research with adults. Conducting studies with children requires different kinds of recruiting, scheduling, interviewing, and observational techniques. They also discuss the added complexity of overeager parents, shy and distracted children, and hectic family homes, and suggest ways to overcome these challenges.

**Chapter 5: Cultural probes, interviews, older adults.** We explore research with older adults in Wallace and Lindley's chapter on using cultural probes with care home residents. These design probes enabled the researchers to creatively engage with the care home residents and supported in-depth conversation that allowed them to learn about participants' lives at the care home. They discuss the use of probes as a tool to facilitate conversation, challenges in conducting research in a communal space, and issues that may arise when dealing with the complex interplay between domestic and work environments in the care home context.

**Chapter 6: Origami maps, behavioral changes, longitudinal study.** Fox's chapter on the Business Origami Technique explores another type of design probe that can be used to facilitate conversations with families. This technique uses tokens to represent key parts of a technology ecosystem to answer "who, where, and how" questions about the ecosystem. This technique is not often used or documented within the HCI literature, yet it can be tremendously useful for studying domestic life. In this chapter, Fox describes using Business Origami to study and track changes in families' use of the Internet in their homes. The chapter also discusses ways to adapt this technique from its traditional paper-based format to a digital format that enables the Origami artifacts to be used for longitudinal studies.

**Chapter 7: Financial tours, sensitive topics, interviews.** The final chapter in this section focuses on using probes and interviews to study sensitive situations like personal finances. In most countries and cultures, one's finances are often considered a very private topic. Kaye's chapter discusses techniques and tools that were used to understand participants' financial practices despite the sensitive nature of this information. These include using financial maps, index cards with financial events, and studying physical financial "tools" such as wallets. The chapter highlights ways to alleviate participant concerns about the privacy of personal information and the ways in which researchers can be cognizant about this issue.

## SECTION 2: TECHNOLOGY DESIGN AND EVALUATION

In the second half of the book, we shift gears to *designing and evaluating* technology for domestic life. Evaluating technology that has been designed for families and the home presents new challenges that are specific to the context of domestic life. The chapters in this section explore ways to address these challenges.

**Chapter 8: Autobiographical design, design research, self-usage.** We begin this section with Neustaedter, Judge, and Sengers' chapter on autobiographical design in the home: a research method that involves detailed self-usage of a technology while one is designing it. Autobiographical design has previously been used within the field of HCI, yet its usage in the domestic setting presents new and interesting challenges. These challenges outlined in the chapter by describing the autobiographical design of the Family Window, an always-on video communications system for families. Through this example, Neustaedter et al. discuss the benefits, challenges, and limitations in using this method as well as more general lessons for successfully using autobiographical design in the home.

**Chapter 9: In-home deployments, field trials, prototype evaluation.** Next we move to Brush, Meyers, and Scott's chapter on in-home deployments, which is a research method that evaluates systems designed for families and the home. Although this method is widely used, as Brush et al. point out, it requires careful planning and considerable effort to avoid common pitfalls and successfully evaluate the usage of a system. They share insights drawn from the in-home deployment of PreHeat, a prototype thermostat that automatically controls home heating using occupancy sensing and prediction. The in-home deployment of PreHeat highlights important lessons, including the value of being able to remotely determine the state of the prototype and determine issues with the system, and the importance of adapting the system to deal with unexpected issues in the home environment.

**Chapter 10: Multi-home deployments, field trials, prototype evaluation.** Broadening the focus from single-home deployments, Judge and Neustaedter discuss ways to conduct in-home deployments with multiple connected households.

They compare and contrast single-home deployments with multi-home deployments by describing the design and evaluation of Family Portals, a multi-home video media space that connects three families' homes in order to promote feelings of connectedness among family members. The field trial of Family Portals highlights an increase in the level of complexity when conducting multi-home field trials due to the interconnection between households and an increase in privacy concerns when connecting multiple homes using always-on video.

**Chapter 11: Prototype evaluation, field trials, intact social groups.** Tang, Junuzovic, Inkpen, and Venolia's chapter explores new methods for studying the design and evaluation of personal communication technologies, including VideoPal, Experiences2Go, and TV2Gether. These technologies focus on connecting close friends and relatives over distance and are not easily studied in lab environments. They describe alternative methods focused on embedding researchers within an intact social group, observing technology usage outside the home, and passively capturing technology experiences through software. The overall lessons focus on the "invisibility" of researchers, privacy concerns, and observing realistic behaviors.

**Chapter 12: Community groups, interviews, design, prototype evaluation.** Massimi's chapter moves away from family interviews and home visits to explore how one can conduct research in community groups. Community support groups are places where family members often talk about their home lives, family relationships, and the challenges they face. Thus, these groups offer a unique avenue in which to gain additional perspectives on home life. In particular, they may allow researchers to explore the difficult times or emotional struggles that family members may face. Massimi describes the study and design of an online support web page called Besupp to explore these topics.

**Chapter 13: Conflict, children, divorce, interviews, prototype evaluation, field trials.** In Yarosh's chapter on conflict in family life, we again explore challenging situations that often arise in domestic life. Through an exploration of the design and field evaluation of the ShareTable, Yarosh documents the challenges in recruiting and conducting studies with adults and children in divorced families, where she draws on several theories of conflict. This chapter explores lessons relating to interviewing one versus multiple individuals at the same time, notions and definitions of family, the negative impacts of technology interventions, and ethical concerns and challenges.

## LOOKING FORWARD

The domestic environment and domestic life are extremely important areas to study and research in the field of Human-Computer Interaction, yet studying them is becoming increasingly challenging. Through descriptions of research projects and case studies, this book reveals many lessons that academics, researchers, designers, and students can apply in their own research. However, domestic life is ever changing, as are the technologies that we use, design, and develop, so this book is also a foundation for thinking about the present and looking forward to the future. As times change, along with culture, technology availability, and technology usage, researchers should develop new and interesting ways to study everyday practices and technology design in domestic life so they can build on the lessons, methods, and practices this book presents. Researchers should continue to create their own learnings, adaptions of methods, and new and interesting ways to conduct research in the fields of domestic computing and Human-Computer Interaction.

## REFERENCES

Beyer, H., Holtzblatt, K., 1998. Contextual Design: Defining Customer-Centered Design. Morgan Kaufmann, Burlington, MA.

Dix, A., Finlay, J., Abowd, G., Beale, R., 1998. Human Computer Interaction, second ed. Prentice Hall, Toronto.

Hartson, R., Pardha, P.S., 2012. The UX Book: Process and Guidelines for Ensuring a Quality User Experience. Morgan Kaufmann, Burlington, MA.

Lazar, J., Feng, J.H., Hochheiser, H., 2010. Research Methods in Human-Computer Interaction. John Wiley & Sons, Hoboken, NJ.

Neustaedter, C., Brush, A.J.B., McDonald, D., 2008. Designing for Families. In: Extended Proceedings of the Computer Supported Cooperative Work (CSCW). ACM Press, New York, NY.

Neustaedter, C., Judge, T.K., Harrison, S., Cao, X., Sellen, A., 2010. Connecting Families: New Technologies, Family Communication, and the Impact on Domestic Space. In: Proceedings of the ACM Conference on Supporting Groupwork (GROUP). ACM Press, New York, NY.

Neustaedter, C., Yarosh, S., Brush, A.J., 2009. Designing for Families. In: Extended Proceedings of the ACM Conference on Computer-Human Interaction (CHI). ACM Press, New York, NY.

Nielsen, J., 1993. Usability Engineering. Academic Press, Waltham, MA.

Oduor, E., Neustaedter, C., Venolia, C., Judge, T.K., 2013. The Future of Personal Video Communications: Moving beyond Talking Heads. In: Extended Proceedings of the ACM Conference on Computer-Human Interaction (CHI). ACM Press, New York, NY.

Rosson, M.B., Carroll, J.M., 2002. Usability Engineering: Scenario-Based Development of Human-Computer Interaction. Morgan Kaufmann, Burlington, MA.

# Understanding Domestic Life

# Conducting Interviews with Remote Participants

*2*

**Serena Hillman\*, Azadeh Forghani\*, Carolyn Pang\*, Carman Neustaedter\*, Tejinder K. Judge#**

*School of Interactive Arts and Technology, Simon Fraser University, Surrey, BC, Canada\*; Google Inc., Mountain View, CA, USA#*

## INTRODUCTION

Interviewing is a common approach for collecting data from people in a lab environment or in the field. It is also commonly used as a data inquiry method in studies of domestic life. In fact, many of the chapters in this book discuss the use of interviews in various settings and contexts. Yet the present-day complexities of study designs and the pragmatics of conducting research mean that it may not always be possible to interview study participants in person.

First, it may not be possible to find local participants for a study, given the demographic that one is interested in. Travel to another location could be cost-prohibitive, especially if potential participants are not located in the same city or within driving distance. This could happen if one wants to interview members of the same family, but they are distributed across different cities or even countries. Second, even if participants are located in the same city, travel time may be onerous, or traffic issues may present significant travel challenges. Third, study participants may be more comfortable without a researcher present at their home, or they may not feel comfortable meeting with a researcher at another location, such as a coffee shop (Weiss 1994). Given alternative options, they may be more apt to participate in a study if they feel safe and comfortable without a stranger (the researcher) physically present. Similarly, sometimes traveling to a participant's home or another meeting place may put the researcher's safety at risk (Weiss 1994). For previous research projects, we have had to travel to questionable neighborhoods (e.g., a crime-ridden neighborhood, a remote rural area) to conduct interviews. We have also interviewed participants in their home where the situation did not seem safe, given other household members in the setting or the mannerisms of the participant. This was even for studies of seemingly mundane topics such as photo sharing. There are also a host of other reasons why it is difficult and sometimes impractical to do in-person interviews.

Historically, phone interviews have been an alternative to in-person interviews, yet the richness of actually seeing a person during an interview can be lost (Weiss 1994). It can also be more challenging to build rapport with a participant, which in the past has sometimes led to shorter, less detailed interviews (Weiss 1994). As a result, interviewing methods often focus on being able to see the person and his or her surrounding as well as any pertinent contextual information. With the increasing ubiquity of video communications systems and the proliferation of free video chat applications such as Skype, Google+ Hangouts, FaceTime, and others, it is now possible to conduct interviews with remote participants. However, based on our collective experience of conducting over a dozen studies using video chat technology, we have recognized that this method is not as straightforward as simply calling a participant over Skype (or other video chat system) and conducting the interview. Many challenges can arise that turn a simple interview into a complicated one. Even worse, these challenges can cause issues when collecting critical data from participants.

The focus of this chapter is on describing lessons learned and best practices in conducting interviews over distance through the use of video chat technologies. We describe these lessons through case studies focused on grandparent-grandchild communication over distance, health information sharing, and mobile commerce (mCommerce) practices. We selected these three studies because they presented broad and varied situations in which we interviewed participants over video chat. The grandparent-grandchild study focused on older adults who were often less familiar with video chat technologies. The health information sharing study focused on a highly emotional topic for many participants. Participants also engaged in paper-based activities that were then discussed with the interviewer. The mCommerce study mostly focused on young adults, who discussed digital artifacts—in the form of diary entries and screenshots—during the interview. For each study, we focus in on the specific challenges that came up from the unique study contexts. These include the issues we faced as researchers when acquiring ethical clearance from our university, the challenges in recruiting and conducting each study, and the issues we faced when analyzing our data. We also share approaches that we took for addressing these challenges.

## CONDUCTING FACE-TO-FACE INTERVIEWS

Before describing our three studies, we first review some basic principles and guidelines for conducting interviews with participants. Readers interested in more detail should refer to the books we cite in this chapter or others focused on interviewing techniques and methods.

First, interviews in Human-Computer Interaction (HCI) research are typically used to elicit qualitative user feedback on design ideas, concepts, or existing technology. These can occur before, during, or after (in a retrospective way) the use of a technology. Interviews can be used to learn about user routines, patterns, and behaviors to determine the need for new technology. This latter style of interview is the type we focus on in this chapter, though the discussion is likely more broadly applicable to other types of interviews as well.

One-on-one interviews with study participants come in several forms, often varying in terms of the amount of direction that the interviewer gives to the participant (Schensul et al. 1999). These range from *structured interviews* to *semi-structured interviews* to *closed interviews*, where each has a slightly different purpose along with associated benefits and costs (Schensul et al. 1999). The three studies discussed in this chapter all utilize semi-structured interviews because the studies are all exploratory in nature, yet they focus on specific topics that we wanted to understand more deeply.

We have also seen the importance of context emerge as a part of HCI interview methods. This relates to a method known as *contextual inquiry* (Holtzblatt and Jones 1995; Beyer and Holtzblatt 1998). The goal of contextual inquiry is to understand the practices of interviewees within their actual environments. Originally, the method was developed for workplace studies, but it has since been used in home environments. By conducting interviews within the context of an interviewee's existing practices, the person is more likely to think about his or her practices and processes than if the interview was conducted elsewhere. This method has been used in domestic settings as part of *technology tours* (Baillie and Benyon 2007).

Physical objects and activities are now present in many face-to-face interviews. These may include design activities that are part of participatory design sessions (Sanders 1999; Sanders and William 2001). They may also include looking at digital or paper-based artifacts in focus groups (Goldman 1987). These techniques highlight the need to see and talk about objects and activities around participants during interviews, which is a focal point in all of the studies presented in this chapter.

During the interview, the interviewer should establish a relationship and rapport with the interviewee, respect the interviewee's perspective, and work to uncover detailed information about the focus of the interview (Weiss 1994). Interviewers must be good listeners, but good listening can be difficult to achieve in practice. There may be *situational* obstacles, such as noise from the environment or challenging topics being discussed (Nichols and Steven 1957; Wood 1996). There may also be *internal* obstacles, such as biases, a lack of focus, or diverse listening styles (Nichols and Steven 1957; Wood 1996). Good listening involves removing distractions from the environment (e.g., background noise), using open body postures (e.g., not crossing one's arms) and making eye contact, sitting attentively (e.g., leaning in toward the interviewee), being patient, and listening rather than talking (Nichols and Steven 1957; Wood 1996). All of these are important to remove internal distortion—problems with the method and environment in which the interview is conducted—and external distortion—problems with the interaction between the interviewer and interviewee (Book 1980). Throughout the interview, the interviewer can use various techniques to move the interview along, change direction, or probe for more details (Book 1980). These include a mixture of verbal statements in conjunction with body language. For example, *flow* techniques can be used to gain more information on a topic. They involve an interviewer making statements such as "I understand" or using body movements such as nodding one's head or leaning forward.

Thus, interviewing is about more than what is being said by the interviewee. It involves the environment in which the interview is conducted. Moreover, it involves complex body language, facial expressions, and gestures from both the interviewer and the interviewee. For the interviewer, these techniques set up the structure of the interview and can help transition topics, show interest, and gain deeper insight. In a similar nature, seeing the interviewee provides valuable details beyond what the person is saying. These can include valuable emotional information such as a participant's discomfort with certain topics or questions. This illustrates the importance of both the interviewer and interviewee being seen by each other and also the importance of seeing the context or environment in which the interview is taking place to understand what distractions or other internal distortion threats may be present.

As one moves to interviewing participants remotely over video chat, it is important to ensure that the interviewing suggestions, techniques, and methods we have described above and those that are documented elsewhere continue to be thought about and applied as needed.

In the next section, we describe the ethics of having people participate in interviews over video chat. Following this section, we move into specific descriptions of each of our three studies and the lessons we learned about interviewing over video chat. Some challenges and lessons overlapped between all three studies and, for this reason, our first case study goes into more detail than the latter two.

## THE ETHICS OF CONDUCTING STUDIES OVER VIDEO CHAT

The first challenge we experienced with conducting remote interviews over video chat happened before our studies even began. As is the case with nearly every university, one has to obtain clearance from an ethics review board (e.g., The Institutional Review Board [IRB] in the United States) for studies involving human participants to ensure the studies present minimal to no risk to them, including ensuring that data is kept confidential and anonymous.

For all of our studies, our university's ethics board was concerned that participants' identities and data would be transmitted electronically over the Internet during a video chat call. This created the small possibility that the video transmission could be intercepted by other individuals (e.g., hackers) and the person's identity and data could be revealed to a third party. Thus, the ethics board at our university had a concern about us guaranteeing the confidentiality of our participants' identities and associated data if the participants took part in a study over video chat. To circumvent this issue, we first explained to our ethics board that many data transmission protocols found in communications software (e.g., Skype) use secure connections that encrypt the data being transmitted. Yet despite this security feature, our ethics board still had concerns that encryption and secure connections may not be 100% reliable. As a result, and in agreement with our ethics board, we instead included a statement in our study protocol and consent forms that the confidentiality of participant identities and data could not be guaranteed for those participants who participated in our study over video communication tools such as Skype, as our ethics board does not consider it to be a confidential medium. We also stated that participants could decide if they were willing to take this risk or not as part of their consent to participate in the study. To date, this has not presented any issues to our study participants. Yet, we caution that other ethics boards may have different policies than ours, and certainly one should learn about and understand what concerns may exist for participants as they relate to studies conducted over video-mediated communication systems.

> **LESSON**
>
> Conducting studies over video chat may introduce new ethical and confidentiality concerns for both participants and ethics review boards. Be cognizant about these concerns and address them in participant consent forms and the study's protocol.

## CASE STUDY 1: GRANDPARENT AND GRANDCHILD COMMUNICATION

In the spring and summer of 2012, we conducted a diary and semi-structured interview study with grandparents and parents of children aged three to ten. The goal was to explore how grandparents and grandchildren conversed over distance using the phone, video chat, and other technologies. The study was primarily conducted by Azadeh Forghani, a PhD student, within her broader dissertation research. Full results from the work can be found in Forghani et al. (2013) and Forghani and Neustaedter (2014).

### STUDY METHOD

In order to recruit our ideal participants with varying demographics (e.g., children's ages, technical abilities, occupations) and various amounts of distance separation, we tried several recruitment methods, including snowball sampling through friends and family, posts on Facebook and Twitter, emails to teachers and parents at a local elementary school, and advertisements on Craigslist (a North American-based online advertising site). Finding eligible participants was challenging, which is a common situation for most studies that we conduct. In this case, it was hard to find participants who were interested in being a part of a research study, had children or grandchildren in the desired age range, *and* experienced distance separation between the grandparents and grandchildren. We also wanted to balance our participants to ensure we had a range of children's ages.

Eventually, we recruited eighteen participants; half of them were grandparents while the other half were the parents of children between the ages of three and ten. Because we broadened our recruitment efforts to meet our demographic needs, participants tended to be spread out geographically. Eight participants were from Greater Vancouver, a city that spans approximately 100 kilometers in the province of British Columbia, Canada. Five participants were from within Canada but outside of Vancouver, one was from the United States, three were from Iran, and one was from Australia.

The study consisted of two stages: a diary study and a semi-structured interview.

1. **Diary Study:** Participants were asked to record diary entries for a period of three weeks through a study web page. We asked grandparents to record information after each instance of communication with their remote grandchildren and asked parents to do the same after each time their children communicated with the remote grandparents.

2. **Semi-Structured Interview:** After the three-week diary portion of the study, we conducted a semi-structured interview with each participant. Naturally, it was not easily feasible to conduct face-to-face interviews with participants who lived in another country. Hence, we decided to interview them over either the phone or video chat. Given the large geographic spread of Greater Vancouver, the participants who lived in the city were asked if they preferred an interview over the phone, over video chat, or in person at home. Overall, across remote and local participants, only four interviews were done in person, while the remaining interviews were done remotely: five via the phone and another nine via video chat.

When using video chat, participants were asked to choose a video chat application they were most familiar with. This turned out to be Skype for all remote participants. Some local participants preferred the phone because they felt they were not familiar enough with video chat. Others preferred the phone because it allowed them to multi-task and watch their (highly mobile) young children during the interview as opposed to being stuck in front of a computer. While local participants did not give reasons why they chose not to do in-person interviews, we suspect this had to do with a researcher coming to their home, feeling somewhat uncomfortable with this person being a stranger, and also feeling obliged to clean up their home beforehand.

Next we address several challenges we faced while conducting interviews over video chat.

## SCHEDULING

We found that connecting with participants at a designated time to conduct a video chat interview was often difficult. Participants were willing to schedule an interview, but last-minute cancellations happened far more often for video chat interviews than for in-person interviews. In general, participants felt less committed to a video chat interview and would routinely contact us on the day of the interview and ask to reschedule. Participants were told ahead of time that interviews typically took an hour to complete. Thus, they knew we would be committing only an hour to the interview as opposed to taking the extra time to drive to meet them, and as a result, they were more likely to reschedule at the last minute.

We could not completely overcome such situations, but we learned that when we sent reminders by email the day before an interview and verified that the participants were still available during the scheduled time, they tended not to reschedule. This additional reminder and confirmation solidified commitments from both the participant and the interviewer to participate as previously scheduled.

### LESSON

Participants may feel less committed to participate in a video chat interview and may cancel or reschedule more frequently than for an in-person interview. Remind participants of scheduled appointments and the interview's importance to increase their commitment.

When participants lived in a different time zone than we do, we faced additional challenges in trying to understand what days and times they were available to participate. We were very careful to figure out what the time zone difference was between our location and the participant's and explicitly detail this when talking about days and times. We also sent reminders to participants specifying the interview's time and date in their local time zone to make sure they were still available at the scheduled time. Even still, some participants were easily confused by the time zone differences, and this caused additional challenges when scheduling remote interviews as well as rescheduling ones that needed to be moved or were missed because of a mix-up in time zones.

## TECHNICAL ISSUES AND SCAFFOLDING

Six interviews were conducted over video chat with grandparents between the ages of sixty and seventy-three. All were well educated and had basic computer knowledge; however, their experience with video chat applications varied widely. Some participants frequently used video chat systems for academic or work purposes, while others were less familiar with them and had to ask another family member (e.g., an adult child) to help with the application before we could start the interview. This meant that sometimes an additional adult was present at the interviews. This may not seem to be an issue, but some interview questions asked about communication challenges and social tensions that might arise between grandparents and parents. Having another person present and privy to hearing the participant's interview responses could compromise what was said, causing participants to hold back on their concerns or issues and not report them. We did not notice any instances of this in our study, but it is certainly something important to consider.

Setting up video chat calls was also a challenge with those who were less experienced with the technology, because it usually meant that the first ten to fifteen minutes of the interview involved making sure the connection was working and that both parties could see and hear each other. If there were problems, the setup had to be changed or we had to troubleshoot. This additional effort caused some participants to have a hard time concentrating on the interview questions, as they were noticeably worried about the connection and whether or not they were using the application correctly. For example, one participant repeatedly told us that it was her first interview over Skype and she was not really 'into' video chat. We noticed this caused her to be distracted, and it was much more difficult for her to recall information about the times she communicated with her grandchildren. As a result, she often answered our interview questions with simple 'yes' or 'no' answers. With other participants, technical issues arose in the middle of interviews, which caused them to lose focus and let their attention wander. Some participants were also overly distracted by the ability to see their own preview window in Skype.

To circumvent such issues, we included additional setup time in our study protocol and expected that it was needed for each and every video chat interview. We tried to relieve our participants of any anxieties they might have had about video chatting by focusing on ice-breaking conversation during the first part of the interview. We talked about how, like the participants, it was difficult for our own family members to use video chat systems. This typically helped participants feel more comfortable.

---

**LESSON**

Participants may feel anxious when using video chat for interviews because of their inexperience with the technology. Try to reduce such anxiety by providing simple yet detailed instructions for first-time participants and engaging in ice-breaking conversation.

---

We recognized that both technical and social issues that arose about the video chat application could easily make participants feel negatively toward the technology. This was a challenge because we asked participants how they did or did not use video chat with their grandchildren, yet we did not want to create negative associations about video chat as a way to communicate with grandchildren because of a poor experience during the interview. We tried to circumvent this by minimizing technical issues with the video chat application; however, it is certainly not something that one can completely control.

## BUILDING RAPPORT WITH REMOTE PARTICIPANTS

In this study, we found it more challenging to establish rapport with remote participants over video chat as compared to an in-person interview. In-person interviews often involved natural 'small talk' at the onset of the interview. For example, we might discuss how we each traveled to the coffee shop to conduct the interview or how we navigated to the participant's home and understood the directions given. At coffee shops, we often discussed the weather while we ordered or waited for our coffee to arrive. Because we were both in the same location, we could discuss the effects of the weather on our activities and empathize with each other. These informal exchanges helped to create an initial sense of trust between the participant and interviewer.

On the other hand, making informal small talk at the beginning of a video chat interview was more difficult. There was less shared context to talk about because we were in different locations. Small talk about the weather typically felt awkward because there was no common ground. We felt it was also rude to talk about what might be seen in the background of one's video window (e.g., the room, a painting on the wall); however, this was really the only other piece of information that might be commented on. The only truly shared context we could talk about informally was how we had set up the video chat call and whether or not it was working correctly. Yet this in itself was often a frustrating issue and not a good ice breaker.

To try to circumvent this issue, we asked less challenging questions during the first half of a video chat interview in order to ease the participant into the topic of interest, and moved the more challenging questions to the end. This is a common interview strategy for building rapport with participants (Weiss 1994), and we believed it was especially important when conducting video chat interviews.

---

**LESSON**

Building rapport with participants may be more difficult over video chat than it is in person. Prior to an interview, read about the participant's background (e.g., number of children, occupation), if available, and use this information as part of ice-breaking conversation. Then, when interviewing, sort the questions from easy to challenging.

---

## INTERRUPTIONS AND ENGAGEMENT

We often faced various interruptions and changing levels of participant engagement during video chat interviews. We found controlling the flow of a video chat interview more difficult compared to in-person interviews. Participants who were parents would often be interrupted by their children, which would make regaining their focus more difficult. Such interruptions can certainly happen during in-person interviews, yet because the interviewer was not physically present during video chats, it was easy for children to not understand that a formal interview was occurring. When we conducted in-person interviews, older children most often understood the presence of the interviewer and tried not to interrupt. Over video chat, this was more difficult to notice and understand.

One challenge was maintaining eye contact with participants to ensure they were engaged and focused on the interview. For example, one participant took long pauses during the interview, and it was hard to tell if she was trying to remember something related to the questions or if she was doing something else on her computer, such as checking email or browsing the web. When using video chat, participants would typically see the interviewer's face but not the hands, so if the interviewer looked away from the computer screen to record notes (a second laptop was used to type notes during the interview), the participant would not necessarily know what the interviewer was doing. This was explained by saying things like, "Great, let me just make a quick note on that" so the participants would not feel as though the interviewer was disinterested in their answers.

During the interviews, we raised questions relating to diary responses that participants had previously filled out and that were recorded on a study web page and stored in a text file. This meant that during the interview, we would have to open the file and switch our focus between the participant on Skype and the diary answers in the file. While we have no data to understand the effect of this activity, we suspect this could have been challenging for the participants, as they would likely have recognized that we were not maintaining continuous eye contact with them. They could have easily wondered if *we* were the ones checking email or browsing the web. We tried to mitigate such situations by telling participants what we were doing; however, it could still have been easily misconstrued.

---

**LESSON**

Challenges when conducting interviews over video chat may include distractions from others in the participant's home, a lack of eye contact, multi-tasking during the interview, and a limited view of body language. Try to mitigate these problems by clearly communicating with participants ahead of time that they should attempt to remove any likely distractions that may occur. Also, let them know what will be done to collect data so they do not think the researcher is distracted during the interview.

---

## SUMMARY

The first case study illustrates the manner in which we conducted interviews over video chat with parents and grandparents. It was especially challenging to schedule interviews with participants (and keep those scheduled times), build rapport with participants in order to talk about social issues, and maintain constant engagement during the interview process.

The next study builds on several of these themes and explores the context of sharing health information among distributed family members.

# CASE STUDY 2: HEALTH INFORMATION SHARING

In the spring of 2012, we conducted a mixed-methods (qualitative and quantitative) study exploring family communication routines in situations where a family member had suffered from a chronic illness. The goal of our study was to explore the ways in which people used various technologies to communicate over distance, the benefits people received from each type of technology, and the communication challenges that people faced. The study was primarily conducted by Carolyn Pang, an MSc student at the time, as part of her thesis research. Full results from the work can be found in Pang et al. (2013) and Pang (2013).

## STUDY METHOD

We recruited seventeen individuals through advertisements on social media sites, postings on an online public community, and solicitation to students at our university. Participants were representative of a family network, with participants' ages ranging between twenty and seventy. All participants had an immediate family member (e.g., child, sibling, parent) who had suffered from a chronic illness within the past three years, including cancer, diabetes, leukemia, Alzheimer's, and multiple sclerosis.

The study contained two parts: a semi-structured interview and a design activity. Six people participated remotely because they resided outside the Greater Vancouver region. This was necessary, as it was a challenge to find enough local participants who met our recruiting requirements (e.g., had a family member suffering from a chronic illness) and were willing to participate in a potentially emotional study. Remote participants were required to be in front of their computers to video chat and access links online. They were asked beforehand to have a few supplies readily accessible during the study, such as sheets of paper and a pen.

1. **Semi-Structured Interview:** The semi-structured interview was split into two parts: a paper-based activity and interview questions. The paper-based activity required a pen and blank sheets of paper. Participants were asked to create a social map specific to their health situation. They were asked to think about any individuals with whom they shared health information about the patient, and then draw a diagram or map depicting this network, identifying and grouping individuals in any way they wished. Interview questions elicited more details about the family and social map along with details about the health situation and technology use. Figure 2.1 shows an example diagram created by a participant. This activity took between thirty and forty-five minutes to complete.
2. **Design Evaluation:** The design evaluation activity comprised two parts. Participants were first asked to draw and/or list tools or features they would use in a system to facilitate health information management and sharing. The second part of the activity involved an evaluation of user interface screens from existing health information sharing systems. In-person participants were asked

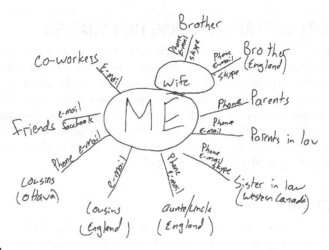

**FIGURE 2.1**

A participant's drawing of his family and social map.

to mark up the screens, which were on printed pieces of paper. Participants circled features they liked using a green marker and features they did not like using a red marker. Figure 2.2 shows an example screen marked up by a participant.

We could not provide printed screenshots of the interface to remote participants, so we sent them a URL that contained images of each screen. We asked them to view the images at the appropriate point in the study and to then describe their thoughts to us. The interviewer then marked up printed copies of the screen using red and green markers accordingly. This activity took between thirty and forty-five minutes to complete. In hindsight, we could have used Skype or Google+ Hangout's screen-sharing feature to help support this activity; however, such features were new or unfamiliar to our participants, and we did not fully recognize the challenges we would face with our chosen study approach. In essence, our approach felt adequate at the time.

## EMOTIONAL CONTENT

Given the study's focus on health issues and communication surrounding them, we quickly found our study sessions to be highly emotional. During the drawing activities and interviews, many participants were required to talk about very difficult times, either currently or in the recent past, where a loved one was near the end of life, had already passed away, or faced a grim and unknown future. Because of the emotional nature of the topic, we felt it was especially important to build rapport with the participants in order to make them feel comfortable enough to open up about their personal experiences and emotions. As in the previously described study, we found it was much easier to build trust and rapport with participants in person. It

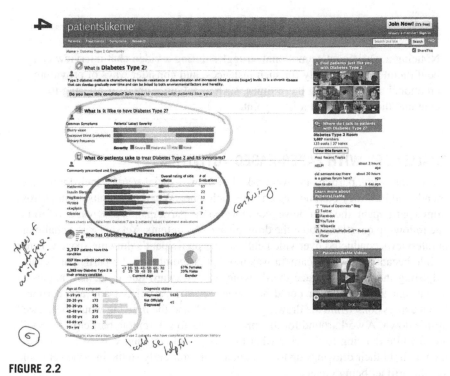

**FIGURE 2.2**

A sample marked-up screenshot of the existing health information sharing system, PatientsLikeMe.

was easier to break the ice with small talk and show compassion through body language and facial expressions. Our remote participants seemed less willing to deviate from the interview questions and often waited for the next question rather than offer to expand on their responses. This contrasted with in-person participants, who were more willing to expand further on their answers and continue the conversation.

It was evident that some participants did not expect to experience pain and sadness as memories of their experiences with chronic illness surfaced. In-person interviews allowed for small, yet important, physical gestures in times like these, such as handing over a tissue box when a participant began to tear up or cry. For remote interviews, these small physical gestures were not possible. The interviewer had to be especially tuned in to the emotions of the participants and offer small breaks for them to compose themselves. This was often difficult to notice over video chat because of video resolution or audio quality. Despite instances of emotional breakdowns, all of the participants were able to complete their interview in one sitting. However, researchers in similar situations should be aware of this challenge and consider continuing at a later point for interviews that become too emotionally challenging in order to respect the participant's well-being.

> **LESSON**
>
> Noticing a participant's emotional struggles during a video chat interview can be difficult. Watch closely for such instances, and consider ways of providing emotional support during these times, such as taking a break or offering to continue the interview at a later point.

## CHALLENGES WITH PAPER-BASED ACTIVITIES

During the study, participants were asked to draw a social map of their family and friends and how they communicated with each other. When physically sitting across from a participant, the interviewer could watch the participant's progress and formulate follow-up questions about the drawing and its contents. Yet this was a challenge in interviews conducted over video chat, as the participant's drawing space was not visible because the video camera was most often pointed at the participant's face. Adjusting the camera to face the drawing was awkward due to camera angles; it meant that the interviewer could no longer see the participant and any pertinent facial expressions while the drawing was created, and the drawing would be viewed upside down. A workaround for this problem was to ask remote participants to talk aloud while drawing to describe what they were drawing and why. We also asked them to hold their drawings up to the camera intermittently so the interviewer could see the artifact being created.

Asking participants to hold up their drawings led to a few other issues. For example, it became noticeably awkward for them to coordinate the position of the drawing in the frame of the camera. They also had to flip the sheet of paper back and forth between showing it to the camera and looking at it themselves in order to ensure they were pointing at the correct items in the drawing. After a few occurrences of this, participants quickly became frustrated with the process and many appeared to rush through it. Shared drawing tools and screen-sharing features could be a way to address this challenge; however, at the time of the study, these types of technology features were far too complicated for our participants, given their limited experience with video chat.

We found workarounds for some participants. For example, one participant who was tech savvy took a picture of his drawing and emailed it to the interviewer during the interview so he could talk through the diagram. This participant's drawing is shown in Figure 2.3.

Figure 2.4 shows a screen capture of a participant holding up a piece of paper in front of a webcam while using Skype.[1] This participant was not comfortable using a

---

[1]The participant's image has been blurred for anonymity. We note that the image is of a poor quality. This is not an artifact of the book's printing. It directly points to the challenges of capturing data from participants holding up their paper-based artifacts during a study.

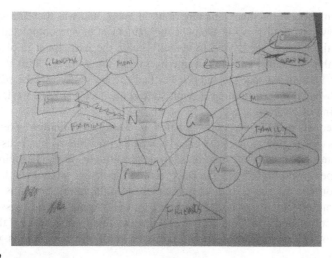

**FIGURE 2.3**

Remote participant's drawing captured by the participant by taking a photo of it and emailing it to the interviewer.

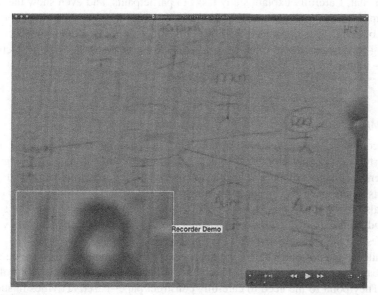

**FIGURE 2.4**

Remote participant's drawing captured by the interviewer using screen capture. Due to the low bandwidth of the video connection, the drawing appeared blurry to the interviewer.

camera or smartphone to share a picture of her drawing and was therefore asked by the interviewer to hold it up in front of the camera after she completed it. This resulted in the interviewer having to verbally guide the participant in placing her drawing within the video camera's frame by saying things like, "Shift it upwards an inch." It also meant that the interviewer had to repeatedly ask the participant to confirm what she was pointing at with statements such as, "Are we looking at your grouping of close friends?"

In the second stage of the study (labeled as "Design Evaluation" previously), participants took part in more paper-based activities, this time with a focus on evaluating commercial health information sharing systems. In-person participants annotated paper printouts of the interface screens to show what they liked and disliked about the interface. Remote participants told the interviewer this same information, and she annotated her copy of the printouts. Again, we faced issues with the placement of items in front of the camera, but this time it was by the interviewer, who was trying to verify the correctness of the annotations with the participants.

---

**LESSON**

Conducting paper-based activities can be challenging when interviewing over video chat. Carefully explain study tasks to participants, and even show them examples of a completed artifact so they know about the desired content and level of detail. If using screen-sharing applications is not possible, consider asking participants to use cameras or scanners to capture and share the artifacts created during the interview.

---

## SUMMARY

Our second case study reveals how video chat can be used to conduct an interview-based study on deeply emotional topics, such as communication between family members in instances of chronic health situations. This requires interacting with participants in a respectful way while building a level of trust that allows them to open up. It also highlights issues in noticing discomfort and emotional pain. The study included paper-based activities, which were especially cumbersome to do over video chat, despite the valuable data that they provided.

While we did not find suitable workarounds for all participants when conducting paper-based activities over video chat, we identified challenges that arose for these tasks. They point to the need to carefully construct paper-based activities in such a way that both local and remote participants can have a similar experience when completing the task so as to avoid (or minimize) frustrations. The challenges also suggest that there may be value in considering digital, on-screen activities that are comparable to paper-based activities.

The next study moves away from family communication to explore another situation in domestic life: shopping and purchasing items using mobile devices.

# CASE STUDY 3: MOBILE COMMERCE

In the spring and summer of 2011, we conducted a diary and interview study that investigated how people shopped and purchased products on mobile devices, including shopping for items using an eBay phone app and searching for new apps in the Apple App Store. This type of shopping activity is called mobile commerce, or mCommerce for short. The goal of our study was to investigate user behaviors and trust concerns while participating in mobile commerce shopping. The study was primarily conducted by Serena Hillman, a PhD student at the time, as part of her dissertation research. Full results from the work can be found in Hillman et al. (2012), Hillman and Neustaedter (2012), and Hillman (2014).

## STUDY METHOD

The study involved a total of seventeen participants who frequently shopped and made purchases using a mobile device. Participants' ages ranged from nineteen to forty-four; thus, many participants were of a younger demographic than the previous two studies. We recruited participants using social media applications, online forums, and emails. All but one participant lived in the Greater Vancouver area, though participants were spread across the city or lived in a suburb. The study consisted of two stages: a diary study and a semi-structured interview.

1. **Diary Study:** Participants were asked to record electronic diary entries each day for a period of three weeks. Diary questions asked them to describe their mobile commerce shopping experiences and feelings around their trust of online merchants. Participants were also asked to take screenshots on their mobile devices when shopping or purchasing items to act as memory aids for subsequent interviews. These were uploaded to our server along with the diary entries.
2. **Semi-Structured Interview:** After the three-week diary portion of the study, participants were presented with three options for a semi-structured interview. They could conduct the interview over the phone, over video chat, or in person. Many participants preferred the video chat option rather than a phone or in-person interview; approximately one third of our interviews were done over video chat. Participants told us that a video chat interview was preferred because it afforded greater flexibility in timing the call and had zero travel requirements.

During the interview, participants were asked to review diary entries and the screenshots they had submitted and answer clarifying questions. Questions mostly focused around understanding the shopping activities of each participant. On average, interviews lasted approximately thirty minutes.

## PREPARING FOR THE INTERVIEW

This study revealed that it was critical to be properly prepared for our interviews over video chat. We tried to provide additional levels of comfort for the participants because we did not know if they would be familiar with being interviewed over video chat, and we wanted them to feel comfortable sharing their shopping experiences. For example, the interviewer would make sure that she sent them her video chat username well beforehand so that participants could add it to their contact lists. Despite this, participants would typically not add her as a contact until just before the interview (e.g., five minutes). We found it important to give the participants the power to call the interviewer when they were ready, rather than the other way around. We believe this allowed them to have some control over the interview process and to feel ready before the interview started.

To provide an additional understanding of expectations, we sent participants an email about the general topics that would be discussed and let them know they could contact the interviewer whenever they were ready to start the video chat interview. The questions we sent were general enough to prevent priming the participants but provided some context for the types of questions we would be asking. We also recognized that they would need access to the diary entries and screenshots they had previously uploaded to our online diary form, as these items would be discussed in the interview. We made sure to send the items to participants via email ahead of time, with a clear explanation as to why they needed the information. These preparations gave the participants insight about what the interview might include.

We believed it was important to respect each participant's chosen level of privacy in this study. We found that some participants did not want to share their camera's view and wanted to use the video chat system as a voice-only application, yet for reasons unknown to us, they still selected to use video chat instead of the phone. This was surprising, but made us realize that even if someone chooses to participate in a study using a video chat system, the way the participant wants to use system and its features may vary. Naturally, having the video channel turned off limits one's ability to share and view body language and facial expressions. However, respecting a participant's desired level of privacy is likely more important than the additional contextual information obtained through video.

---

**LESSON**

Adequately prepare for a video chat interview by exchanging contact information and familiarizing participants with an understanding of the study's focus. Respect participants' chosen levels of privacy in terms of how they use the video chat tool (e.g., audio only versus audio plus video).

---

## AUTHENTICITY

This study brought to the surface issues of authenticity for some of our participants, perhaps because they were a slightly younger demographic than the participants in our other two studies. Nearly all of the participants were new to participating in research studies. Because of this, some participants were unsure of the authenticity of our study and its process. In other words, they did not know if we were conducting a real research study. They had never met the interviewer or anyone from the project prior to the study, and they had only communicated with us online through email. In hindsight, we think that participants might have assumed that, after they completed the diary portion of the study, they would come to a university for the interview. Finding out they did not have to caused them to feel hesitant. While trust in the authenticity of the study did not seem to affect their involvement, we believe it might have had an impact on the quality of the data they provided. Generally speaking, participants who felt uncertain about the study's legitimacy tended to remain shy and would rush through the interview. We did our best to pace the interviews and to get more details from these participants, yet at times their hesitancy was difficult to overcome.

After reflecting on the face-to-face interviews we conducted in the same study, we better understood why remote participants may have questioned the legitimacy of our study. With some face-to-face interviews, participants are required to come to a research lab, university, company, or organization. The act of coming to such locations, along with the business-like appearance of the location, fosters a sense of institutional trust. This trust transfers to the specific study for which a person is being interviewed. In the case of video chat interviews, institutional trust and, in turn, trust in the legitimacy of a study can be more difficult to create because participants are not entering a known location of academic research. Instead, they are connecting to another user over video chat, whose username and on-screen image may easily look less than professional. This suggests that interviewers should consider ways that institutional trust can be created as part of a remote study. For example, one could consider using a video chat account that is set up with professional information, including a professional-sounding handle, or username, and a business-like image of the interviewer. We build on this idea more in the next section.

---

**LESSON**

Participants may be concerned with the authenticity of a study when an interview occurs over video chat, as they are not required to visit a research institution or a company. Consider ways of providing additional degrees of institutional trust, such as using a professional-looking video chat account.

---

## ENVIRONMENTAL CONTEXT

In this study, we found that the view through the video chat window often provided a more contextualized understanding of our participants and their situations than interviews conducted over the phone, at a coffee shop, or at our university campus. We could often see into participants' homes or workplace environments and observe the everyday, mundane things that occupied these spaces, such as dogs, art, furniture, etc. Similar to in-home interviews, this allowed us to see contextual information that helped us to better understand participants and their life situations, which often related to their shopping habits (e.g., what types of items they purchased).

Sometimes participants even commented on the other activities or things happening at their home. For example, here is the first portion of one of our interviews:

<Participant answers video chat call>
*Participant*: Let me get the dog out.
*Interviewer*: Go right ahead.
*Participant*: So I apologize right now in case you might hear any barking in the background. I got my daughter in Iraq right now as a contractor so I am babysitting her Australian cattle dog and British bulldog.

The above situation illustrates how the participant very quickly opened up to the interviewer as a result of the daily life events going on around him. The participant knew the interviewer could see him dealing with a dog and so provided an explanation. This gave us an opportunity to engage in small talk before jumping into study questions. We had similar situations arise with other participants as well.

Just as we could see a participant's surroundings, we realized that video chat interviews revealed details about our own environment, and participants certainly noticed this aspect, sometimes even commenting on it. For example, one participant commented on the art hanging on the interviewer's office wall. This reveals the importance of being willing to share and talk about the interviewer's own environment. It also suggests carefully thinking about one's own appearance on video chat and what surroundings are visible. These visuals should certainly match the image that a person wants to project as a researcher. In some cases, it may mean projecting the appearance of a close confidant, and in other situations, it may mean projecting the appearance of a more formal figure. Even though discussions about one's environment may not focus on anything relevant to the study, by sharing these details with participants, a better rapport could be developed and used to improve the quality of data reported by participants and their interest in opening up during interviews.

---

**LESSON**

Video chat provides views into both the participant's and interviewer's environments, which may be helpful for ice-breaking conversations. It also means constructing an environment that projects a desired appearance to the remote participant.

---

## SUMMARY

This case study revealed the importance of what participants see over a video connection and the level of professionalism the view conveys. This relates to participants' trust in the authenticity of a study, which is tied to the institution conducting it, and relates to the appearance of the environment and how the interviewer looks and portrays himself or herself. As with any study, being prepared before the interview is also important.

## DISCUSSION AND CONCLUSIONS

This chapter describes a variety of challenges and situations we faced when using video chat for conducting interview-based studies. There are likely many more situations that one might face and many ways to overcome the difficulties that might arise. The most important thing is to recognize potential challenges before interviewing over video chat so undesirable situations can be avoided. If challenges do arise during a study, it is important to understand their effects on the study and how one can mitigate them in the moment. As people around the world become more familiar with video chat technologies and have greater access to them, researchers are likely to increasingly use them as tools for conducting research studies. Along with this adoption and proliferation, new challenges will surely arise. Only through continued review and critique of this method will we be able to fully understand its unique benefits and challenges.

As a culture, we are still adopting video chat technologies and understanding what roles they play and for what situations they are useful. This means we are still developing norms of usage for the technology. Not everyone will understand these norms, and some people will likely have to learn about them over time and through firsthand experience. Our studies illustrate situations occurring in current culture and society with existing norms as they are still developing. They may continue to evolve and eliminate some of the issues we have described as well as introduce new challenges. We encourage others to think about and build on the lessons we have presented in this chapter.

## ACKNOWLEDGMENTS

We are grateful to all the participants in our studies, who were comfortable enough to participate over video chat technologies, allowing us to explore our research topics and also learn about conducting interviews over distance.

## REFERENCES

Baillie, L., Benyon, D., 2007. Place and Technology in the Home. In: Journal of Computer Supported Cooperative Work (CSCW), 17. Springer.

Beyer, H., Holtzblatt, K., 1998. Contextual Design: Defining Customer-Centered Design. Morgan Kaufmann, Burlington, MA.

Book, C.L., 1980. Human Communication: Principles, Concepts and Skills. St. Martin's Press, New York.

Forghani, A., Neustaedter, C., 2014. The Routines and Needs of Grandparents and Parents for Grandparent-Grandchild Conversations over Distance. In: Proceedings of the ACM Conference on Computer-Human Interaction (CHI). ACM Press, New York, NY.

Forghani, A., Neustaedter, C., Schiphorst, T., 2013. Investigating the Communication Patterns of Distance-Separated Grandparents and Grandchildren. In: Extended Proceedings of the ACM Conference on Computer-Human Interaction (CHI). ACM Press, New York, NY.

Goldman, A.E., 1987. The Group Depth Interview. Prentice Hall, Upper Saddle River, NJ.

Hillman, S., Neustaedter, C., 2012. Trust in Mobile Shopping: An Empirical Study. User Experience Magazine 11 (4).

Hillman, S., Neustaedter, C., Bowes, J., Antle, A., 2012. Soft Trust and mCommerce Shopping Behaviors. In: Proceedings of the International Conference on Human-Computer Interaction with Mobile Devices & Services (MobileHCI 2012). ACM Press, New York, NY.

Hillman, S., 2014. Social Issues, Behaviours and Routines of Ubi-Commerce Users in North America, PhD Dissertation. Simon Fraser University.

Holtzblatt, K., Jones, S., 1995. Conducting and Analyzing a Contextual Interview. In: In Human-Computer Interaction. Morgan Kaufmann, Burlington, MA, pp. 241–253.

Nichols, R.G., Steven, L.A., 1957. Listening to People. Harvard Business Review 35 (5).

Pang, C., 2013. Technology Preferences and Routines for Distributed Families Coping with a Chronic Illness. In: Master of Science Thesis, School of Interactive Art & Technology. Simon Fraser University. April 2013.

Pang, C., Neustaedter, C., Riecke, B.E., Oduor, E., Hillman, S., 2013. Technology Preferences and Routines for Sharing Health Information During the Treatment of a Chronic Illness. In: Proceedings of the ACM Conference on Computer Human Interaction (CHI). ACM Press, New York, NY.

Sanders, E., 1999. From User Centred to Participatory Design Approaches. In: Symposium on Design and the Social Sciences: Making Connections. University of Alberta, Canada.

Sanders, E., William, C., 2001. Harnessing People's Creativity: Ideation and Expression through Visual Communication. In: Langford, J., McDonagh-Philp, D. (Eds.), Focus Groups: Supporting Effective Product Development. Taylor and Francis.

Schensul, S., Schensul, J., LeCompte, M., 1999. Essential Ethnographic Methods: Observations, Interviews, and Questionnaires. Altamira Press, Lanham, MD.

Weiss, R., 1994. Learning from Strangers: The Art and Method of Qualitative Interview Studies. The Free Press, New York.

Wood, J.T., 1996. Everyday Encounters: An Introduction to Interpersonal Communication. Wadsworth Publishing Co, Belmont, CA.

# "Rainy Days Work Best for Us": Lessons from Home-Based Family Interviews

# 3

**Gilly Leshed\*, Maria Håkansson**[§]

*Cornell University, Department of Information Science, Ithaca, NY, USA\*; Chalmers University of Technology, Gothenburg, Sweden*[§]

## INTRODUCTION

It was a sunny late spring evening, and I was driving through winding rural roads, trying to find the correct address. As I arrived at an old two-story country house surrounded by big trees, with a few vegetable garden plots, a hoop house, a barn, a fenced area with sheep, some cats, and a border collie, I was greeted by lots of kids running around. Julie,[1] mom of nine children between the ages of ten months and eighteen years, came out of one of the garden plots, peeling mud off her hands. Dave had just arrived home from work as I pulled in. I was given a tour of the farm and shown the sheep, rams, rabbits, fields, irrigation system, vegetable gardens, bed and breakfast, and play structure. Afterward, we sat in the backyard. The kids shoveled in the pizza I had brought as the parents signed off on consent forms for everyone. About forty-five minutes after I arrived, I started the audio recorder to begin the interview—one interviewer with eleven interviewees.

This was the beginning of an interview carried out as part of a study of coordination practices among farm families (Leshed, Håkansson, and Kaye 2014). As two mothers in academia who sit at desks and work on computers during the day and take care of families and households in the evenings, we had no idea what life is like for families who have a completely different lifestyle. Furthermore, we suspected that many of the families studied and designed for in the human-computer interaction (HCI) field were too much like us: white-collar, middle-class professionals in single- or double-income families that consist of mom, dad, and a small number of school-aged children all living in the same household. But what happens in other kinds of families? Single-parent families? Families impacted by a network of divorces and remarriages or families that are dispersed across households? Low-income or blue-collar families? Immigrant families? Gay parent families? As we were digging

---

[1]Names of people and farms who participated in the study are pseudonyms.

through the HCI literature, we found a few notable examples of papers that looked into family practices that are different from the middle-class model (Odom, Zimmerman, and Forlizzi 2010; Wyche and Grinter 2012; Yardi and Bruckman 2012; Yarosh, Chew, and Abowd 2009), but most did not.

We therefore sought to learn from other kinds of families, who organize their lives differently, as a way to expand our understanding of family practices around coordination and organization as well as the design space for family technologies. In search of a family demographic that is less represented in the HCI literature, we were inspired by the vibrant agriculture community surrounding our university, Cornell, located in the town of Ithaca, in a rural area of New York State in the United States. Seeing farmers as vendors in the local farmers' market (Figure 3.1), we realized that we did not know much about this demographic. We guessed that they might face challenges, for example around finances, but we were also enchanted by an idealized view we had of these families living off the land out in the countryside. Although farm families had not been studied before in the field of HCI, rural and farm life has long been the focus of studies by sociologists (e.g., Woods 2011), as have modernization and technological development in rural life (e.g., Kline 2000). Within the diverse forms of rural life, small-scale farm families have been characterized by owning, operating, managing, and working on their farms by a seasonal rhythm of production and by integrating work and home (Strange 2008). With our access to a community of small-scale organic farm families through the local farmers' market, we chose to study this group of families.

In the spring of 2012, we carried out interviews with farm families in Ithaca, New York. We drove to their houses, went on farm tours, and sat in their back yards and homes as we listened to stories of coordinating family and work life in and outside of the farm. Choosing to study farm families who merge home and work meant that the scope of our study extended beyond what may be considered to be "family" or "domestic"; we explored our participants' lives holistically, including their work, school, volunteer, and extracurricular activities, as well as their family and home practices. The seasonal patterns that dominated the families' lives also impacted our ability to meet with them and carry out the study. And the ongoing togetherness experienced by living, working, and studying on the family-owned farm revealed—and sometimes concealed—emotions around family conflicts and tensions that we had to deal with during and after the study.

Our choice to interview farm families in their homes implies certain particularities and challenges that may seem relevant only to this demographic and the specific setting of our study. However, our study offers insights that may extend beyond interview studies of farm families. Drawing on the challenges we ran into and our experiences in dealing with the farm families, we learned lessons for running family studies that go beyond this specific group. In this chapter, we discuss the following four lessons:

1. The temporal rhythms of domestic life—those related to natural rhythms, such as seasons and growth, and to structural rhythms, such as school, work, and

holidays—matter to families and may affect running the study and its outcomes. Researchers should therefore take those temporal rhythms into account when planning and conducting a study.

2. Interviewing a large family with many participants can be overwhelming and exhausting for a single interviewer. Consider interviewing as a team of two or more researchers to make it more manageable and to increase the opportunities for taking in as many perspectives as possible.

3. Hearing everyone's voices—including children—is more than being polite or respectful to all participants. It is a way to gain a more holistic understanding of family life and individuals' perspectives.

4. Emotions, tensions, and conflicts are part of everyday life and may come up during a family study, even if not directly relevant to the research questions. Be generous with time when planning a study in order to allow people enough time to tell their stories.

## AN INTERVIEW STUDY OF FARM FAMILIES

The interview method, which we used for a family study, is quite common in the HCI field (e.g., Davidoff, Zimmerman, and Dey 2010; Neustaedter, Brush, and Greenberg 2009). After researchers choose to conduct family interviews, they must recruit the families and coordinate the interviews, meet the families, get family members to participate in the interviews, document their responses, and, after leaving the interview site, analyze and interpret the data into meaningful findings. In this section, we describe details of the method we used and decisions we faced throughout the study. In the section following this one, we dive deeper into some challenges we faced during the study, how we overcame them, and more general lessons for family interview studies.

## CHOOSING INTERVIEWS OVER OTHER METHODS

Our choice to run an interview study stemmed from several factors. The goal of our study was to understand the everyday practices of families, where they live and work, and various ways they use and appropriate organization and coordination tools such as calendars, to-do lists, and other tools we hadn't thought of. We believed that in-depth interviews in families' homes could give us the complex data we were interested in collecting. More lightweight methods, such as surveys, might not have provided us with the depth in which we were interested. On the other hand, a full-fledged ethnographic study that would give us a long-term, fuller view on the families' relationships and practices was infeasible, given our limited time and resources, and we had to devote attention to other activities besides this study. Finally, we both had experiences in running interview studies, making the interview method a natural choice.

**FIGURE 3.1**

The local farmers' market scene gives an idealistic view of farm family life, with farmers appearing happy and healthy, and dedicated to growing and selling organic produce.

We therefore built on our previous experiences and studies: Håkansson was in the process of studying simple-living families, in which she visited the homes of families who voluntarily live simply, out of concern for the environment and their own well-being, and interviewed them about their sustainability practices (Håkansson and Sengers 2013). Leshed had completed an interview study with individuals about their everyday practices of organizing and managing their time and tasks (Leshed and Sengers 2011) and an interview study with college students on their use of communication technologies with their remote parents (Smith et al. 2012). We combined elements from these studies: Håkansson was familiar with visiting families in their homes, interviewing the family as a whole, and going on home tours to get a deeper understanding of the everyday practices; Leshed was familiar with interviews that explore time and task management tools and practices, and those that involve show and tell of tools, such as calendars, to-do lists, and other organizing and coordination tools. While learning and practicing new research methods is invaluable for expanding one's own skillset, building on the researchers' strengths could help to construct and run a solid, successful study.

> **LESSON**
>
> When choosing which method to use, in addition to considering the goal of the study and the available resources, consider the research team's research methods skills: those methods they are comfortable with or those they would like to develop.

## RECRUITMENT: THE FARMERS' MARKET

To start, we had to find farm families to interview. Located in a rural area, Cornell University has a history of maintaining relationships with the agriculture community, including having an agriculture school, a veterinary medicine school, and a cooperative extension unit. We contacted the university's cooperative extension, and one employee told us she was in contact with farm families and could help us make connections. Then the ball started rolling. She contacted a few families who were interested in participating in the study and gave us their email addresses or phone numbers.

We also went to the town's farmers' market to recruit. One weekend morning early in the spring, we met with the cooperative extension representative at the farmers' market. She introduced us to farmers she knew who had families, and some of them guided us to others at the market. Not knowing any farmers personally, we had difficulty knowing which farmers at the market had families unless they had a child standing with them at the stall. We introduced ourselves, handed out printed flyers, told them about our study, and exchanged contact information if they expressed interest. With 150 vendors at the market, we could not reach many of them in one visit, and so we returned at a later date to continue recruiting. On another weekend, we went to a smaller farmers' market in a nearby town to recruit more families.

We also recruited by asking the families themselves, at the end of each interview, to give us contacts of other farmers they knew who may be interested in participating. Overall, we recruited thirteen families who participated in the interviews. These methods of recruitment—through the cooperative extension representative, the farmers' markets, and snowball recruiting—meant that the group of families we interviewed was limited to small-scale organic farmers who produce vegetables and fruits; animal products, such as meat and eggs; and other farm products, such as cheese, cider, and fiber, as well as cooked foods. Dairy and grain farmers, along with large-scale farmers and farmers in other countries and climates, remained outside of the group of our interviewees.

> **LESSON**
>
> Local recruitment and snowball recruitment yield a homogeneous group of participants. While these types of recruitment are valuable for getting an in-depth understanding of this group, the results may not allow for generalizing the findings to other groups.

## SCHEDULING, GETTING THERE, AND BREAKING THE ICE

We scheduled interviews mostly via email by contacting one of the parents and asking to schedule a visit. As is discussed more in depth later in the chapter, our timing of the study was not ideal for farmers, as work on farms ramps up in early spring, which is when we first got in touch with them. A few of our participants expressed a wish that we were flexible enough in our schedules to come, not based on arbitrary schedules made ahead of time, but based on the weather at a moment's notice. They preferred that we come during a rainy day, when work outside in the fields was limited and they spent more time indoors doing other kinds of work.

We outlined and printed directions to get to the farms using online map services. Some farmers gave us explicit driving directions, stating that relying on online map services or GPS (global positioning satellites) would take us to the wrong place. We drove between thirty and sixty minutes out of town, navigating small roads and admiring beautiful landscape, woods, and farmland. When we arrived at a farm, we were often astonished by the lovely green fields, the chickens, dogs, barn, vegetable gardens, country house, tractors, and other details that had typically been outside of what we see in our everyday academic lives (Figure 3.2).

The homes were cozy, with a lot of do-it-yourself areas and hand-me-down furniture. We loved seeing how they made the houses work for the family. For example, Hickory Hill Farm had two bedrooms for eight people, so the family built an extra nook as a shared bedroom for their two older daughters. In the kitchen, which they built entirely by themselves, they used old seed catalogs as wallpaper (Figure 3.3). Kane Acres Farm dedicated an area off the kitchen as the farm office (Figure 3.4). We noted that houses were generally colder than what we were used to: farm houses were not as energy efficient and insulated as we expected, and the families we visited were sometimes trying to save on heating costs. We learned to dress warmly for interviews that took place on cold days.

**FIGURE 3.2**

A farmhouse and green fields were among the first impressions we had at the outset of every interview.

Along with the common interview packet with consent forms, an interview protocol, two audio recorders (we used both during each interview to have a backup), and a camera, we brought two additional, important items to the interviews: a light meal and a one-hundred-dollar gift card to a local business of their choice. Gift card choices, made when scheduling the interviews, included grocery stores, a hardware store, restaurants, and a children's clothing store. Compensating families with a one-hundred-dollar gift card was a way for us to not only thank them, but also express our recognition of the value of their time. It might be easy to take for granted that home time is not as financially valuable as work time. For those whose lives join home and work, such as farmers, homemakers, teleworkers, and home business owners, home is the workplace, and vice versa. One farmer explicitly mentioned the gift card as the reason why he had agreed to participate in our study. For him, that amount showed that we had understood and taken seriously that his time is worth money too—he is not just farming at home "for fun." Although our financial reimbursement wasn't exceptionally high for these kinds of studies, we believe it encouraged some families to participate despite being swamped in farm work.

We told the families that we would bring pizza to the interview unless it was scheduled in the morning, in which case we offered to bring bagels. We thought of bringing the meal as a way to make it easier for families to spend a few hours with us and not worry about meal preparation time. We were not sure how organic farmers would respond to our offer of pizza, one of the American staples of unhealthy junk food. Only one family explicitly requested that we not bring any food to the interview, and, of course, we respected their request. The others were

**FIGURE 3.3**

The kitchen at Hickory Hill Farm was built entirely by the family. The wallpaper is made of old seed catalogs.

appreciative of our gesture, even though one pizza was not always enough for the entire family, and the pizza was usually cold by the time we arrived at the family's house. The meal we brought became a social icebreaker to set off the visit. We gave the pizza (or bagels) to one of the parents, who usually made the decision whether to open it up right away or keep it for later, after the interview. Some of the families invited us to join them for the meal.

**FIGURE 3.4**

Inside, homes were cozy and messy, with a lot of do-it-yourself areas and furniture. At Kane Acres Farm, the area off the kitchen serves as the farm office.

> **LESSON**
>
> Recognize the value of participants' time by compensating them appropriately, and think about ways to help them participate in the study. A light meal is low cost and goes a long way to establish rapport and reciprocity between the researcher and participants as well as breaking the ice at the outset of the session.

## THE INTERVIEW SESSION

Overall, fifty-three individuals were present in thirteen farm visits, including babies, toddlers, school-aged children, teens, adult children, parents, and grandparents. In ten of the visits, we interviewed as a team. We took turns with one of us leading the session by being responsible for following the interview protocol and the other assisting with follow-up questions and taking pictures. In the other three visits, only one of the researchers was present. Our visits to the farms lasted two to four hours each.

Our method of studying farm families included qualitative, semi-structured interview sessions, in which we sat with the family, usually in the kitchen, living room, or outside in the yard, and asked about practices, strategies, and tools they used for coordinating the work on the farm and for family life. We covered questions about the farm business, everyday activities on the farm and within the family, how all of these activities were coordinated among family members, and how participants felt about and valued being in a farm family. Throughout the interviews, we asked interviewees to show us objects and tools they used for their coordination, organization, and time and task management. We saw many different forms of tools, including calendars hung on kitchen walls; to-do lists written on backs of used envelopes; notebooks with details about seeding, harvesting, and financial transactions; digital spreadsheets that mapped vegetable plots; and chalkboards in barns with lists of projects written on them.

The visits included farm tours, where we asked the families to tell us about the farm business by showing us their farms. As we arrived at the farms, we decided whether to have the interview first and then the farm tour, or the other way around. For example, if the family was already outside, we often asked them to first show us the farm and tell us about the farm business, and then sit for the interview. We did not get a farm tour on a few occasions, for example, if the weather was bad, or if the interview had taken a long time and we sensed that the family was tired.

We had initially planned to interview each family member separately, but after the second interview we found that families preferred to be interviewed together, with some individuals coming in and out of the interview: someone might be coming back from work, going out to take care of animals, attending a crying baby, or the kids were getting tired or going out to play, and so on. The families we interviewed couldn't simply stop their lives and dedicate full attention to us. Other interruptions included neighbors stopping by and children offering us answers to questions we did not ask. These interruptions and the dynamic nature of who is in and who is out of the interview sometimes made following a semi-structured interview protocol difficult. On occasion, the interviews felt chaotic or filled with irrelevant data, and given the time limitations, at times we had to skip questions, rush through the interview, or not get everyone's perspectives on a topic.

At the same time, what initially seemed like irrelevant data sometimes proved to be valuable for a deeper understanding of the family. For example, on the farm tours, we saw vegetable fields and fruit orchards, garden plots and greenhouses, animal shelters and pasturelands, barns and storage areas, farm machinery and food processing equipment, and children's sand boxes and swing sets. Learning about how members of a farm family organize their everyday lives came not only from their wall calendars and to-do lists, but also from how they organize their homes, fields, and barns. At White Birch Farm, for example, a separation between two vegetable garden plots—one tangled and disorganized with chickens roaming inside, and the other well lined up and weeded—indicated the two personalities of Wanda and Jim, the married couple who owned the farm. Observing the difference between the two plots started a conversation on how they can work together on the farm harmoniously without getting on each other's nerves. At Singalong Farm, the play structure was intentionally installed by the greenhouses to keep the children in sight while the parents work. Having families tell us about these aspects (for example, by flipping through a children's book and looking at the children's drawings) was a way for us to build rapport, respect the family, and achieve a better understanding of the dynamic family interactions in a holistic way.

> **LESSON**
>
> Sticking to the study plan can be difficult when dealing with changing family dynamics. One solution is to build in flexibility by having modules that can be asked in different orders. Another is to mark core questions or topics of the study; if the interview ends up being rushed, at least these core questions can get asked. Finally, what initially seems irrelevant to the study can later prove valuable for a deeper understanding of the family.

## POST-INTERVIEW AND DATA ANALYSIS

After each interview, we carried out an informal debriefing session in the car on the way home or in the office the next morning, during which we talked about our observations, early impressions, and feelings following the interview. We also compared and contrasted the most recent interview with previous interviews and started to synthesize our understandings from multiple interviews. Although we did not initially plan for this, talking in the car on the way back turned out to be valuable, because it was the first opportunity for us to reflect on our initial impressions. These discussions were about our personal experiences during the interview, what we had seen, whether it had gone well, what the atmosphere felt like, and feelings that we wanted to share with each other. It also allowed us to let off steam built up from running the interview and taking in a lot of impressions, and sometimes hearing about or observing hardships and conflicts.

The conversations about our early observations, impressions, and feelings were typed into rough, uncensored fieldnotes as we discussed them or immediately afterward. They proved valuable later on; we used them in our analysis, and they helped us recollect our thoughts and feelings immediately following each interview. In addition to these fieldnotes, our data included audio recordings of the interviews, which were later fully transcribed using a transcription service. We also took photographs of objects that families showed us during the interviews. We analyzed the data—transcripts, photographs, and fieldnotes—using open coding, where we read the transcripts and fieldnotes and looked at the photographs over and over, marked them with our thoughts, and looked for common emergent themes.

> **LESSON**
>
> Take some time after each interview to talk about and write down first impressions, observations, and thoughts. This helps researchers let out stress from the interview, documents observations that were not audio recorded or photographed for initial synthesis of multiple interviews, and provides a way to recollect how researchers felt during the interview.

## CHALLENGES AND LESSONS

As we see throughout this book, doing open-ended research in the dynamic, rich context of domestic life poses a number of challenges. In this chapter, we present the unique challenges of studying the specific context of farm families. Next, we discuss the lessons we learned from these challenges and how they could be relevant to a broader set of domestic situations beyond farm life.

## TEMPORAL RHYTHMS AFFECT FAMILY LIFE

We heard from more than one family that they were happy to talk to us, especially on a *rainy day*. Most other days mean a workload of accomplishing as much outdoor farm work as possible, which sometimes does not even allow for lunch breaks, let alone participating in a four-hour research interview. As we were scheduling the interviews through email exchanges, one participant wrote that "*rainy days work best for us.*" This introduced new challenges for us as researchers, who are rarely affected by weather and seasons when we try to recruit participants and schedule interviews.

As we report in Leshed, Håkansson, and Kaye (2014), natural rhythms such as seasons and growth (e.g., vegetables, animals, children) and structural rhythms such as weekly farmers' market days play significant roles in the lives of the farm families we talked to. We conducted our interviews between mid-April and late June, which, in the northeastern United States, coincides with the emergent growing season. In retrospect, we realize this was not an ideal time to talk with farmers. Katie at Kane Acres told us:

> "In March, when it's nice weather you spend every daylight hour out there, because you know all of a sudden it could turn worse."

We learned from the study that as the days get longer and the weather gets better after a dark, frozen winter, farm work gets more intense every week, until it slows down in late fall. As a result, as our study shifted from spring into summer, we noticed that scheduling interviews with the families became increasingly harder; they were simply too busy growing and harvesting, sometimes almost around the clock. During this season, most of our participants were also involved in selling produce at local farmers' markets. These markets often take place on the weekends, which means that farm families are busy preparing for, selling at, and cleaning up after the market on Saturdays and Sundays, when many other families have time off. For us, this unfortunate planning with regard to the seasons meant that we had to be very flexible with our own time and schedule the interviews whenever the families had a gap in all their activities, which for most interviews meant evenings or mornings, sometimes with short notice.

The takeaway lesson is that the *rhythms of particular activities in domestic life matter* (as well as in other contexts, like scientific research, as shown by Jackson et al. [2011]). Life rhythms are likely to affect the running and outcome of a study and are therefore important to take into account, when planning and scheduling short-term studies and when embarking on long-term research endeavors. In our case, the busy growing season likely made it more difficult for us to recruit families.

On the other hand, we had the chance to talk to them when they were particularly busy and therefore had plenty of recent stories to share with us about the challenges of merging family and farm work. One limitation in our study was that we gathered data *only* during the busy season and not, for instance, during the winter, which, the farmers told us, is the season their daily lives are usually slower, and the kinds of activities they engage in are substantially different than in the summer: more finances, accounting, and planning; more indoor activities; and more vacation time. If we had wanted to say something about domestic life in a farm context over the longer term, we would have needed to return to the families on several occasions in order to fully understand how their lives change throughout the seasons.

Farm families are not the only ones influenced by various temporal rhythms. In fact, most families are affected by structural temporal rhythms related to work schedules, school calendars, religious and national holidays, and so forth. Such temporal structures help bring order to a society and at the same time introduce the need for coordination mechanisms to synchronize activities in multiple schedules and calendars (Zerubavel 1981). This also impacts decisions about designing a study with families. Daily work, school, and extracurricular activity schedules are likely to impact when the family is available to interact with the researcher. For instance, school calendars define school days versus vacations and summer breaks and are likely to change the kinds of family activities that take place in different times of the year. Families are also influenced by natural rhythms, and not only those from being on a farm. Big life events, such as birth and death, drastically change the rhythms and routines in a family. For example, one family we tried to recruit was about to have a baby, and with the busy growing season, participating in a study was simply not going to work. On a daily level, mealtimes are dictated by hunger and fullness as opposed to predetermined meal times, and young children are put to bed early in the evening, and some need a daytime nap.

> **LESSON**
>
> When planning a family study, pay attention to families' temporal rhythms at the long and short terms to identify times more suitable to conducting the study. After the study has been completed, it is crucial to understand the temporal context in which it was carried out and how structural and natural rhythms played a factor in the data collection and the findings.

## FAMILY INTERVIEW DYNAMICS

Picture a large wooden kitchen table where multiple family members sit, eat, play, do homework, prepare food, talk, get up, walk away, and come back as neighbors come by to pick something up or drop off their baby for babysitting, dogs bark, the phone rings, and babies cry. In the midst, two researchers are trying to conduct a family interview. This was not an unusual situation for us during the study.

Our original intent, which we expressed when scheduling the interviews, was to have all family members present during each interview, as we wanted to hear a variety of stories and perspectives on farm family life from adults and children alike. However, this did not always happen: in some cases, family members were away for school or work, and in other cases, adult children no longer lived on the farm. Often, we did not know until we arrived how many would be present and who would participate. Further, the number of participants changed over the course of our visit, with people coming and going (having previous commitments) or because of family and farm needs—going to cover the hoop houses before the night frost, or going upstairs to take care of the twin babies waking up from their naps. In two cases, the interviewees explicitly requested an individual interview, not wanting to have their family members involved in the study. These turned into emotionally loaded interviews, with serious tensions emerging around the family and the farm. In other cases, we met people during the interviews who were not direct family members. One family invited their employee to be part of the interview, expanding our concept of what "family" means to them. In other interviews, neighbors, friends, or employees made spontaneous visits. They did not stay for more than few minutes, and the interview was partly on hold during these interruptions. These encounters opened our eyes to, and often brought up discussions around, the strong local ties in these families' lives.

How does one manage and make sense of an interview that involves a group of dynamically changing interviewees in various ages and relationships with the family? It was helpful that we were parents ourselves, as we weren't taken by surprise by what could sometimes look like a minor chaos of activities and children. Furthermore, we tried to be as flexible as possible and talk with whoever was with us at the moment. This made the interviews more manageable time-wise, and they often felt more like relaxed family conversations than formal interviews. At the same time, we had to accept that we probably missed some family members' views while gaining others', and we tried to make the most out of the limited views for our analysis.

As mentioned earlier, we conducted the majority of our interviews together, and we took turns throughout the visit being a "lead" interviewer and an "assistant" interviewer. Having two researchers made it easier overall to remember and manage all the practical details before the interview (picking up a meal and gift card, bringing documentation and equipment, driving, reading driving directions, finding the right place, etc.) and during the interview (organizing consent forms, operating the audio recorders, and photographing objects for documentation). Having two of us was also useful in remembering to ask the important questions, following up on stories, and even continuing the interview with one researcher when a young child was seeking attention from the other. Finally, it was helpful for recalling important and nuanced interactions, discussing what they meant, and supporting each other in the more emotional interview sessions. Therefore, one lesson from our study is to have a higher ratio of interviewers to family members. The numbers do not have to be equal—it would not make sense to bring eleven interviewers to a family of 11—but it is indeed helpful and less overwhelming to interview as a team when meeting large families. On the other hand, one should be cautious about bringing too many researchers, which could overwhelm or intimidate a small number of interviewees; more is not always better.

Of course, not everyone has the resources to bring a team of researchers to a family study. In the cases where only one of us conducted an interview, recording devices were extremely helpful. We audio recorded all sessions and took many pictures of various objects in homes and on the farms, not knowing what was going to be relevant for the analysis as conversations and sights were captured. We simply tried to take everything in during the interview and later, in the analysis, attempted to make sense of all that we had captured and recorded. If during the interview we found it difficult to pay attention to multiple voices simultaneously, recording everything allowed us to return to the interviews later and assemble the voices and perspectives into a fuller picture of the family. An alternative strategy could be to return for multiple visits with the same family to get at aspects that were not covered in previous visits.

---

**LESSON**

Getting multiple views on dynamic family situations can ease the burden of taking in and remembering all the details. Consider having multiple researchers, multiple recording techniques (fieldnotes, audio/video recordings, and pictures), or multiple visits.

---

## HEARING EVERYONE'S VOICES

The families we visited were diverse in terms of number of children (between one and nine) and their ages. For instance, Naomi and Toni from Oak Ridge Farm had a toddler and a baby. Linda and John from Halfmoon Farm had five children: one adult who was married and lived forty minutes away, another child who was attending college and lived at home, and three teenage children. Mary and Don from Spirit Hill Farm had three married daughters with their own young children living about one hour away. This diversity of ages and family situations played a crucial role in managing the interviews.

Although the infants and toddlers were too young to actively contribute by answering questions, their presence at the interviews and their occasional need for attention and care were important sources of information for us. We saw how the families run their lives, and valuable discussions were triggered around the topics of our study.

The young children—preschool and school-aged—were usually enthusiastic about talking with us and did so in their own ways. They wanted our attention and shared their drawings, magazines, toys, schoolwork, garden plots, farm animals, pets, etc. We politely interacted with everyone and looked at everything they shared with us, but at the same time, we were worried that some interview questions were not being answered and that time was taken away from other valuable parts of the interview. After a few interviews, we recognized that the children's participation was valuable to our understanding of practices around merging home and work. For example, farm work was often integrated as hands-on elements in the children's schoolwork, such that the children contributed to running the farm. At Halfmoon Farm, as part of her math education, twelve-year-old Megan was in charge of the finances from selling chicken eggs. For their homeschool science project, the children at Foxtail Farm designed and built a lever to pull down a stairway to a loft bed in the bed and breakfast cabin.

We recognized that children's spontaneous contributions to the interviews, such as showing us objects that at first seemed irrelevant, playing with our recording devices and cameras (Figure 3.5), or taking us on a farm tour, were gateways into stories that proved useful later on. This insight did not make dividing the time we had during the farm visit easier, but it changed our perspective on the children's participation in the interview.

One critical challenge was running a family interview with teenage and adult children. When we were sitting together for the interview, we sometimes (but not always) felt that these children were not comfortable sharing their experiences, thoughts, opinions, and feelings, especially in the presence of their parents. In some cases, the older children participated very little or were excluded from the interview either voluntarily or by the parents scheduling the interview when the children were away. For example, at Greenwood Farm, the parents portrayed a positive picture of a family in which everyone happily collaborates in running the farm.

**FIGURE 3.5**

Five-year-old Micah at Hickory Hill Farm wanted to play with our camera. He took this picture of his Lego set on the kitchen table. Behind the Lego set is the audio recorder. Allowing children access to our equipment was one way we interacted with them, which built rapport that served as gateways into stories that proved useful later on.

The three adult children living at home were present at the interview, but hardly contributed. We sensed a tension "under the hood" that implied the children's opinions were different from their parents', but we couldn't get a hold on the source of this sense, because we did not get the children to talk with us openly and honestly. In other cases, parents talked about conflicts with teenage children. We would have loved to hear the children's sides of these stories, but unfortunately, the parents scheduled the interviews to times when the children were not at home.

These experiences demonstrated the importance of letting everyone share their stories, independent of age and role in a family. Sometimes we felt that we failed to reach some of the personal aspects of experiencing farm life. This was either because of the time-consuming aspects related to young children's need for attention (from parents and researchers) or because of the difficulties in talking with teenage and adult children in the presence of their parents. Yet, recording the aspects related to babies' needs, young children's experiences, and older children's independent opinions are crucial to getting a fuller understanding of a family as a whole. Hearing everyone's voices is more than being polite or respectful to all participants; it is a way to gain a deeper understanding of their everyday lives.

With multiple family members present and wanting to take part (essentially a pleasant difficulty), we struggled with how best to divide our time within the family to make sure that we covered the main themes, at the least. Longer visits would not have solved the problem of letting everyone share their experiences, because spending two to four hours with a family was already taxing, both for the family and for us. Instead, we believe that having more researchers, who could split up between the parents and the children, or returning to the families for multiple visits, would have given us the opportunity to be more thorough in our interviews. We wish we had dedicated special times, and perhaps a separate gift card, to interview increasingly independent older children privately, with the hope that they would open up to tell us about their perspectives.

---

**LESSON**

Dedicate ample resources to get everyone's perspectives: spend more time with the family, return for multiple visits, or bring more researchers to the interview. Pay special attention to getting older children's views; they might not feel comfortable sharing around their parents and other family members.

---

## TENSIONS AND EMOTIONS

How to deal with emotions that come up in interviews is related to the challenge of hearing everyone's voice and showing respect to all participants. In a few interviews, participants shared accounts that were deeply emotional in different ways. We heard stories about a severe work accident that radically changed the situation for one family, and the stress involved for someone whose living depends on physical farm work.

Another interview brought up emotionally draining financial struggles, family conflicts, and bitterness around division of labor and lack of cooperation in the family. Other issues that emerged in our more emotionally loaded interviews were social isolation in a rural environment, loneliness, work overload, parent-teen conflicts, and home maintenance problems. In two separate cases, we interviewed only one participant. The interviews were particularly emotional and felt confession-like, as though they were outlets for participants to talk about things in their lives that worried them and which they might not be able to talk freely with other family members present.

For example, the interview with Nina at Forest Creamery revealed many tensions that leaked out throughout the visit. When we scheduled the interview, we were explicit about wanting to meet and talk with the entire family as much as possible, and that we would be asking about the family and farm coordination practices. Yet, when we arrived at the farm, we were surprised to find out that Nina did not plan to include in the interview her husband, a school teacher, or her two teenage children. She invited us to sit outside in the yard for the interview; it was a beautiful spring afternoon. When her husband and children stopped by the outdoor table later, Nina hardly even introduced them to us. Nina then opened up, delving deep into serious difficulties she was facing with the cheese business operations, finances, and her family relationships. As she spoke to us sincerely about her family conflicts, we understood why Nina wanted to talk without her husband and children present. Throughout the interview, we felt that Nina had a deep need to talk to outsiders and pour out her emotions, conflicts, and fears. She also told us that her house was messy and dirty and that she was too embarrassed to bring us in, explaining why she wanted to have the interview outside in the yard.

In these cases, the emotions, conflicts, and tensions caught us off guard; we were not surprised they were brought up, but we were not exactly prepared for them. We planned an interview protocol that asked ordinary questions about time and task management in a realm where home and work are merged, and it was sometimes difficult to know how to react to a cascade of emotions. It was particularly challenging to move on with the interview without interrupting something we sensed the interviewee felt was very important to them, even if what they were sharing was of little relevance to our study. Our strategy was mostly to listen, confirm that we were following their story, and allow them to talk freely. When we sensed that they had covered a story, we gently steered them into talking about our original themes again. In especially emotional interviews, the participants explicitly thanked us afterward for taking the time to let them talk about their lives, which in these cases felt rewarding to us.

As with the previous challenges we faced, we later recognized that learning about the dark side of these people's lives was valuable for us to gain a fuller picture of who they are, even if some of the tensions, conflicts, and emotions were not always directly related to our research goals. They helped us see beyond the positive stereotype of healthy farmers growing organic foods in lovely green meadows, and we felt closer to them, seeing them as real people with real struggles, fears, and hopes. Chapter 13 goes into more detail about conducting studies in situations where conflict is present in a family and ways for managing this conflict.

> **LESSON**
>
> Emotions and conflicts are unique in each family, and whether one is a novice or an experienced interviewer, preparing for them in advance can be difficult. Be generous with time both when planning the study—have fewer questions to reduce the risk of having to rush through them—and in allowing people to take their time when telling their stories.

## SUMMARY

Some of the challenges we faced in the study are just part of dealing with human participants. People don't show up, or they don't respond as expected, or they are sidetracked and take the interview in different directions. Researchers need to be prepared that these events might happen and respect their participants in such cases. As mothers, we were prepared for crying babies, interruptions from hungry children, and family conflicts, which we expected to see when visiting family homes. At the same time, we were struck by challenges we did not expect, which came about from interviewing families in a setting we were not familiar with and that we were trying to make sense of in a short time. Although we knew that farmers' lives are shaped by the weather and seasons, their work is physical in nature, and they live in rural areas, we did not know exactly how these would affect not only the findings of our study, but also running the study itself.

In some cases, we were left wondering how we could have gained more out of some of the interviews. We were surprised to get to a farm and find out that only part of the family was participating in the interview, although we had specifically requested beforehand to have all of the members present. We were concerned when we sensed some family members were hiding conflicts that showed up in their interactions. And we were worried as the time for the interview went by, when children were getting tired, or it was getting too dark outside to carry out a farm tour. At the same time, we tried to look at these challenges as sources for better understanding our interviewees' lives, identities, and values. In the end, we believe that we were able to get the most out of many of the family interviews with the limited time and resources we had and despite the challenges we faced.

Although some of the challenges might seem relevant to farm families only, we drew lessons from them that extend beyond the farm to many kinds of families in a wide range of situations:

1. Families have prior commitments and needs, which shape their temporal rhythms and the synchronization between those rhythms. Researchers need to recognize and respect those rhythms and minimize friction that may be caused by trying to tap into the families' everyday lives.

2. With multiple people at various ages and changing needs, a family study could become highly dynamic and continually changing. Dedicating more resources, such as a bigger research team, more recording devices, and possibly multiple visits, could be effective for capturing an overall picture of the family.

3. Families are composed of individuals, each having their own views and perspectives that can deviate from each other, seem irrelevant, or sidetrack from the main themes of the study. Hearing everyone's voices is not only a way for the researcher to demonstrate respect for the family, but can also provide valuable insights that emerge only in the analysis.

4. Every family has tensions and conflicts, and when going into a study that involves families, researchers have to be aware that those may come up. Participants letting off steam, even if not directly related to the study, provides a more holistic picture and allows for building rapport with the researcher.

We were driven to study farm families by our goal to learn about a group of families that had not been previously examined in the HCI field. By merging home and work on a farm, this group exhibited family coordination practices that had not been examined and designed for in previous family technologies. Interviewing farm families helped us identify blind spots in how we understand family life in the HCI field and gave us insights into new ways of designing family technologies.

Studying farm families not only expanded the design space of family technologies, an important aspect in the HCI field, but it also expanded the methodological space of running family studies. By deviating from the kind of family we expect to see in a family study and studying one that is *not* like our own family, we were also able to gain valuable insights into carrying out a family study in general, the opportunities it brings, and the challenges we would face. In other words, studying farm families expanded our methodological thinking about conducting studies with families. Would we do things differently if we had the chance to repeat this study? Definitely, but this would not guarantee overcoming or leaving out challenges. After all, with challenges come opportunities, insights, depth, and rigor in research.

## REFERENCES

Davidoff, S., Zimmerman, J., Dey, A.K., 2010. How Routine Learners Can Support Family Coordination. In: Proceedings of the SIGCHI Conference on Human Factors in Computing Systems (CHI '10). ACM Press, New York, NY.

Håkansson, M., Sengers, P., 2013. Beyond Being Green: Simple Living Families and ICT. In: Proceedings of the ACM Conference on Computer-Human Interaction (CHI '13). ACM Press, New York, NY.

Jackson, S.J., Ribes, D., Buyuktur, A., Bowker, G.C., 2011. Collaborative Rhythm: Temporal Dissonance and Alignment in Collaborative Scientific Work. In: Proceedings of the Computer Supported Cooperative Work (CSCW). ACM Press, New York, NY.

Kline, R.R., 2000. Consumers in the Country: Technology and Social Change in Rural America. Johns Hopkins University Press, Baltimore, MD.

Leshed, G., Håkansson, M., Kaye, J., 2014. "Our life is the farm and farming is our life": Home–Work Coordination in Organic Farm Families." In: Proceedings of Computer Supported Cooperative Work (CSCW). ACM Press, New York, NY. To appear.

Leshed, G., Sengers, P., 2011. "I lie to myself that I have freedom in my own schedule": productivity tools and experiences of busyness. In: Proceedings of the ACM Conference on Computer-Human Interaction (CHI). ACM Press, New York, NY.

Neustaedter, C., Brush, A.J., Greenberg, S., 2009. The Calendar Is Crucial: Coordination and Awareness through the Family Calendar. ACM Transactions on Computer-Human Interaction (ToCHI) 16 (1), 1–48.

Odom, W., Zimmerman, J., Forlizzi, J., 2010. "Designing for Dynamic Family Structures: Divorced Families and Interactive Systems." In: Proceedings of the Designing Interactive Systems (DIS). ACM Press, New York, NY.

Smith, M.E., Nguyen, D., Lai, C., Leshed, G., Baumer, E., 2012. "Going to College and Staying Connected: Communication between College Freshmen and Their Parents." In: Proceedings of the Computer Supported Cooperative Work (CSCW). ACM Press, New York, NY.

Strange, M., 2008. Family Farming: A New Economic Vision. The Institute for Food and Development Policy.

Woods, M., 2011. Rural. Routledge, New York, NY.

Wyche, S.P., Grinter, R.E., 2012. This Is How We Do It in My Country: A Study of Computer-Mediated Family Communication among Kenyan Migrants in the United States. In: Proceedings of the Computer Supported Cooperative Work (CSCW). ACM Press, New York, NY.

Yardi, S., Bruckman, A., 2012. Income, Race, and Class: Exploring Socioeconomic Differences in Family Technology Use. In: Proceedings of the SIGCHI Conference on Human Factors in Computing Systems (CHI '12). ACM Press, New York, NY.

Yarosh, S., Chew, Y.C., Abowd, G.D., 2009. Supporting Parent–Child Communication in Divorced Families. International Journal of Human-Computer Studies (IJHCI) 67 (2), 192–203.

Zerubavel, E., 1981. Hidden Rhythms: Schedules and Calendars in Social Life. University of Chicago Press.

# Wear Nice Socks: Guidance for Conducting In-Home Studies with Children

# 4

**Elizabeth Foss, Mona Leigh Guha, Allison Druin**
*Human-Computer Interaction Lab, University of Maryland, College Park, MD, USA*

## INTRODUCTION

In 2008, our team at the Human-Computer Interaction Lab (HCIL) at the University of Maryland, USA, formed a research partnership with Google when we were granted a Faculty Research Award to investigate how children search on the Internet. The goal of this partnership was loosely defined; we believed that children's interactions with open-Internet search interfaces (i.e. interfaces with uncurated and unrestricted content) were poorly researched, and so we wanted to more deeply understand how children behaved as searchers. Although a body of research had developed around children as searchers, none of the existing research approached children in their homes as users of the unrestricted Internet or had attempted to understand children searching holistically in the context of other tasks. We thought that, with children as a growing segment of search interface users, there was an opportunity to study child searchers from a fresh-slate perspective. In order to achieve this, our data collection strategy combined elements from several methods, which are explained in the following section.

## EMPIRICAL APPROACH

We approached our research without any preconceived notions or theories of how children search online. The goal of our initial exploratory study was to allow our collected data to point us toward conclusions and theories regarding children's search behaviors rather than attempt to prove an existing theory. Our data-driven approach was consistent with the Grounded Theory method. In Grounded Theory, researchers begin studies by empirically exploring a particular phenomenon. After collecting only a small amount of data, researchers initiate analysis, seeking to uncover similar patterns across sources. Armed with initial patterns as directions for continued research, researchers return to data collection to further explore these patterns in an iterative pattern, driven by data (Strauss 2003). Grounded Theory differs from experimental research, where researchers approach their study with the goal of testing an already-formed hypothesis (Lazar, Feng, and Hochheiser 2010).

Within Grounded Theory, researchers can use any number of data collection techniques. For our study of how children searched in the home, we decided to conduct semi-structured interviews. This style of interview can be broadly defined, but our research context meant that we followed a prepared interview script while deviating freely as needed to clarify or explore ideas more deeply. Semi-structured interviews allow researchers to pursue unique or novel lines of inquiry or to ask for clarification (Lazar et al. 2010). We thought that both of these allowances would be useful, given the lack of in-home and open-Internet research on children searchers and the young ages of the participants in our studies.

The remaining aspect of our empirical approach was our participant-observation data collection technique, drawn from ethnographic research. Participant observation allows researchers to be more interactive with participants when exploring phenomenon, clarifying participant actions, and—most advantageous to our research context—checking that participants actually do what they believe and report they are doing (LeCompte and Preissle 1993). As part of our semi-structured interviews, we requested that the participants demonstrate their search behaviors by giving them search tasks that ranged in difficulty and included self-generated as well as imposed tasks. By asking our child participants to conduct searches while we observed, we were able to uncover aspects of their behaviors that they might otherwise have forgotten (Lazar et al. 2010).

## CHILDREN'S SEARCHING IN THE HOME

From the outset of our productive partnership with Google, we wanted to gain a clearer understanding of the problems, skills, and typical behaviors children displayed when searching in the home. At the time we began our research, much of the existing literature surrounding children and search had been conducted in schools or public libraries (e.g., Chelton and Cool 2004). Educational settings can impose restrictions on children when searching (Gross 2006; Selwyn, Potter, and Cranmer 2009). However, prior research has found that children are most likely to go on the Internet in their homes (Rideout, Foehr, and Roberts 2010). There are two key distinctions for search in the home environment versus the school environment: at home, there is more time available to children for exploring the open Internet (Rideout et al. 2010), and for older children especially, there is less-restricted access to the open Internet (Livingstone, Bober, and Helsper 2005). Figure 4.1 illustrates an example home search environment for a pair of male siblings in the children's Internet search studies. The differences from a school or library setting are apparent: the boys' computers are paused on different online games, there are numerous alternate activities present, a couch provides a high level of physical comfort, and there are headphones for immersion and a mouse that supports that child's preferred method of input.

**FIGURE 4.1**

A typical home search environment.

In this chapter, we describe our experiences during our in-home research studies, detailing the processes of recruiting, scheduling, interviewing, and following up with participants. We discuss the challenges we encountered, both expected and unexpected, and we give our approaches to ameliorating the complications of conducting in-home research with children. The chapter is divided into major sections presenting our research method, our preparations before the in-home visits, and events during data collection in the field.

## METHOD

This chapter draws on our experiences during three separate in-home studies conducted with children aged between seven and seventeen. For each study, we visited the homes of participants and interviewed children as well as parents in order to understand children's Internet search behaviors in the home. The child interviews were planned as semi-structured and observational; we often broke away from our script to understand responses more deeply, and we asked the child participants to complete search tasks while we observed. Our interviews with parents aided us in constructing a more complete picture of each child by establishing early childhood computer use and household rules and norms surrounding digital media. Over the course of the three studies, we conducted 341 in-home interviews with 236 unique parent and child participants. The first study captured the search behaviors of young children. Following the initial study, we investigated the search behaviors of adolescents using a separate group of participants. During the final iteration of this research, we revisited participants from the first study to understand changes in search behaviors over time. All studies were conducted in the United States.

## PARTICIPANTS

In 2008, our child participants were seven, nine, or eleven years old (Druin et al. 2010; Foss et al. 2012). At least one parent of each child was also interviewed. We enrolled a total of eighty-three children in the study, with an even gender distribution. Our participants lived mainly in suburban Maryland, with a small number living in rural areas in Virginia.

For our study of adolescents in 2011, 38 participants, fourteen to seventeen years old (Foss et al. 2013), agreed to be interviewed while they conducted searches. As in our earlier study, a parent of each adolescent participated. The majority of our adolescent participants lived in suburban Maryland, with a slightly higher percentage than in the 2008 study residing in rural Virginia.

In 2013, we returned to our participants from the 2008 study in order to conduct a longitudinal study. We were able to reengage fifty of the original eighty-three participants. In the time elapsing between the studies, the children had aged to between ten and fifteen years old (Foss 2014).

## DATA COLLECTION

During each home visit for all three studies, we first interviewed the parent, asking the child participant to be somewhere in the home where he or she could not hear the interview. Asking the children to remain out of earshot enabled parents to more naturally respond during their interviews and ensured that parental interview responses did not bias the children. We asked parents about their household rules and the child's searching habits in order to obtain context for the child interview. Parent interviews were recorded using audio as well as handwritten notes. After completing the parent interview, we interviewed the child participants as they used their preferred device, such as an iPhone, a tablet, or computer to search. Children also used their preferred search interface until the final search tasks, when they were all directed to use Google in order to allow for the uniform analysis of approaches to search tasks.

We began the interview by asking general questions such as the amount of time the child spent using the computer, then moved into search tasks. (There were five during the 2008 study, with a more difficult sixth task added in 2011 and 2013 due to the older ages of the participants.) We concluded the interview by asking for opinions on the Google search interface and the challenging aspects of searching. In order to record the spoken and interface interaction events, we videotaped the children from a wide angle (see Figure 4.2), capturing the participant and their device, and we also kept detailed handwritten notes of queries entered and clicking behavior. Across all three studies, interviews with children ranged between fifteen and fifty-four minutes. In keeping with our Grounded Theory approach, we iteratively

**FIGURE 4.2**

Camera positioning during the Internet searching studies. The wide angle captures the child, the computer screen, and the environment.

analyzed the data collected during each study, allowing our theories about children's search to emerge naturally.

## LESSONS AND CHALLENGES

### PREPARING FOR AN IN-HOME STUDY

At the beginning of our children's study, we tried to anticipate differences between lab-based and home-based research and determine practices that would ease shifting from the lab to the home for our research. Our approach included acquiring explicit ethical permissions for all of our planned research, reflecting on the qualifications of researchers before involving them with the study, approaching families as respectfully as possible, and considering our own comfort and safety while working in the field. Scheduling interviews and anticipating issues with recruiting participants proved to be more challenging. In this section, we describe our planned approaches and our responses to recruitment and scheduling challenges.

#### *Ethical Considerations*

Participants under the age of eighteen in the United States are considered a protected population by the U.S. Department of Health and Human Services. Researchers working with this population are subject to more ethical regulations than for studies with adult participants. These ethical guidelines exist to protect the welfare of vulnerable populations (e.g., children and people with disabilities). For academic researchers, these guidelines are enforced at the university level by institutional review boards (IRB). In the context of the children's Internet searching studies, we were careful to gain pre-approval for all the recruiting, protocol, data collection, and data management strategies we used, as well as plan our research studies to prevent any harm to the participants.

While our university's IRB required us to obtain parental consent for each child's participation, it did not require us to obtain signed assent forms from our child participants. Even though we did not need the forms, we obtained verbal assent from each child for participation in the study and for recording via video camera prior to beginning each interview. In cases where a parent had given us permission to record but the child objected to the camera, we did not tape the interview, and instead relied on handwritten notes. We believed that our presence in the home space required us to respect the children's decisions to participate or abstain and ensure their comfort with videotaping.

### Researchers Experienced with Children

Because of our lab's focus on designing new technologies for children, we were able to populate our initial research team with researchers who already had experience working with children. Their experiences prior to working in our lab included leading after-school programs, teaching in early childhood or elementary settings, being camp counselors, and working in clinical settings for children and adolescents with mental health issues. After joining our lab, researchers spent two afternoons a week and two weeks during the summer working with children to design new technologies. These researchers learned co-design techniques that emphasized the importance of elaboration during ideation; the careful balance of child-to-adult leadership in communication during ideation; and the informality of dress, names, and working on the floor.

Many skills we had learned from working with children in the lab or other settings were useful when we interviewed children in the home. First, the children responded well to researchers who had learned to communicate equitably and without judgment despite age differences, which is one of the main tenets of our work with children in the lab. For example, we found it was useful to admit when we did not understand a child's response. Instead of asking the children to restate, which would frustrate some of them, we asked them to correct our restatements of their thoughts, placing the children in the position of expert. Second, children's behavior toward us was not universally polite, and some children were easily distracted. We were able to respond to these situations in a patient, friendly, and encouraging manner rather than take offense or attempt to rush children to respond to our questions. We believe that our ability to do this came in part from logging many hours working with children before beginning this research. Finally, some children gave unexpected responses to questions, and we accepted these answers, attributing the misunderstandings to our protocol rather than pressing them for other answers and assuming that a misunderstanding was their fault. For example, we asked a seven-year-old girl about the design of the search engine results page. Rather than getting an evaluation of the usability of the page as we had asked for, we received her thoughts on the content of the page:

> **Researcher**: Well, what do you think is good about that page?
> **Seven-year-old girl**: It's helping dogs. It puts on sale that sometimes you can buy to take care of it like it's your own baby.
> **Researcher**: Okay. And then so that's something good. Is there stuff that's bad about that page?
> **Seven-year-old-girl**: Well, if they get married, that's a little bit bad.
> **Researcher**: If they get married that's a little bit bad?
> **Seven-year-old-girl**: Mm-hmm.
> **Researcher**: Okay.

With this particular child, a novice and unsure searcher, researchers thought that pressing her toward a "right" answer could not only make her uncomfortable, but also influence her candid responses to our remaining questions.

---

**LESSON**

When working with children, involving researchers with previous experience working with children is advantageous. If researchers without prior experience with children are involved, modeling an encouraging and empowering interview style can result in better experiences for participants and better data.

---

## Respect for Participants and Family Norms

From the outset of our research, we attempted to remain as open as possible in the language we used when communicating with families. To this end, our interview script asked parents to discuss their "spouse or partner" instead using of gender-specific terms like husband or wife, and we only inquired about other adults in the home if there was some preceding indication of the presence of a co-parent. When we emailed potential participants, we were careful to refer to their "home" rather than "house"; house implies a stand-alone structure, and we did not want to make assumptions about the family's living situation. During the multi-year span between the 2008 study and the study with the same participants in 2013, we found that many families had experienced divorce. This affected our communication with parents. We generally had the contact information for only one parent, and many parents would copy their ex-spouse into our email exchanges, causing complications in scheduling as the parents worked out which home the children would be in at the time of the interview and whether both parents would attend.

Conducting research in the homes of participants required us to be aware of community values and differing household norms. Many families remove their shoes before entering the home because of cultural customs or young children playing on the floor, and we could usually spot these homes by the shoes piled up on the front porch or inside the front door. We made sure to wear socks and shoes instead of stockings or sandals and to ask if we should take off our shoes before crossing the threshold into the home. Some parents expected their children to call us "ma'am" or "sir," which interfered with the more informal tone we attempted to maintain during the interviews with children; this was usually easily solved by saying to the child, "Oh, you don't have to call me ma'am!" Finally, many families insisted that we stay and eat dinner with them as guests after the interview, and this invitation felt impolite to decline, especially when parents prepared extra food for us while we interviewed their children. During a home visit to interview siblings, a ten-year-old girl and a twelve-year-old boy, the mother not only popped popcorn to snack on, but also baked chocolate chip cookies, offering both mid-interview to the researcher and the children. We generally accepted mid-interview food, but as graciously as possible refused offers of dinner after the interviews were completed.

> **LESSON**
>
> Be prepared for participants' norms and customs to be different from the researcher's, and adapt behavior in response. Don't make assumptions regarding participants' homes or family structures.

### Curiosity, Safety, and Trust

When conducting in-home research with children, there is a need to establish trust between researchers and the participating families, as participants allow researchers who are strangers to enter their homes. We attempted to have a high level of transparency for the goals, motivations, and funding source of the Internet searching studies as well as personally for each involved researcher. Throughout the studies, we maintained an updated website containing not only the purposes of our research, but also a complete listing and email addresses of all faculty and students involved with the study. Through our website, participants could verify our affiliation with the university and with the HCIL and contact us via our professional emails and phones, if needed. We shared the link to our website with potential participants in our recruitment flyers and initial contact emails. Prior to each interview, we informed participants of the names of the researchers who would be coming to their homes, as, occasionally, email exchanges would be with one researcher, yet a different researcher conducted the interview. During the 2011 study, a parent remarked to us that her daughter had been curious about us prior to the interview, and rather than use our website to find our university profiles, the adolescent had looked us up using Facebook.

For future studies, perhaps including photos and brief biographies for each researcher on the study website and in recruitment emails would alleviate some of the curiosity felt by adolescent participants about researchers who are visiting their homes.

> **LESSON**
>
> Maintain transparency of the research to allow participants to verify researchers' credentials.

In addition to facilitating trust from participant families, we also considered the need for our own physical safety in the field, as we were entering the homes of people we did not know. We did not have the ability to investigate our participants in the same way that they could verify us. We traveled to largely unfamiliar neighborhoods and homes, and many of our interviews took place after dark, particularly during the winter months, when the sun sets earlier. During the 2011 study, interviews were scheduled even later in the evenings, as older children have later bedtimes and more after-school commitments. For safety reasons, when visiting study homes after dark, our team often felt more comfortable working in pairs. We also made sure to visit gas stations close to our university or our own homes and to lock our cars, especially when we parked on the street. During the 2013 study, as participant families were familiar to us and we had visited their neighborhoods during the 2008 study, we felt more comfortable in the field, even late in the evening.

> **LESSON**
>
> Working in unfamiliar field locations requires additional planning to ensure researchers' safety.

### Recruitment

Accessing children for in-home research is not easy. Parents and schools act as gate-keepers for children and adolescents, ensuring children are not contacted by unfamiliar adults. As a result, recruiting children is indirect, as recruitment is not aimed directly at the participant group, but rather at parents. Our recruitment methods were not all successful, particularly at the beginning of our research. In 2008, we began recruiting by using campus-based emails and posting flyers. After three months, we had conducted only 8 percent of our planned 120 interviews, so we employed broader recruitment methods. The in-person strategy of recruiting at a public library led to only two interviews and required a significant amount of effort and time to coordinate. We also recruited in a rural location to broaden the demographic profile of our participants. However, the name of our university and lab carried little to no weight in this location, and this effort resulted in only a small percentage of our interviews. Adolescents proved to be especially difficult for us to recruit. We noticed a number of parents of adolescents contacting us to ask if we planned to offer incentives for participation, a much more common question than during the 2008 study. We were, in fact, offering a ten-dollar Amazon.com gift card or a study t-shirt, but it is possible that the value of these incentives was not great enough to provide external motivation for participation. Upon finding out we were offering only ten-dollar gift cards to adolescent participants, one mother relayed her son's reaction: "Thx but son says Google makes billions and could give him 40"

A more successful recruitment strategy was to reach out to our personal networks and organized parent groups. We contacted our networks of friends, family, acquaintances, and coworkers, asking anyone with children of our target ages to participate. This strategy led to nearly a third of our 2008 study interviews. Our personal networks provided much of our adolescent sample. Almost half of the families participating in the 2011 study were personally known by a researcher on our team. The personal connections likely aided us by lowering the barrier of entry into homes; potential participants were more likely to welcome us into their homes as trustworthy acquaintances than as unfamiliar researchers. Parent-Teacher Associations (PTAs) also proved to be extremely helpful to our recruitment efforts. These parent groups, which were associated with public schools, had existing channels for distributing information; each PTA had monthly newsletters, monthly meetings, and email mailing lists, and comprised involved parents who were willing to distribute our message. PTA contacts resulted in 30 percent of all our interviews.

> **LESSON**
>
> Recruitment should be ongoing, multifaceted, and responsive to strategies that work while discarding those that do not. Personal networks and existing groups are particularly useful in disseminating information.

### Scheduling

The task of scheduling our in-home interviews with both children and adolescents proved difficult. From our perspective, the research was work, and we wanted to contain the interviews to business hours as much as possible. For the participating families, the research was extra-curricular, and as it would take place in their homes, would need to be conducted during leisure time. From the outset of the studies, we were at odds with the participants when scheduling the in-home interviews, and we quickly learned that we needed to adjust our scheduling expectations. When doing research in homes, it has been our experience that being flexible with our time has been quite necessary.

Scheduling in-home research with children is challenging, as not only must the child's schedule be accommodated, but parental presence is needed, as well. In the context of our search studies, we needed to find times to visit homes that worked for us, for the children, for at least one parent, and often for siblings as well, as other children in the household depended on their parents for transportation to after-school activities. During the school year, children were not available until late in the afternoon, and often had homework assignments, sports practices, scouting, and other commitments, and adolescents in particular had busier schedules than younger children. One mother illustrated the trials of scheduling in an email:

> If I'm not needed much, he ends camp at 5 Mon and Wed and could work with you at my office. Otherwise we would have to make it Tuesday 7:15 at my house. We have something at 7 on Thursday night. I usually work until 7 Mon and Wed. Friday traffic is terrible. So let me know.

At the outset of the studies, we thought that national and religious holidays and school breaks would provide us with periods of rapid data collection, as children's availability would not be constrained by their school attendance. Instead, we found that families were likely to be traveling during these times. Even if families remained local, parents communicated to us that school breaks and holidays were particularly busy times for their family, and would ask us to contact them at later dates. During all three studies, even when we successfully found times for interviews, sometimes illness, snowy or icy weather, and simply forgetting that researchers were coming all made rescheduling the sessions necessary.

We adopted strategies to ease the scheduling difficulties early in the 2008 study and continued our practices through the adolescent and longitudinal studies. After experiencing trouble with communicating with parents in the weeks surrounding school breaks, we learned to check the schedules for the local county, city, or private schools prior to emailing PTAs or parents. We attempted to have a researcher available every weekday afternoon and evening, beginning around three in the afternoon when children would arrive home from school, and lasting until around eight at night, the latest we expected to be in participants' homes.

We coordinated our personal schedules by using a cloud-based shared calendar. Although we each experienced a slight loss of privacy by sharing our personal schedules, any member of the research team was able to see at a glance our available times, regardless of which researcher was emailing with a potential participant. Through the practice of sharing calendars, we were able to schedule each other to conduct interviews with minimal time lapses in email exchanges with potential participants; we found that rapid response times led to a much higher rate of successfully enrolling participants. Our busiest time turned out to be around four in the afternoon; for all three studies, we completed 28 percent of the interviews immediately as children returned home from school. We made an effort to not conduct interviews on weekends, as even the most avid researchers need days off. However, despite our attempts to confine interviews to weekday evenings, we conducted 17 percent of the interviews for all three studies on either a Saturday or a Sunday, as weekends provided families with unscheduled time in their homes. Chapter 3 goes into more depth about considering families' temporal, structural, and natural rhythms when scheduling interviews and planning studies with families.

## LEAVING THE LAB BEHIND

As we transitioned from our in-lab preparations to fieldwork, we encountered several unforeseen challenges. Parent and child participants were occasionally hesitant regarding our use of video recording equipment, and we found that parents could derail or facilitate our interviews with their children. The home environment had effects on our studies, as children could be easily distracted, and our presence in the home altered the families' normal schedules. Finally, we came to understand that addressing the needs of our own team allowed us to be more effective researchers. The following section describes our approaches to alleviating these events.

### Oh, You're Recording?

During our email communications with parents prior to the interviews, we were explicit that we planned on video or audio recording our interactions if the family was comfortable. During these initial communications, a few families indicated that they would be uncomfortable with the use of recording devices. As one mother replied in an email, "We are NOT comfortable with the videotaping of the children but if you can proceed without that, that's fine." Another parent was unsure about how we would maintain the recording: "Not sure about videotaping, unless it is required for the study and won't be publicly available." Based on these reactions, we amended our standard email to include assurances that families could participate without recording if they preferred. Once we were in homes, several parents hastily cleaned off the desk space that would be in the camera frame, not wanting the clutter or personal documents such as bills to be recorded.

In all three studies, upon our arrival at the home, we asked parents to consent to audio recording their interview. All of our parent participants agreed to audio recording, except for one father near the end of the 2013 study. This father was very forthcoming regarding his daughter's overuse of her iPad and stated that he would not have been as open if he were being recorded.

We obtained written consent from the parents to interview their children. A section of the child consent form contained two options: we could either use or not use photo and video clips in future presentations or publications. While the younger participants in the studies showed little interest in the consent process, some of the older participants were curious about the forms and weighed in on whether to allow us to use their interviews in academic forums. As soon as we understood that the adolescent participants were concerned about the use of their data, we altered our consent form to include a third option, which required us to allow families to review and approve any photos or videos to be shared with a larger audience. Based on the number of parents initialing their agreement to this option over the blanket permission or non-permission, our perception is that participants appreciated and preferred the increased control over the use of their data. The experience with consent in the search studies leads us to implications for future studies. Due to the home setting, the adolescents were more comfortable and assertive than they might have been in the lab setting, which encouraged their self-advocacy. In future research, we will include detailed consent options to facilitate the empowerment of our participants, regardless of the context in which the study is conducted.

During the three studies, only six of the 171 child interviews were not video recorded due to child or parental preference. Since we were in the homes of participants, we did not have any macro recording software installed on the participants' computers as we would have had in a lab setting, so our only source of data for non-videotaped interviews was our handwritten notes. We asked for participants' patience as we would be slow in recording their responses and actions, although by working in pairs, with two researchers taking notes on the same interview, we were able to minimize data loss.

> **LESSON**
>
> Participants of all ages care about the protection of their personal information. Providing them with detailed options for the future use of their interview data is important, as is being prepared to rely on non-digital methods of preserving interactions with them.

## Parents Observing Interviews

After we concluded interviews with parents, we gave them the option of observing their child's interview and asked them not to aid their child in any way. Some parents relayed to us that they thought their presence would interfere with their child's participation and remained out of the room; some sat nearby and attentively listened; and others would busily fold laundry, work on another computer, or begin preparing dinner nearby. These occupied parents were clearly listening, but for the child, they faded into the background of normal household activity.

Of the parents who remained physically present and attentive during the interviews, many were asked direct questions by their children. We generally intervened prior to the parent responding by saying, for example, "We asked your dad not to answer." However, in-context redirection by parents was much more difficult. Some parents would directly answer their child's questions despite our request that they remain uninvolved, and others would prompt their children into "right," alternative, or lengthier answers. One mother observing our interview with her seven-year-old son was particularly notable. The mother repeatedly told her son to focus, asked him if he was experiencing spelling difficulty, and directed him to answer researcher questions when he was non-responsive. We learned to stress the importance of non-interference to parents prior to beginning the child interview. It was occasionally helpful to explain our research to the parent using the same words that we used with the children; anything the children demonstrated was showing us how children approach Internet search, and we were not looking for right or wrong answers.

---

**LESSON**

Parents can be overly invested in their child's performance during research studies, and minimizing parental interference can be difficult to do politely. Preparing friendly redirection statements that are appropriate to use in the presence of the child participant can avoid problems with parental interference.

---

### Corroboration

We interviewed parents prior to interviewing children and asked the children to leave the room when we talked with their parents, although we invited parents to observe interviews with their children. We posed some of our interview questions to both parents and children during their separate interviews in order to obtain not only a complete picture of the child's search habits, but also to establish a gauge of the accuracy and honesty of the child's responses. The most banal of the duplicate questions pertained to the amount of time spent on the computer in terms of days per week, sessions per day, and session length. We expected our younger participants to experience difficulty answering these questions, and in the case of the children ages seven or nine, asking parents to answer these questions provided us with accurate responses. However, we found that during our 2011 study, parents would profess to house rules regarding short permissible lengths of time for computer, television, or video game use, while adolescents would occasionally contradict parental statements by relaying that they used the computer for many hours per day. In these cases, we believe the adolescents provided more accurate responses, as adolescents were more likely to use computers independently. During our time in the homes, we did not observe any tensions arising between the adolescents and their parents due to our questioning.

For our child participants in particular, we received unlikely responses to some interview questions. For example, consider this exchange between a nine-year-old boy and a researcher:

> **Researcher**: How much do you search the web for fun?
> **Nine-year-old boy**: Ten hours, maybe.
> **Researcher**: Like in a week?
> **Nine-year-old boy**: Oh, no, like in day.
> **Researcher**: Ten hours in one day! Alright. You search a lot.

Another participant, also a nine-year-old boy, when asked what made him use the computer, responded, "I usually use Mozilla Firefox," while his parents relayed that his usual computer use was to play games. We accepted such answers during the course of the interviews and did not challenge the participants on their responses. In these cases, the corroboration of the parent interviews was extremely helpful.

> **LESSON**
>
> Corroboration is helpful. Young children are not always accurate in their responses, and parents can provide clear information. Adolescents are generally more independent and able to describe their own habits more accurately than their parents can.

### What Was the Question Again?

Conducting in-home research has inherent distractions for young participants that are not present for research conducted in the lab setting. Other people were often the source of interruptions during the search studies. As an unusual occurrence, our presence in the homes sometimes drew rowdy siblings into the rooms where we were conducting interviews with participants. Many parents proceeded with their normal routines of cooking dinner or starting loads of laundry while we interviewed their children, so we often talked over the noise of blenders, vacuum cleaners, and loud conversations in the next room. To compensate for household distractions, we learned that asking the participant if they needed a question repeated would redirect their attention, and we also took breaks from the interview for long interruptions such as discussions with parents about homework or visitors to the family home.

Other people in the home environment were not always the causes of distraction during the interviews. Many children were already on their computers when researchers arrived at the home and did not want to stop playing games and transition into being interviewed. As we entered homes with the intention of collecting naturalistic data on children's computer use, we felt that directing children to focus their entire attention on the interview might create an artificial scenario, so we allowed children to engage with us however they were comfortable. When it was necessary for children to conduct searches, we showed them how to pause and minimize their games to return at a later time rather than insisting on their full attention. Adolescents and especially the older longitudinal participants had their cell phones present in the home. Although no participants sent messages or answered their phones while being interviewed, they did receive texts, notifications, and phone calls. Background events in the home environment not only caused distraction as they occurred, but also caused difficulty when we later watched and transcribed the interviews, as the voices of our young participants were easily drowned out by their surroundings.

During our research, we accepted these distractions and the later difficulties they caused with transcription as necessary when researchers desire the natural environment as the context. If we had chosen to alter the normal environment by asking parents to lock up pets, send siblings away, and remain aware of our recording devices, we would have created an artificial setting. In our pursuit of real-world computer use behaviors, we believed that minimal intervention was more important than uniform and quiet interview settings.

> **LESSON**
>
> Accepting the distractions in the home environment is necessary when seeking naturalistic data. To help children focus, researchers can allow breaks, repeat or restate questions, or ease the transition away from a preferred activity.

### How Much Longer Are You Staying?

During the searching studies, we found that we had to manage our time to accommodate the routines of the family. Our arrival time in homes often coincided with the end of the school day. We found that many parents would complete our brief interview about their child and then move to the kitchen to prepare dinner for the family. As a result, toward the end of our interview with the child, smells of dinner would permeate the house, causing children to rush to finish the interview and researchers to worry that we were disrupting the family schedule. For interviews conducted after dinner, we found that participants were sometimes sleepy; their normal bedtime preparation routines were sometimes disrupted by our presence. Ideally scheduled interviews, occurring when the participants were neither hungry nor sleepy, overlapped with time the children would normally spend engaged in free time on the computer or other self-directed activities. We suspected some participants resented the time spent responding to questions when they might otherwise have been playing computer games. In retrospect, conducting interviews on weekend afternoons when possible might have alleviated conflicts with routine activities, and directing parents of young children into early afternoon interview times could help to avoid hungry or sleepy interviewees.

> **LESSON**
>
> Busy families schedule in-home interviews at all hours without serious consideration for the focus of their children. Balancing researcher availability with proposed ideal times to interview children of varying ages can be difficult but will result in more attentive participants.

### Interviews Gone Awry

Our interviews did not always proceed smoothly. Because we were in participant homes, we accepted the family's default browser settings when we asked children to search the open Internet. On one occasion, while searching for "dolphins eat," one nine-year-old girl encountered a pornographic web page. While the participant displayed no reaction, the researcher conducting the interview immediately blocked the screen from the participant's view using the interview script and pressed the backspace key, returning the participant to the search engine results page. Fortunately, this was the only incident during the series of studies to result in a participant accidentally viewing explicit content, and in the laboratory setting, we could have blocked such sites from the search engine results.

An interview with a novice seven-year-old participant was entirely derailed when the participant declined to answer any questions at all. We had prepared for participants to indicate to us that they wanted to end the interview early, and we ensured that we would not push the participants to answer questions unwillingly, but we had not anticipated complete silence. After encountering the camera-shy seven-year-old, we included contingencies for such events. We placed a five-minute time limit on interviews with children who were entirely unengaged, after which we would stop the interview even if the child did not verbally indicate to us wanting to stop. We agreed that a different researcher might be able to draw out a particular participant, so we also planned to switch researchers after several minutes if a participant did not respond to one of us.

---

**LESSON**

Even with experience and meticulous planning, unexpected events will occur during field research with children. Rapidly reacting to unplanned situations and revising protocols prior to continuing research can help to protect child participants.

---

### Awareness of Our Own Needs

For some researchers on our team, the home environment caused us to become acutely aware of our own personal needs. During the 2011 study, one researcher had severe allergies to pet hair. We found that this researcher was uncomfortable in participant homes with pets, sneezing and coughing throughout the interviews. While we did not raise the issue of pet ownership with families prior to arriving at homes, we ensured that this researcher acted as a note taker instead of as the primary interviewer when we found ourselves in homes with pets, as his sneezes were less disruptive from behind the camera. Another researcher had congenital deafness in one ear, making hearing the quiet voices of young children difficult when seated to the left side or in noisy environments. Given the varying layouts of furniture and placements of computers, it was not always possible for this researcher to sit on the right side of the participant. Rather than overburdening participants with explanations of her difficulty hearing, this researcher adopted the strategy of asking questions such as, "Can I make sure I heard you correctly?" and repeating the children's comments for confirmation.

> **LESSON**
>
> A research team can circumvent difficulties that might arise due to researcher needs through awareness of those needs and minor adjustments to the interview protocol.

## CONCLUSIONS

In this chapter, we have outlined the challenges inherent in conducting in-home research with children. We have also described our approaches to and strategies for solving these problems when we found good solutions, although some challenges were unforeseen or remain unsolved. Even though in-home research with children is difficult, we believe that such research is invaluable to understanding children's behaviors and factors affecting their behavior in their natural environments. Children are able to respond naturally, may be more assertive, and are more comfortable in their own homes. In the context of our studies on Internet search, had we conducted research in the lab or school, we would have uncovered very different search behaviors than we observed in the less-restricted home environment.

## REFERENCES

Chelton, M.K., Cool, C., 2004. Youth Information-Seeking Behavior: Context, Theories, and Models, vol. I. The Scarecrow Press, Lanham, MD.

Druin, A., Foss, E., Hutchinson, H., Golub, E., Hatley, L., 2010. Children's Roles using Keyword Search Interfaces at Home. In: Proceedings of the 28th International Conference on Human Factors in Computing Systems (CHI '10). ACM Press, New York, NY.

Foss, E., 2014. Internet Searching in Children and Adolescents: A Longitudinal Framework of Youth Search Roles. In: Doctoral dissertation. Retrieved from drum.umd.edu.

Foss, E., Druin, A., Brewer, R., Lo, P., Sanchez, L., Golub, E., Hutchinson, H., 2012. Children's Search Roles at Home: Implication for Designers, Researchers, Educators, and Parents. J. Am. Soci. Inf. Sci. Technol. 63 (3), 558–573.

Foss, E., Hutchinson, H., Druin, A., Yip, J., Ford, W., Golub, E., 2013. Adolescent Search Roles. J. Am. Soci. Inf. Sci. Technol. 64 (1), 173–189.

Gross, M., 2006. Studying Children's Questions: Imposed and Self-Generated Information Seeking at School. Scarecrow Press, Inc, Lanham, MD.

Lazar, J., Feng, J.H., Hochheiser, H., 2010. Research Methods in Human-Computer Interaction. John Wiley and Sons, Chichester, UK.

LeCompte, M.D., Preissle, J., 1993. Ethnography and Qualitative Design in Educational Research. Academic Press, Inc, San Diego, CA.

Livingstone, S., Bober, M., Helsper, E., 2005. Internet Literacy among Children and Young People: Findings from the UK Children Go Online Project [online]. LSE Research Online, London. http://eprints.lse.ac.uk/397/1/UKCGOonlineLiteracy.pdf.

Rideout, V.J., Foehr, U.G., Roberts, D.F., 2010. Generation M2: Media in the Lives of 8- to 18-Year-Olds [online]. A Kaiser Family Foundation Study, Menlo Park, CA: Henry J. Kaiser Family Foundation. http://www.kff.org/entmedia/upload/8010.pdf.

Selwyn, N., Potter, J., Cranmer, S., 2009. "Primary Pupils' Use of Information and Communication Technologies at School and Home." Br. J. Educ. Technol. 40 (5), 919–932.

Strauss, A.L., 2003. Qualitative Analysis for Social Scientists. Cambridge University Press, Cambridge, UK.

# The Flexible Realities of Using Design Probes: Reflections from a Care Home Context

# 5

**Jayne Wallace\*, Siân Lindley**[§]

*Duncan of Jordanstone College of Art and Design, University of Dundee, Dundee, UK\*; Microsoft Research, Cambridge, UK*[§]

## INTRODUCTION

A good deal of research in Human-Computer Interaction has considered how to support "aging in place," yet there are many circumstances that result in older people either choosing to or finding themselves relocating in later life. These can include downsizing one's home, moving into sheltered accommodation, and moving into a care home. The research we describe in this chapter is part of a broader program in which we wanted to focus on *placing in age*. We follow Leith (2006) here, who has argued that aging in place does not mean remaining in the same space forever, for example by equipping a home with assistive technologies. Instead, it can entail working toward a feeling of being "in place" in a new environment. Leith highlights preparedness to change the manner in which one shapes one's living environment, to pare down possessions, and to look to the positive side of living with others, for example when moving to congregate housing, as part of this process.

In the study we focus on here, we aimed to explore how a sense of being in place might be accomplished in a residential care home. We used the probe method (Gaver, Dunne, and Pacenti 1999) to learn about and from a small group of residents, and in this chapter we document some of the dynamics of the process as it evolved. We present an account that offers less of a neat, rigid process of gaining responses to questions posed through objects, but more a dialogical engagement centering on creative processes that, at points, can be directed away from the individual probes by participants to other creative activities and conversations that arise as meaningful to them. Throughout, the engagement remains scaffolded by the probes and the environment maintained by them.

This study was part of a wider project (see Lindley and Wallace [under review]), the first phase of which comprised interviews with people who either were planning to or had recently downsized their homes. We were interested in the decisions that people would make in relation to downsizing: where they would relocate to, how they would deal with their possessions, what they imagined the use of space to be like in their new home, and so on. The second phase of the project was to involve people living in a residential care home. However, we felt that relying on interviews would not be appropriate here. While the downsizers we interviewed had chosen to move, this is unusual for those transitioning to care. Instead, moving into a residential care home may be triggered by an unexpected event, such as a period of ill-health, or prompted because of an inability to cope with living alone or being widowed. This meant that interviews directed toward understanding what had motivated the transition and whether expectations had been fulfilled would be misdirected. Yet, we anticipated that many of the topics that emerged in our study of downsizing, and especially those relating to possessions and space, would also resonate with people living in care. Indeed, prior work has shown that personal possessions can support exploration and facilitate presentation of self in the context of care homes (Wapner, Demick, and Redondo 1990) and, on the flip side, that the expectation that possessions must be given up and space shared with others is cause for considerable apprehension when imagining what it means to live in a care home (Peace, Holland, and Kellaher 2006). We wanted an alternate way to understand what these topics meant for care home residents and how they formed the backdrop to the residents' experiences of living in care.

The approach we decided on comprised creative engagements with care home residents, centering on the use of design probes (Gaver et al. 1999). These would, we hoped, support a depth of conversation as well as allow us to simply spend time at the care home, getting a sense of how residents spent their time in communal areas. Such an approach resonates with other studies of care homes, in which observation unfolds around a central activity. For example, Blythe et al. (2010) worked with an artist, who drew portraits of care home residents, as a way of structuring the time spent with them and to serve as a "ticket to be silent" as well as the more familiar "ticket to talk" (Sacks 1992). Müller et al. (2012) noted how familiar care home residents were with organized activity and so used probe-like stimuli in activities that involved both researchers and residents. Because the creative sessions in our study took place in the shared spaces of the home, they allowed us to closely engage with a small group of residents as well as observe the residents' interactions with care home staff and other residents, and to more generally understand the social dynamics of these spaces.

However, the probes were not simply vehicles to support our spending time at the home; they were also designed to raise questions, facilitate explorations of the research questions, and help us get to know the residents we were working with. Probes have been used in this way in a number of studies by the first author of this chapter; they are a means of building relationships with participants over time and exploring biographical and experiential aspects of their lives with them. In this study, understanding the residents' experiences of possessions, space, and home more broadly was central to our goal. Through the use of probes, we hoped to start a conversation mediated by objects and acts of "making," and to be able to represent abstract notions of "home" in physical items in order to facilitate gentle explorations around residents' experiences of home within residential care.

In this chapter, we give some background on the use of probes in HCI, describe the probes we designed as part of this project, and discuss the atypical ways in which our use of probes played out in relation to the challenges that are inherent to the dynamics of the care home structure. We focus in particular on the ways in which we adapted our engagements as events unfolded, what this revealed about the method, and the benefits and lessons we took from being flexible. These lessons are bound up with our use of probes in a group setting, which, although unusual, nevertheless underpinned a framework that allowed relationships and reflective conversation to develop over time. We especially emphasize the importance of reciprocity and genuineness in allowing for this development; rather than deploying a standard probe pack or asking neutral questions, the probes were carefully designed (revealing an investment by the researchers) and encouraged participants to speak openly rather than attempt to give the "right" answers.

## DESIGN PROBE METHOD

Since their creation in 1999 by Gaver and colleagues, the adoption of probe methods in HCI has become wide in both scope and divergence (as discussed by Boehner et al. 2007) and heterogeneous in use and misuse (as detailed by Gaver et al. 2004). Cultural probes, initially developed as part of the Presence Project (Gaver, Hooker, and Dunne 2001), were born out of the pragmatic motivation to overcome the challenge of researchers not being able to work consistently in person with their participants, as those participants lived in several European countries. Probes, as a series of small, provocative and creative artifacts each embodying questions, provided the means for the researchers to intrigue, stimulate, and encourage their participants from a distance to reflect, act, and respond in thoughtful, lateral, and creative ways. Initial probes included a disposable camera with prompts such as "Take a picture of something beautiful" or "Take a picture of something boring" and maps that included surreal imagery printed on envelopes asking for indications of a participant's emotional topography of a location. Probes give researchers the "designerly" means to pose sets of questions through objects and the ability to create scaffolds that help participants reflect and respond (Wallace et al. 2013a). Through probes, researchers are able to extend themselves into their participants' lives and, in turn, invite participants into the researchers' design processes. Probes are curious objects that lead to the sharing of unobvious and real aspects of the participants' lives that attend to details within experience and individuality.

In the Presence Project (Gaver et al. 2001), the probes enabled the relationships between researchers and participants to endure despite them not being together physically, and for an enthusiasm and involvement in the project to continue in each community. There was a deeper motivation beyond the pragmatic, however: a need for a new design-centered approach to engage with the complex and multilayered realities of experience. Ideologically, approaches to design in HCI in the 1990s were creating an imbalance in the designer-user relationship and, as Wright, Blythe, and McCarthy (2006) describe, the term "design" in HCI meant a focus on engineering usability rather than creative interaction or design-led methods for participant engagement. Approaches to understanding people foregrounded use, work, and working environments and were only just beginning to register other areas of life through the so-called "third wave" of HCI (Bødker 2006). The dominant perspective was of people as "users," and subsequently, the methods employed to understand these contexts were rudimentary in design terms and limited in their framings of what it means to be a person.

Gaver et al. (1999) saw the creative fine art processes of the Situationists, Dadaists, and Surrealists as holding suitably subversive yet playful methods to both unsettle the HCI status quo and provide creative, agile, practical methods for the exploration of richer layers of human experience. Examples of Gaver et al.'s Domestic Probes (2004) include a drinking glass to be used as a listening device to amplify sounds in the home, a piece of photogram paper with which participants could capture impressions of domestic objects placed on it, a pack of labels on which to write the idiosyncratic rules of a participant's home, and friends and family maps with which to plot the roles people play in the lives of participants.

As such, initial probes were designed objects that brokered a dialogue between researchers and participants that judiciously used "tactics of ambiguity, absurdity, and mystery throughout, as a way of provoking new perspectives on everyday life" (Gaver et al. 1999, 26). They were intended to "subvert or undermine, rather than supplement, traditional HCI methods" (Boehner et al. 2007, 1080) and, importantly, design was central to the method. We (Wallace et al. 2013a), along with Gaver et al. (2004) and Boehner et al. have discussed how the method has become somewhat of an umbrella term, in which design has ceased to be a central focus, and have considered how to re-engage with design in relation to the materiality, form, and character of probes. In this chapter, we want to focus on another aspect of the method, and by doing so, highlight its flexible nature and scope. We wish to consider the use of probes as vehicles for conversation and relationship building when spending time *with* participants, rather than *away* from them. We consider how this plays into issues of trust and reciprocity, which is often highlighted in discussions of cultural probes (e.g., Boehner et al. 2007). In the following, we outline the study in more detail before describing how things played out in the care home and the lessons we took from this.

## STUDY AND METHOD

The care home (which is given the pseudonym "Green Oaks") is a purpose-built residential care home with approximately thirty residents in the South of England. Residents each have a private room and share communal bathrooms and several large communal spaces that serve as living rooms and dining rooms. We worked with this care home because, when we approached the manager (Helen[1]) to describe the research goals and show examples of previous creative methods we had used with elderly people (Wallace et al. 2013b), she was supportive and enthusiastic and expressed that she saw potential benefits for her residents. She felt that a number of residents would enjoy the engagements, conversations, and opportunity to contribute to a piece of research.

We left it completely open to Helen to approach residents who she felt would be interested in participating, and she introduced us to four residents (Grace, Lily, Amy, and Emily, all between the ages of seventy and ninety) who she felt might enjoy working with us. We did not specify criteria for inclusion other than that the residents needed to be capable of giving informed consent to participate. Helen also selected residents knowing they would have to spend time together regularly, and so chose people who were known to get along reasonably well. The women she selected had either lived locally or in neighboring towns for most of their lives. They were widowed and had family living nearby. All had limited mobility. We did not specify that participants should be women; however, women made up a higher proportion of residents than men, and this may have been reflected in the fact that we ended up with an all-female group.

We used a space in one of the shared areas of the home to work with the women as a group in a format that echoed existing activities run in the home (small numbers of people sitting around a table to make something). Helen arranged this, and staff were aware of our use of the space and the fact we would be using audio recorders within it. Our engagement spanned five weeks, with one or two sessions of approximately three hours per week. However, and as hinted at above, fitting into the existent pattern of activities and, perhaps more significantly, the dynamics of the care home led to some methodological departures from our typical way of researching. Rather than working with individuals on a one to one basis (Wallace et al. 2013b), giving them probes to live with and complete over a number of weeks, we worked with all four residents collectively and designed probes to make and complete *with* them during the sessions themselves. Probes in this context were conversational agents, stimuli around several conceptual themes, and scaffolds for creativity that enabled us to inquire about points of continuity with the women's previous homes, how and in what ways they had been homemakers, and their feelings about home more generally. In practical terms, probes facilitated us in getting to know one another and were the tools for us to encourage the women to act as *creators* in the ethos of homemakers once more.

## PROBE DESIGNS

A key motivation for us in designing the probes was creating ways of exploring the complexities of home with the care home residents while being sensitive to the fact

---

[1]All names are pseudonyms.

that they were no longer living in their own homes. By using the probes, we were not only concerned with the women's reflections on things past; the study was also forward facing in that we were exploring aspects of the present, such as the tension between shared and private space, as well as the future, by orienting the women toward imagining their own dream spaces and how these could be created. To maintain a connection between the literature that was informing our thinking and the probes, we developed probe design ideas around four themes: "home and continuity," "living in and through objects," "home as sanctuary," and "home as a journey." These are detailed further in a separate paper (Lindley and Wallace, under review) but will be described briefly here.

We wished to focus on "continuity", as it was highlighted in our research with downsizers and is a theme that runs through research into cherished possessions as transitional objects (e.g., Wapner et al. 1990 and Sherman and Dacher 2005). Facets of the probes built on this theme by inquiring about how possessions can serve to anchor, help transition, and provide comfort in the context of living in residential care. The second theme, "living in and through objects," had been signaled in several of our earlier related projects with older people. In this theme we include the practical aspects of homemaking as well as the divesture of possessions. "Home as a journey" related to the literature on home as an ongoing construction, and we were motivated by Rowles and Chaudhury (2005), who draw on Dovey (2005) in discussing how being at home assumes meaning only in relation to being away from it. This relates to an ongoing tension in life between wanting to remain in the known and familiar and an imperative to venture forth and reach out, which has clear implications for people who live in care homes and for whom travel and mobility may be compromised. "Home as a journey" foregrounds connections to things "without" and opens up a dialogue around ideas we had in which design could support connections to places, things, and people external to the care home. In contrast, the final theme, "home as sanctuary," enabled a focus on home as something within and private, relating to notions of safety, comfort, and security, both physical and emotional.

Our four probe designs (Figures 5.1 through 5.4) were the products of multiple sketch developments and alignments between emergent probe design ideas, the

**FIGURE 5.1**

Wallpaper House probe.

**FIGURE 5.2**

Welcome Mat probe.

**FIGURE 5.3**

Door Handle probe.

**FIGURE 5.4**

Chair probe.

literature that had informed our approaches, and our early design aspirations for the design work to follow. We now describe them with very broad strokes. (See Lindley and Wallace [under review] for more detail.)

*Wallpaper House* related to continuity and living in and through objects; *Welcome Mat* inquired about the ritual of coming home, the feeling of home, and continuity over time; *Door Handle* explored both sanctuary spaces and home as a journey; and *Chair* explored home as a point of departure and return.

The *Wallpaper House* probe (Figure 5.1) comprised a series of plain, flat-pack models of houses made from lining paper that could be decorated, collaged, and drawn or written on, and was accompanied by a series of wallpaper samples. We asked the women to make, with our help, a series of houses that represented different rooms from homes in which they had lived in the past. We asked about their changes in taste over the years and some of the most significant rooms from homes in which they had lived (favorite rooms, rooms from their childhoods, their first homes as adults).

The *Welcome Mat* probe (Figure 5.2) asked residents how they had made a home feel welcoming. The probe was intended to be a discussion point and could be written or drawn on. Our aim was to stimulate reflections of the details of what coming home feels like and how the women created their particular ambience of home, homeliness, and comfort, both for their own families and for visitors.

The *Door Handle* probe (Figure 5.3) leveraged connotations of doors leading into different spaces. It invited the women to use their imaginations to visualize turning the handle to open a door into their dream room. It encouraged fantasy and ideas untethered to practical, financial, or conventional constraints.

The *Chair* probe (Figure 5.4) built on the imagination element of *Door Handle* by asking the women to envision where, if anything were possible and their armchair were a transportation device, they would like to travel to. The fabric cover could be written onto and the cushion could be embroidered, but again, the key creative act here was the women being imaginatively open and active in conceiving of places they would visit. Knowing that most residents in Green Oaks seldom left the home and that asking questions about travel and connection to other places may be insensitive, we used gentle humor (for example, the comedic form of oversized tractor wheels connected to a conventional armchair in the *Chair* probe) to diffuse the possible negative dynamic connected to our theme of inquiry. Indeed, the design of all of the probes was guided by a desire to ask our questions sensitively and in gentle ways that could be led by the women and flexible for them to take them as far as they wanted to (or not).

We wanted to use our probes as an opportunity to open up conversations about home, design possibilities, and the potential of technology to support the women in new ways within the care home through the ideas that developed. We endeavored to use the probes in a very personal, conversational, and non-detached way with participants, and to do so by keeping design at the center of the method. Design enabled us to bring a rich tactile and aesthetic language to our engagements through the physicality of the probes, and to judiciously use the power of metaphor to inquire about contexts of home in gentle but unusual ways. Probes enabled a dialogical interview to occur supported by and through objects. In many instances, conversation and talking through responses to the questions posed by the probes became as important as physically completing them.

Each session typically began with reflections on the previously completed probe and the introduction of a new one, but then could be guided by what the women wanted to talk about or what they physically brought to the sessions themselves. In raising design-centered questions about home, we were able to gently shift the women into spaces where they were having creative ideas and asserting design preferences, and to this end the probes functioned as participatory design tools. Each of the conversations was recorded, transcribed, and analyzed, but not the probes themselves. The content of probe responses is something that we usually respond to through more designerly means, such as building up a visual language of imagery that corresponds to the probe response or sketchbook development of ideas, which, in our use of the method, often involves further conversations with participants to clarify and refine them.

## CHALLENGES AND LESSONS

In the following sections, we consider challenges that emerged in our study in greater depth. The first section highlights some of the dynamics of the care home context that we needed to adapt to in order to work within this space. The second reflects on the nature of the probes method and the need for open, adaptive behavior in its use in order to fully utilize what a probe stimulates for participants. The third develops some of the ideas expressed already, which relate to how we used the probes to develop trust and build relationships with a group. The fourth section considers how we drew on our findings in considering opportunities and challenges for the design of technologies when our probes were far removed from being technological in themselves.

### FITTING IN WITH THE PATTERNS OF THE CARE HOME

As noted earlier, this study's use of probes differs from our previous experiences with the method. Instead of being tailored for individuals, the probes were made for a group of people we didn't know. The probes were then used to ground group conversation. Furthermore, this group setting meant that the activities we had designed resonated strongly with the existing program of activities for residents, and while we had expected that this would make the activities more readily accepted, in fact it did not necessarily work to our advantage. At the beginning of our first creative session, as we spread out wallpaper samples and the wallpaper houses, Amy asked us, "What's being put in front of us again now, then?" The way she posed the question suggested that, rather than being excited or even curious about the session we had in mind, she was used to partaking in activities that carried little meaning for her. This impression gained further weight when we noticed some freshly painted plastic containers near the table where we were working. These were to be made into a totem pole, but the women were unable to tell us what this would be used for, or where it would be placed: "We don't know, but it keeps him (the activities organizer) happy."

> **LESSON**
>
> Group activities suggest a different dynamic to time spent with an individual. Time was needed to build relationships with the women before rich personal insights could be gained.

A second feature of these early sessions was our sense of the care home as a workplace. Of course, care homes sit across the spheres of home and work; our participants lived at Green Oaks, but it was also a site of work for managers and staff. We often saw residents deferring to the care home as a workplace: "How long are you here today, Simon? (...) That's a very long day. What about you, Joanne? (...) I think they're too long a day for you girls and boys." The rhythm of the home was set by meal times, tea times, and sessions (including the activity sessions) organized by staff, who also made appointments with chiropodists or hairdressers on behalf of the residents. These routine features of care home life produce mundane problems; for example, we often found ourselves working against a backdrop of vacuum cleaning, tea making, routine toilet breaks, or table laying, and we found it difficult to schedule our visits directly with the women, as they were largely unaware of the appointments that had been organized for them. Again, this was problematic in terms of building a relationship directly with them; it seemed that scheduling had to be facilitated by the care home staff. Helen had introduced our participants as residents who, she believed, would enjoy the activities, and she also scheduled our follow-up visits by necessity to fit around the other uses of the communal space in which we were working. However, these issues were also revealing, and they eventually became essential to our analysis, as they highlight issues of control and agency that were important to our understanding of life in the care home.

> **LESSON**
>
> Settings for fieldwork are multifaceted. Attending to aspects of an environment that are not, at first glance, relevant to research aims can be important.

While this mixing of home and work may seem, at first glance, to be specific to the context of living in a care home, there are power dynamics in all domestic arrangements, and it may often be the case that one family member signs up to partake in a study on behalf of others, especially children. Developing an atmosphere that draws in those whose participation was initiated by others, even where consent has been given, is essential.

## UNDERSTANDING THE NEED FOR FLEXIBILITY

Despite the challenges of the care home context and routines, we had faith in the method. The first author has used it many times in a variety of situations, and we understood that, through applying it in a different context, the relationships between all parties would develop in different ways. We gave the method time to progress, continuing to work with the women each week. Our relationships with them developed, and as we began to know them better, we let the women divert conversation and activity away from the completion of probes to themes (albeit related) that held meaning for them. For example, in one session we drew on a conversation with Grace, in which she had talked about being able to crochet. This being a skill neither of us possess, we asked her if she would teach us, and she agreed to lead our third creative session. We provided wool and crochet hooks, as did Grace, and the dynamic altered significantly as a result. Rather than the women being participants completing an activity, they were sharing skills and teaching *us*. Interestingly, this shift was evident not only in *our* relationship with the residents, but also, during the session, in the dynamic between them and staff members.

As mentioned above, the backdrop to these sessions could be chaotic, with staff talking to one another, preparing cups of tea, vacuuming, and interrupting residents for toilet breaks. Yet, here, staff were drawn into the session, showing an interest in Grace's abilities and what she was teaching us. One staff member even picked up a crochet hook and yarn to show us what she could do. The activity became a relaxed backdrop to natural conversation, in which earlier topics, suggested by the probes, began to resurface. As such, this "diversion" was not a marker that the probes method wasn't working, but quite the opposite. The method had begun to create a conversational space scaffolded by creative artifacts, which were wholly different to the usual activities in the care home; the artifacts supported a personally meaningful connection. In this altered space, the women began to share stories and opinions that were reflective, considered, and spoke of both happy and difficult times in their lives in relation to home. The tangents remained connected to the notion of home but were led by the women, and there was a notable shift from "doing an activity" to using probes and creative processes like crocheting to reflect on genuine feelings about the complex issues of what home means over the course of one's life.

> **LESSON**
>
> Be prepared to let a method unfold and, when tangents emerge, consider whether they can allow the researcher to address the research aims in alternative ways.

When the probes method was initially developed (Gaver et al. 1999), it was designed to stimulate unobvious and genuine reflection in participants and to elicit creative tangents that would inspire design ideas. Its wider adoption in HCI often shows a much more reductive framing, whereby researchers have been far more rigidly tethered to gaining responses to questions posed through probes. We hope to illustrate here that tangents instigated by participants are not a problem, but are exactly what the method was initially designed to elicit; they are what we as researchers should strive to stimulate. This means researchers need to engage with the method in a flexible and open way in order to go with the flow and improvise in a creative and adaptive manner. The tangents are where a participant wants to go, and it is often here where we discover the most authentic and significant information.

The dynamics of the sessions and care home brought into focus how agile we needed to be to run the sessions, especially in light of the various challenging factors of the particular environment. It was necessary for us to be able to adapt to what was most appropriate in the moment, which meant being proactive at times and passive at others, such as when we relinquished control and the planned format of a session in order to seize an opportunity that presented itself, and let the participants lead. The character of the method is such that, when probes are used to explore personal contexts, they take on unique dynamics with each use. The probes are there in part as a support structure not only for the participants, but also for the researchers, enabling a constant connection to the focus of the study and a range of means to draw participants' reflections to certain aspects of the theme. They can be used in a cyclical manner to refocus attention, but essentially they act as keys for a participant to unlock reflections and new ways of thinking about a topic. A flexible approach to using probes is central to the understanding of their use as a design method.

## DEVELOPING TRUST

When working with probes, particularly around biographical and experiential contexts, a sense of trust is extremely important between researchers and participants as well as among participants themselves. In our study, trust developed gradually as the group dynamic shifted from being somewhat stilted in the initial session to one in which biographical stories and creative skills were easily shared. Of course, the women did not know us until the sessions began, and this had an impact on how comfortable they felt in the first session, and we have mentioned how their initial assumptions were led by previous experiences of creative activities in the home. But what was also interesting was that, although they all knew each other and two of the women described themselves as friends, it quickly became apparent that they knew very little about what each other's lives were like prior to coming to live in the home. A sense of trust needed to be nurtured between the women so that they felt comfortable sharing things not only with us but also with each other. The probes helped a sense of trust develop that enabled the women to share things about themselves in a deeper way than they were used to in the home, and also to be adventurously creative (for example, in sharing dream ideas for imagined rooms) in a number of ways.

The probes, as physical, designed manifestations of questions, conveyed to the women that we had made them in a considered manner, with effort, and especially for them, in ways that would hopefully intrigue and inspire. This dynamic can be an easily overlooked yet incredibly valuable quality in the method; it communicates that we regarded what the women had to say and share as valid and valuable. The probes themselves, and the ways in which we introduced them, emphasized that there were no right or wrong answers. This can be very freeing, and the women knew that we weren't testing them or looking for specific things, which meant that they could talk about whatever they felt was relevant to the topic of a probe. As this cadence, or feel, to the process became more apparent as we worked through initial probes, the women gained confidence and shared things more easily and deeply.

Relatedly, each person could bring something creative to the process regardless of skill or whether they perceived themselves to be creative or not, and the probes gave each participant a variety of ways into this. For one person, this meant talking about the aesthetics of her collection of dolls; for another, this meant recollecting childhood stories related to beauty, along with creative visualizations of her imagined dream room; and for another, it meant teaching us to crochet. There is a leveling to this creative process, both across the participant group and between researcher and participant. Everyone was able to contribute and take turns leading activities and conversation. We had purposefully designed the study to include us completing the probes with the women, not only to spend time with them and in the care home itself, but also to help them overcome physical limitations in completing the probes themselves. As such, from the outset, we took turns taking the lead; sometimes we introduced a new probe, and sometimes the women took the lead by diverting us back to a previous one, teaching us skills, wanting to show us things in their rooms, or directing us in how they wanted particular probes to be completed. A feeling of trust, a sense of creative exploration and purpose, and reciprocal turn-taking developed. The probes helped us create a shift in dynamic from "creative activity done to pass time" to sessions in which all parties took a genuine interest.

Note that this approach is quite different from that taken in, for example, interview studies, where the aim is to be neutral, to avoid expressing opinions, and to keep things consistent across participants. None of these factors were of importance here; instead, we aimed to create a situation in which conversations unfolded gradually as a relationship was formed, and topics of interest as well as the activities that framed their discussion developed over time. In other words, our use of probes necessitated us to *give* more of ourselves than we would for a series of interviews. By giving, we do not mean only through the bespoke making of probes, but also through revealing information about ourselves and being prepared to hand over control. While crochet in itself does not directly touch on the issues we were probing in our project, the act of facilitating Grace in taking control of the session and engaging in an activity that she enjoyed demonstrated trust, respect, and genuine interest. Indeed, despite the lack of a connection between crochet and our research questions, earlier conversations that had been started around our initial probes resurfaced during this session, but in more depth. The women had come to understand what we were interested in, recognized that our weekly sessions meant picking up on this topic in some form, and did so without prompting as our relationships with them continued. This continuation and development of our conversations over sessions was also essential to our research; that deeper topics of conversation could be broached was essential, given the complex nature of our study. We were not simply asking the residents straightforward questions about their daily lives or what they thought of a particular technology; we were asking them to imagine what a different set of living circumstances might be like and to be both creative and honest.

---

**LESSON**

Studies run over a number of sessions give space to establish and return to topics that are of interest to all parties. Reciprocity is key here; participants must feel they can speak openly, rather than try to "please" the researcher.

---

We want to highlight that, as well as giving participants a focus or range of different ways to approach a question and structures for them to respond through, the probes and sessions were *fun*. The women began bringing things to the sessions (crochet hooks, colored pencils, and personal photographs), and they looked forward to the sessions. This was hugely significant to us and a giant leap forward from our initial session. Things like this are what give a study momentum so that interesting things can happen despite the challenges of a particular environment. This meeting halfway is a key component in running the method successfully.

A more general lesson here is that, while building trust and allowing for new insights may not be expected to feature when researching families and couples, it is quite possible that, in these instances too, probes could elicit new conversations, new realizations, and work to open up topics that are rarely discussed in the context of everyday life. Of course, this needs to be caveated by the fact that family members may not wish to share everything with one another, but by creating a framework for a continuing discussion, researchers should expect conversation to reveal insights that are new even to members of the same family.

## LINKING TO TECHNOLOGY

In this section, we consider a final challenge we needed to face in this research: how to use the sessions as a basis for designing digital technologies for use in a care home when the women we were working with had little experience with computers. Of course, user-centered design means understanding a situation and then designing technologies based on that understanding, rather than simply asking users what they would like. However, understanding whether technology would be accepted or appropriated by the women, in the context of a care home, was not something that could be easily reached simply by spending time there. Furthermore, the women's lack of experience with technology meant that conversations about it would have little grounding. We took two approaches here. The first was to gently introduce the women to a technology, once again by tailoring an activity to their interests and biographical experiences, and once again based on conversations that had occurred in earlier sessions. Here, we worked on the basis that two of the women had lived in places of interest; one in a house that is now a local art gallery, and another next to an opera house in London. In our fourth session, we brought in our laptops to show the women what these places look like now, enabling them to direct us on a "walk" around the area through Google Street View. Of course, by responding to the women in this way, we were able to touch once again on the topic of home while also gauging their reactions to technology when presented in a particular context.

Similar to experiences reported by Blythe et al. (2010) and Müller et al. (2012), we found the residents to be fascinated by Street View, directing our journey to take us to key sites around their old homes and describing what had changed since they lived there. Emily remembered how "The opera singers (from the theater next to her home) used to come out where the gardens were, and my mother had a canary, and it always used to sing lovely. We used to hang on the wall, and they used to hang them outside the window. And we used to say, 'Why do they keep coming?' But they were listening to the bird!" Technology performed as a bridge between the past and the present, and rather than being alarmed by changes to particular streets, they were interested in seeing what was different, using the tool as a resource to describe how things used to be. By using the laptop in this way, we were able to introduce some of the possibilities that technologies could offer without bringing to the fore concerns around accessibility or being hampered by the women's lack of confidence. We were able to begin unpacking what technology might *do* in the context of a care home.

The second approach we took was to create something for the women that incorporated some of the same decisions we'd have to make if we designed a personalized digital artifact for them. We wanted to make something that was mobile, reflected shared experiences in the home while being aesthetically personal to each woman, could be foregrounded in conversation, and could equally become part of the background. We were also interested in exploring concepts where we thought technology could play a role in addressing the small amount of personal space and lack of possessions in a care home context, such as through supporting the appropriation of space, being able to reveal and also conceal personal possessions, and being able to draw on possessions to act as tickets to talk (Sacks 1992).

As part of this approach, we decided to create a ceramic mug for each woman. We worked with the participants to make personal decal transfers for plain white mugs, similar to those that the residents already used, liked, and could easily handle to drink from. The mugs were designed to reflect topics that had emerged during the sessions: Lily's mug showed photographs of dolls, representing a collection she had built (and given up when she moved into Green Oaks), countries where she had lived, and patterns from décor that she had loved in her previous home; Emily's mug featured fantasy elements, including decorative teacups and the coins that would be discovered in the garden of her dream home, as well as depicting a story from her past; Grace's mug showed photographs of and drawings by her granddaughters, as well as favorite flowers and a sample of crochet.

Once completed, the mugs were objects of pride to the women and also of great interest to staff, who were unaware of many of the women's experiences that were alluded to by the images on the mugs. While the women were reticent to show off the mugs at first, saying that no one would want to know about them, the curiosity that staff members showed both surprised and encouraged them. Yet, while the mugs enabled the telling of new stories and suggested a means of cultivating relationships between residents and staff, they also highlighted complexities around their use. For example, the women were reluctant to drink from their mugs, let alone leave them in communal areas, lest something should happen to them. We might expect similar findings to arise around digital artifacts, there being a seeming tension around leaving personal possessions in shared spaces, where they may be used by others, or worse, become damaged or lost. Indeed, such concerns may be magnified for people who have few belongings. Yet, we did want to design ways of giving residents a presence in communal areas by, for example, leaving possessions within them. This motivation came from the observation that these spaces often seemed designed to give a homely aesthetic, for instance, through the display of a wedding photo, but without drawing on personal possessions (the photo was of no one the residents knew). The resulting generic spaces were little used and associated with no one in particular. The women's reactions to the mugs hinted at some of the tensions we might encounter if we create technologies to be left in shared areas and suggested a different set of design opportunities, which relate to building objects that fall between private and public, personally owned and shared. These objects could generally reflect the people who tend to use a space, representing them via personal displays of photos or their taste in artwork, music, or film. We present these ideas in greater detail in our research paper (Lindley and Wallace [under review]), but suffice to say for the purposes of this chapter, while we expected the mugs to embody one set of challenges (how to design personal, technological tickets to talk), they came to suggest another, that of how to reposition communal areas as belonging to everyone rather than as belonging to no one.

> **LESSON**
>
> Probes, whether digital or physical, can lend insights into what new technologies might do when introduced to a space. The insights they foster are not about evaluating a concept, but they do suggest how a particular setting might raise implications or challenges for design.

## CONCLUSION

This book is about designing and evaluating technologies that intersect with domestic life, and the various chapters within it, this one included, highlight how the circumstances in which people live vary radically, giving rise to a plethora of experiences and definitions of the "domestic." Research of domestic life as it unfolds in a care home necessitates alternate approaches to those that might be called upon when studying the home life of nuclear families, couples, or, as noted in the introduction, downsizers. Yet the lessons we draw from our study reflect not only the challenges of studying what it means to live in a care home, they also generalize to other contexts, where participants are asked to consider issues that they normally may not, where creativity could prove valuable, and where power dynamics are of interest. We have shown how, with time and space, the probe method worked to create a framework in which relationships developed and reflective conversation unfolded.

Relationships were built not only between us and our participants, but among themselves, too. We have argued that underpinning this was a quality of genuineness in the research. This study required us to be genuinely willing to let our participants lead the way, to let them direct a relationship that we had framed through the probes. We enabled them to give back to us not by answering questions or even necessarily by completing the probes (as is typical of the method), but by overcoming their initial apprehensions about the sessions we had organized, engaging in open conversation with us, and responding to our efforts to make the sessions meaningful for them.

Reflecting on how the first author has become more skilled in the use of the method over a series of projects, it is apparent that, in first use, the desire to be faithful to the method was interpreted as the need to be somewhat absent personally from interactions with the probes so that the objects themselves would illicit responses. While this is true (and this approach certainly worked in the Presence Project, where researchers were not able to be with participants often), her experience is that probes work far more richly when she invests and gives of herself in the process and builds a relationship with participants that is facilitated, extended, and cemented by the probes. In short, it is not all about the objects; it is also about the relationship between participant and researcher. The depth of participant reflection that is brokered by the objects is in part attributable to the sense of being supported and valued that a participant feels in consequence. Through making and using objects, we were able to be reflexive and flexible, proactive and passive, and this is what our participants responded to.

# REFERENCES

Blythe, M., Wright, P., Bowers, J., Boucher, A., Jarvis, N., Reynolds, P., Gaver, B., 2010. Age and Experience: Ludic Engagement in a Residential Care Setting. In: Proceedings of the ACM Conference on Designing Interactive Systems (DIS). ACM Press, New York, NY.

Bødker, S., 2006. When second wave HCI meets third wave challenges. In: Proceedings of the Nordic Conference on Human-Computer Interaction (HCI). ACM Press, New York, NY.

Boehner, K., Vertesi, J., Sengers, P., Dourish, P., 2007. How HCI Interprets the Probes. In: Proceedings of the Conference on Computer-Human Interaction (CHI). ACM Press, New York, NY.

Dovey, K., 2005. Home as Paradox. In: Rowles, G., Chaudhury, H. (Eds.), Home and Identity in Late Life: International Perspectives. Springer Publishing Company, New York, pp. 361–369.

Gaver, W., Dunne, A., Pacenti, E., 1999. Design: Cultural Probes. Interactions 6 (1), 21–29.

Gaver, W., Hooker, B., Dunne, A., 2001. The Presence Project (RCA CRD Projects series). RCA Research Publications.

Gaver, W., Boucher, A., Pennington, S., Walker, B., 2004. Cultural Probes and the Value of Uncertainty. Interactions 11 (5), 53−56.

Leith, K.H., 2006. Home is Where the Heart Is… Or Is It? A Phenomenological Exploration of the Meaning of Home for Older Women in Congregate Housing. J. Aging Stud. 20, 317−333.

Lindley, S. and J. Wallace. "Placing in Age." Under review.

Müller, C., Neufeldt, C., Randall, D., Wulf, V., 2012. ICT-Development in Residential Care Settings: Sensitizing Design to the Life Circumstances of the Residents of a Care Home. In: Proceedings of the Conference on Computer-Human Interaction (CHI). ACM Press, New York, NY.

Peace, S., Holland, C., Kellaher, L., 2006. Environment and Identity in Later Life. Open University Press, Maidenhead, UK.

Rowles, G., Chaudhury, H., 2005. Home and Identity in Late Life: International Perspectives. Springer Publishing Company, New York.

Sacks, H., 1992. Lectures in Conversation: Volumes I and II. Oxford, UK: Blackwell.

Sherman, E., Dacher, J., 2005. Cherished Objects and the Home: Their Meaning and Roles in Late Life. In: Rowles, G., Chaudhury, s. (Eds.), Home and Identity in Late Life: International Perspectives. Springer Publishing Company, New York, pp. 63−79.

Wallace, J., McCarthy, J., Wright, P., Olivier, P., 2013a. Making Design Probes Work. In: Proceedings of the Conference on Computer-Human Interaction (CHI). ACM Press, New York, NY.

Wallace, J., Wright, P., McCarthy, J., Green, D., Thomas, J., Olivier, P., 2013b. A Design-Led Inquiry into Personhood in Dementia. Proceedings of the Conference on Computer-Human Interaction (CHI). ACM Press, New York, NY.

Wapner, S., Demick, J., Redondo, J.P., 1990. Cherished possessions and adaptation of older people to nursing homes. Int. J. Aging Hum. Dev. 31 (3), 219−2358.

Wright, P., Blythe, M., McCarthy, J., 2006. User experience and the idea of design in HCI. In: Interactive Systems. Design, Specification, and Verification. Springer, Berlin/Heidelberg, pp. 1−14.

# Using the Business Origami Technique to Understand Complex Ecosystems

# 6

**Doug Fox**

*Google Inc., Mountain View, CA, USA*

## INTRODUCTION

Imagine you have an Internet service that is one hundred times faster than traditional cable or DSL services. What would you do with that type of speed? Stream HD movies without fear of the dreaded "buffering spinner" on Netflix? Dominate your friends on your favorite online video games? Or just upload hundreds of videos of your cat being cute and mischevious to YouTube?

These were the questions we were faced with on the Google Fiber User Experience Research team. Google Fiber is a fiber-optic Internet service that provides Internet download speeds up to one hundred times faster than cable or DSL services, with a 1-gigabit connection. These speeds are currently rare within the United States, and we were interested to learn how the behavior of Google Fiber users would evolve as a result of this high-speed Internet connection.

Because of the high costs of installing fiber-optic cabling in multiple locations, Kansas City, Kansas, USA, was chosen as the first market for Google Fiber. We wanted to make sure it was worth Google's investment to build this network, so we started with only one market and planned to extend the service based on the uptake and demand. Kansas City was a market that was highly eager for a better Internet experience. Its citizens even held marketing campaigns encouraging Google Fiber to build the fiber optic network there, and the city government was a good partner in helping us get the permissions we needed to build the infrastructure for the network.

We wanted to understand the impact of Google Fiber from this installation point onward, so we started exploring the Internet usage patterns of users who were the first in Kansas City to have the new service installed in their homes. By removing many of the constraints and frustrations of today's traditional Internet experiences, such as slow connections, bandwidth caps, and unreliable service, we wanted to know what, if anything, would change about our users' behaviors. Would they come up with new uses for the Internet that we had not imagined, or would they just do the same activities yet more efficiently? The possibilities were seemingly limitless. For the Google Fiber team, it was important to understand how families used the Internet so we could adapt our services to their particular behaviors. From a business perspective, it was important to learn about changes in Internet usage so Google could build services or products that better matched user behaviors with a faster Internet connection.

We adapted and employed a method known as the Business Origami Technique to learn how multiple members of a household used the Internet when connected using Google Fiber. The Business Origami Technique is a method that traditionally uses "pop-up" paper tokens—paper cut-outs folded so they stand upright—as representations of various people, locations, and technologies in an ecosystem (McMullin 2010). It provided us with a way to understand how the Internet was being used in each household, by whom, and in which locations. The method also allowed us to gather rich details of user behavior that we believe would have been difficult to acquire through an interview or survey of users' online practices.

Keep in mind that, in order to learn about the impact of the Google Fiber Internet service, we needed more than just a snapshot of what multiple family members did online. We needed to understand changes over time, and learn when and how behaviors evolved. Thus, this study was conducted over a period of one year. The longitudinal nature of the study provided unique challenges that required adaptations to the Business Origami Technique.

In this chapter, I discuss the steps we took to employ the Business Origami Technique across fifteen multi-member households. I also discuss the benefits and limitations of this method over other research methods, such as interviews, contextual inquiries, and surveys. Throughout the chapter, I share steps and best practices to adapt the Business Origami Technique from the traditional paper format to a digital format so that the origami map may be more easily used for longitudinal studies. I also document the challenges we faced in adapting and employing the method digitally. These challenges included explaining the exercise to remote participants, ensuring they complete the exercise in a timely fashion, and working around technological failures and issues of technology literacy.

## THE BUSINESS ORIGAMI TECHNIQUE

The Business Origami Technique is a paper prototyping exercise for describing scenarios, contexts, and environments (McMullin 2010). The key benefit of the Business Origami Technique is that it is highly visual, representing complex ecosystems that would be difficult for people to communicate verbally or in written form. In the traditional form of this method, paper pop-up tokens are used to represent each part of an ecosystem (Martin and Hanington 2012). The pop-up tokens look like board game pieces and are "mapped out" by participants, usually on a horizontal whiteboard, and represent events or behaviors of interest. The tokens are

**FIGURE 6.1**

An example of a participant creating an origami map in a household ecosystem with pets, to answer the questions of who, where, and how.

designed for the researchers to understand *who* exhibits specific behaviors, *where* the behaviors are conducted, and *how* they are conducted.

For example, Figure 6.1 shows a study participant designing an origami map in a sample study focused on explaining what her pets do during the day. To represent *who*, the participant created two dog tokens representing the two dogs in the house and labeled them "Garrison" and "Lucy." She also created a cat token labeled "Mittens" representing the cat in the house. The tokens are laid on a large white-board. To represent *where* in the house the pets go throughout the day, she used house tokens, which she labeled with the names of the room locations: "living room," "kitchen," and "bedroom." Finally, she created tokens for different activities (a ball for playing, a bed for sleeping, and a bowl for eating), to show *how* each pet behaves. The final step after creating tokens is mapping out who does what and where they do it. The participant placed the Garrison dog token and a bed token by the bedroom token, because that is where that dog sleeps throughout the day. She also placed ball tokens by the living room and kitchen tokens for Lucy, because that is where Lucy plays.

When designing the origami map, interactions between tokens are drawn and represented via lines and arrows using markers or pens (Martin and Hanington 2012). Figure 6.2 shows that the participant has drawn an arrow from Garrison and the bedroom to the living room, because Garrison does not sleep in the bedroom when Mittens, the cat, enters the room.

When designing a paper-based origami map, it may be easiest to have participants concentrate on one specific token at a time. For instance, if a house token is needed for multiple locations in the home, then have the participants label multiple house tokens for the relevant locations in the home. Then, have them spread out the house tokens over a large blank surface like a table or whiteboard. Glue dots or a

**FIGURE 6.2**

An example of using lines or arrows to indicate interactions between parts of an ecosystem.

glue stick work best for keeping the paper tokens in place. This procedure is repeated for the remaining tokens.

A core component of the Business Origami Technique is having the participant verbalize their design thought process while they are mapping out the ecosystem. For example, as study participants create and place the tokens on the large surface, the researcher instructs them to think aloud and explain each token. Ask them to answer questions, such as, "What does this token represent?" "What is the normal state of the token (e.g., do you normally play ball in the living room)?" Or "What are special circumstances of the token (e.g., when would you not play ball in the living room)?" After participants have described and placed all relevant tokens, they may be asked follow-up questions by the researcher to clarify things that may be of specific interest. For example, they could mark which rooms in the household are the pets' favorites. Much like the think-aloud protocol, this technique provides key insights into participants' thought processes and the reasons behind their behaviors. For instance, the researcher could discover that Mittens, the cat, sleeps in the living room only when it is cloudy outside, while at other times she sleeps in the bedroom.

Although "business" is in the name of the method, this does not necessarily mean that the Business Origami Technique is only applicable to studying business systems and settings. The Google Fiber User Experience Research team adapted this method so it could be conducted with households that were consumers of our Internet services. Traditionally, this method has been used only to study complex business ecosystems and how people in different roles interact with one another, but we saw potential in using this method to learn how multiple people in a household used the Internet and Internet-connected devices in their homes. The study and motivations are described in more detail in the next section.

## SELECTION OF STUDY METHOD

As stated, the Business Origami Technique was used within our larger study to learn about the impact of the Google Fiber Internet on our users in Kansas City. In November 2012, we ran an initial survey to establish a baseline of who our users were and what they did online shortly after we installed the service. While the survey provided us with quantitative data on predictable behaviors (e.g., downloading music), we weren't able to easily collect behavioral data on things we couldn't predict, such as impromptu video conferencing with family using the TV, or setting up a server to host networked video game matches.

Part of the overall study plan was to conduct follow-up in-home visits with a subset of survey respondents. We thought this was a good way to investigate some of the details about their behavioral changes that we couldn't get from the survey. However, we knew that simply asking people, "What do you do online?" would not account for the whole story. There were too many variables within each household such as device type, who used the Internet, and how they used it. These variables would make it difficult to collect accurate data during an interview. Relying solely on interviews would have made identifying trends and behavioral patterns very difficult.

We considered doing a diary study, but thought it would be too taxing on participants to have them record their activities throughout the entire year, even if it was only several times per month. Faced with these constraints from other methods, we turned to the Business Origami Technique.

## USAGE OF PAPER-BASED BUSINESS ORIGAMI TECHNIQUE

Our usage of the Business Origami Technique involved creating blank template tokens for various parts of the Google Fiber ecosystem. A safe rule of thumb is to create ten to fifteen tokens for each type of data (e.g., who, where, how). The important thing to keep in mind is that one does not have to be a professional designer to administer or design the pop-up tokens. Custom software isn't needed, either; instead, copies of pop-up tokens can be downloaded from websites of various organizations that use the method. For example, the British Columbia Government website contains a pre-made set of business origami tokens. Our tokens were created in Microsoft PowerPoint by simply copying silhouette images from the Internet and drawing text boxes for the labels (Figure 6.3). After that, it was just a matter of printing and cutting the tokens. A whiteboard or construction paper laid out on a large table can be used during the study to map out interactions between the tokens.

> **LESSON**
>
> Pop-up tokens can be easily created using templates provided online or using standard off-the-shelf presentation or drawing software.

We wanted to know where in the home family members used the Internet, so we created a pop-up "home" token to represent locations within the home. We used three different pop-up tokens for members of the household who used the Internet. These tokens represented an adult male, an adult female, and a child. Finally, we wanted to

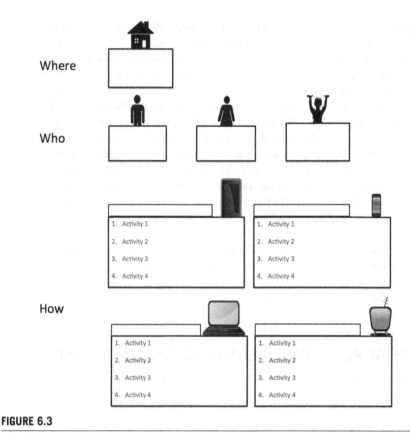

**FIGURE 6.3**

Tokens used in the Google Fiber study to represent where, who, and how the Internet was used in participants' households.

learn how family members used the Internet, so we made pop-up tokens for various types of devices (desktop/laptop, smartphone, tablet, and TV) and had participants write out the top activities they performed on each device. These tokens are shown in Figure 6.3. Participants were given blank tokens during the study and wrote their own labels based on the layout of their homes, the family members, and the devices used to connect to the Internet. Figure 6.4 shows a fully labeled set of tokens.

We first pilot-tested the paper-based version of the Business Origami Technique (as described by Martin and Hanington 2012) internally at Google to make sure it would provide us with the insights we wanted on Internet behavioral patterns. We also wanted to determine if this method could be effectively conducted with only one member of a household. Martin and Hanington (2012) described the Business Origami Technique as a method used in team settings, where multiple members of the ecosystem work together to visually show how they interact with each other. However, we knew from our survey that the households we would be visiting were

**FIGURE 6.4**

An example of a fully labeled set of tokens for one household in the Google Fiber study.

predominantly families with younger children. With this in mind, we knew that not every member of the household would be able to complete the study due to busy schedules or ethical considerations with minors.

After the internal pilot test, we were extremely excited about the potential of the method. The Business Origami Technique provided us with great insight into how an entire household used the Internet. Moreover, the use of one or two "point people" as representatives of the household did not seem to hinder the results. Another advantage was that it took our pilot participants only about an hour to complete the origami map, which we believed was less of a time commitment than having to participate in a diary study.

However, there were some concerns about using this method for the actual study with participants in Kansas City. We planned on visiting participants' homes multiple times throughout the year and have household members use the same pop-up tokens to describe their changing ecosystem and usage. That is, they would show us their existing ecosystem map and simply update it based on any behavior changes. With this in mind, we felt that the paper-based model did not lend itself well to being used multiple times during a longitudinal study. The paper tokens would deteriorate with repeated use.

> **LESSON**
>
> Paper-based tokens can easily deteriorate over time if they are used as a part of multiple study sessions.

We could have asked participants to create new tokens for each visit throughout the year; however, we thought that the hour it took to build the visual map was too long for each and every field study visit. We only had ninety minutes per visit with participants and many other topics to cover beyond the origami map. Hence, we needed a way to either shorten the time it took to create the origami map or think outside the box of how this technique could be implemented in the study while still giving us the time needed for other topics. This led us to design a digital version of the Business Origami Technique, as described in the next section.

## ADAPTING THE BUSINESS ORIGAMI TECHNIQUE TO BE DIGITAL

Due to the aforementioned reasons, we decided to adapt the method of creating the origami map to a digital format. Participants would use the same tokens and visually map them out, but this would be done on a computer rather than on paper. To my knowledge, conducting this method in a digital format has not been previously attempted or documented.

We wanted to make sure that it was fairly easy to create the origami map on a computer, so we had participants use Microsoft PowerPoint. We assumed that PowerPoint would be highly familiar and readily available to most users, thereby making this method almost as easy as creating tokens on paper. The tokens were pre-populated in a template slide, as shown in Figure 6.5. There were ten tokens per type (e.g., ten home tokens). The tokens were stacked on top of each other, like a deck of cards, on the right side of the slide. The top token had examples of how they should be labeled. When creating their origami or ecosystem maps, participants would simply select a token and move it to a blank part of the slide, and then label it. If they ran out of room on the slide, they could create a new slide.

The end product looked similar to the image in Figure 6.6. This is a zoomed-in view of how participants would position and label the tokens. More often than not,

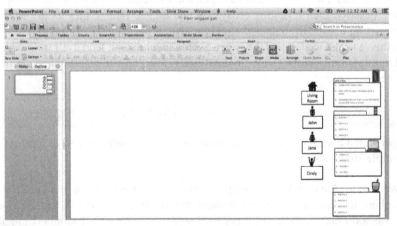

**FIGURE 6.5**

The PowerPoint template used in the Google Fiber study.

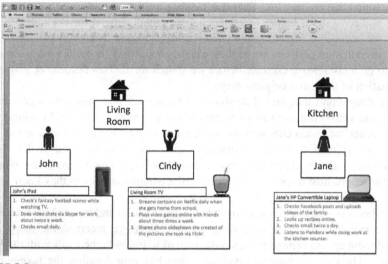

**FIGURE 6.6**

An example of what a digital origami map looked like for the Google Fiber study.

there were many more tokens on the slide, but this was dependent on how many people were in the household, how big the house was, and how many devices the family owned. Typically, there were two to three PowerPoint slides per household.

## SAVING TIME BY GOING DIGITAL

As stated earlier, a major reason for adapting the Business Origami Technique to be digital was to reduce the amount of time it took for participants to create the origami map. The tokens in the map could easily be copied and pasted in the digital form, as opposed to being written out each time. This method actually reduced the amount of time it took to complete the pop-up tokens by roughly half an hour per session in each household. Participants could still talk about the tokens after they were created, so interesting data was not lost. What was removed was the actual construction time needed to make each token during the study. For our purposes, we didn't want to spend too much time in the field visit sessions observing participants creating the tokens, so this was a great way of allowing more time for other things, such as observing and interviewing participants in person as they used the Internet service.

> **LESSON**
>
> The amount of time it takes to complete an origami map can be reduced by having participants create the origami map digitally via software like Microsoft PowerPoint. The ability to copy and paste tokens is a big time saver.

We found that another time-saving measure was to have participants create their tokens and ecosystems before we conducted our initial visit. At the beginning of the study, we conducted screening interviews using Google+ Hangouts, a video chat tool, with potential participants. If they were a good fit for the field visit, we asked them to do a homework exercise before we visited them. This homework involved the creation of their first origami map.

The PowerPoint template slide shown in Figure 6.5 was shown through screen sharing via video chat to show participants how to properly label and position the tokens. After the video chat session, written instructions were then emailed to the participants (Figure 6.7). The instructions reiterated what was said in the video chat session, and served as a reference in case they forgot how to create the tokens. The instructions also displayed an example of a completed map so they knew what the end product should look like.

We then gave them a week to finish the token creation and placement and asked them to email us the completed origami map. Once we received the maps, we cleaned them up and printed them to take with us to the in-home visits with the participants. The cleanup process involved things like repositioning the tokens (for alignment) and fixing misspellings.

During the in-home visit, we had participants describe why they designed the origami map the way they did via the paper printout. As stated earlier, some of the richest data came from participants talking aloud as they completed the map. For example, it was important to understand how each device was connected to the

**Instructions**

Thanks for signing up to help us with the Google Fiber user study. Part of this study is learning how you use the internet at home. To do that, you are going to visually create a diagram that shows how your household uses the internet. Follow the instructions below on how to do this.

1. Open the powerpoint document from the email entitled: "fiber origami"

2. Use the houses to indicate the locations in the home that you use the internet. Reposition the houses so that they are spread out over the screen. Then, label each one the location of the house that you use the internet (e.g. Living Room)

3. Use the people to indicate the household members that use the internet. Then reposition them next to each location in the house that they use the Internet. For instance, if John uses the Internet in both the Living Room and Kitchen, then make two for John and place one near the Living Room and one near the Kitchen.

4. Finally, use the different devices (laptop, tablet, etc.) to show what devices are used to access the internet. For each device provide the top activities that are done on each and how often. Also, use the top box to label what device it is. Finally, reposition the device next to the locations that it is used.

Quick Tip
- Feel free to copy the slide in the Powerpoint document. Often times there is not enough space on one slide.

**FIGURE 6.7**

Instructions given to participants to explain the process for creating an origami map in the Google Fiber study.

Internet and which device was the primary device for accessing the Internet in the home. While we didn't get to hear participants talk during their creation of the origami maps, we obtained similar data by having them discuss the map after it was constructed.

## INCREASING THE LONGEVITY OF THE ORIGAMI MAP BY GOING DIGITAL

The second reason for going digital with the Business Origami Technique was because of our plan to analyze behaviors for one year. An important research goal was evaluating how Internet usage evolved over time with the introduction of Google Fiber in the household. Paper tokens could be damaged or lost, so we wanted a way of easily saving them or having duplicates. Thus, a digital version was ideal.

---

**LESSON**

When planning to conduct a longitudinal study in which the same participants are visited more than once, use a digital process to create the origami map. This will increase the longevity of the tokens and make them easier to update for follow-up visits.

---

After the initial visit, we revisited participants every three to six months. During our follow-up visits, we printed a copy of the original origami map containing the tokens from the previous visit. We would then show the respective maps to the participants and ask them questions as prompts so we could understand updates to the maps and thus understand any changes in the family's Internet usage behaviors. For instance, "Are there any new devices since our last visit?" or "Are there any new locations in the house where you use the tablet?"

In order to remain engaged in the conversation, the field visit interviews were recorded and notes were taken on the paper printout of the origami map. After the visits, we would review the recordings and notes to manually make changes to the digital map. For instance, we would create a token for a tablet if a tablet was added to the household. This would then be saved, and the process was repeated for any return visits.

## ANALYZING THE RESULTS

There is no straightforward way to analyze the results of a business origami session. Similar to other qualitative methods, such as usability studies and interviews, analysis requires the researchers to derive insights from verbal comments made by participants and recognize patterns of behavior. In the Business Origami Technique, data includes written descriptions of the tokens and origami map, participants' verbal descriptions of the tokens, and behavior changes based on the change in placement and location of map tokens.

Having multiple team members attend the origami map interview sessions can help derive these insights. We had two to three people from multiple focus areas in our company, such as product management, design, and engineering, attend our sessions with participants. After the field visits, we hosted debrief meetings to document the things we learned. Having additional team members present in the debrief sessions provided fresh perspectives and insights that may have been overlooked by having only one person in the field.

To recognize patterns of behavior, think of your research questions before running the study. However, thinking of every question prior to the study is nearly impossible. For example, a researcher might learn something new and unexpected during the study. Research questions are often derived from debrief sessions and from stakeholders. Keep an open mind when interacting with these stakeholders. Know that you may have to revisit the origami maps in order to answer questions that arise later.

> **LESSON**
>
> For effective data analysis, have predefined research questions or goals so that the change in specific behaviors of interest can be accurately understood.

We created posters of themes that came out of the data analysis (e.g., the top five Internet-related activities done in the garage). These were useful for sharing the insights from the study with stakeholders. These posters can also be presented in the team's workspace to help them remember some of the key findings from the research.

## CHALLENGES WITH THE DIGITAL BUSINESS ORIGAMI TECHNIQUE

While we conducted our field study using the digital version of the Business Origami Technique, we faced several additional challenges. We outline each here along with the lessons learned in an effort to help researchers conducting future studies that might use a similar technique.

### COMPREHENSION OF THE EXERCISE

As stated earlier, we did not want to take too much time away from the in-home visits with the origami map exercise, so we decided to have participants create the map beforehand. However, this presented us with some unique challenges.

First, it was somewhat challenging getting participants to understand how to complete the exercise. Traditionally, the origami map design sessions are conducted in person, which means additional instruction and correction can be done in real time. Since we wanted participants to create their first maps on their own time before we visited them, we had to provide them with instructions ahead of time to compensate for the fact that we could not correct any mistakes they made while creating the map. As mentioned, we tried to alleviate these issues by showing them how to design the map over Google+ Hangouts and by providing written instructions via email (Figure 6.7). Yet participants would sometimes not understand how to properly label tokens or how to position them. This was especially true for tokens that required more detailed feedback, such as the activities the participants did with specific devices (e.g., streaming Hulu videos on a tablet every evening before bed). Thus, even with our efforts to explain and inform the participants on how to design the maps, we learned that they would most likely not be created accurately. Mistakes were made, such as mislabeling tokens or not including information that was critical to understanding user behavior.

The video chat sessions were critical in teaching participants of how to create the origami map. Unfortunately some participants were unable to conduct video chats with us and their origami maps were not as well designed as those created by the participants who were shown via screen sharing on Google+ Hangouts, how to create the origami map.

> ### LESSON
> Having participants create origami maps on their own time can be efficient when combined with other methods, such as field visits. However, explaining how to design the map may be difficult when a moderator is not in person. Detailed instructions and examples can help alleviate this challenge.

For this reason, the team should build in enough time to review the origami maps before conducting the in-home visits. Instead of asking participants to fix their mistakes, we took what they had submitted and tried to correct mistakes in person during the in-home visits. We prepared a list of questions for each participant in order to fill in any knowledge gaps. Since it is easy to make mistakes when creating an origami map, it is recommended to only use this method when you have enough time in the home visits to do a follow up discussion with participants.

## GETTING PARTICIPANTS TO COMPLETE THE EXERCISE ON TIME

Another challenge with having participants complete origami maps on their own time is getting them to turn the maps in by a given deadline. Many people will wait until the last minute to do so—it is human nature. We assigned a deadline of one week before the home visit, but a few participants waited until the day of their scheduled visit to turn in their maps. This made it difficult for us to have enough time to review the map so that we could ask informed questions during the visit. It also made printing out the map a challenge. For example, I had to rush to the nearest Kinko's (a local printing store) to print two participants' maps right before their in-person study sessions.

Many of our participants were families with young children, which meant busy lifestyles. For example, asking a mom to complete a thirty-minute homework assignment while juggling the schedules of three kids might be a challenge. For this reason, researchers' study schedules must be accommodating. Providing participants with a full week to complete an assignment is a necessity. Reminders should be built into the weekly plan. Initially, we only reminded participants the day before the deadline that their origami map was due. Often, this was not enough notice. In retrospect, we should have given more reminders to prompt participants to complete the exercise prior to the deadline.

---

**LESSON**

It is best practice to give participants a week to complete their origami maps. Make sure to have a week after the maps are submitted to review them so you can ask more informed questions about participants' behaviors. The second week also creates a buffer before the home visit if participants are late in turning in their origami maps.

---

## TECHNOLOGICAL FAILURES

Introducing and relying on technology raised challenges that are not typically experienced with paper-based origami maps. Instead of building our own tool or using lesser-known tools to design the exercise digitally, we used PowerPoint because we assumed most people were already familiar with and comfortable using this software. However, it turned out that two of our participants did not have access to PowerPoint. For these participants, we had to do the exercise with them using video chat and screen sharing; we created the tokens and map in PowerPoint while participants provided us with information on where to place the tokens and draw the arrows.

Of course, one must realize that any time video chat is used, there is a chance for technological issues or failure. Participants may have incompatible software or a slow Internet connection because they choose to participate from work or other locations. There were instances where we had to resort to the tried and tested method of using the telephone. This made the written instructions for how to design the origami map even more important because we were not able to visually show participants how to do the exercise.

Many of our participants were not tech savvy; thus, trying to teach them how to use video chat was a challenge. (Refer to Chapter 2 to learn more about conducting interviews with remote participants via video communication technologies.) For example, after trying to teach a sixty-five-year-old retired teacher how to use video chat, one may appreciate the design challenge that the Google+ Hangout team had for its range of users.

We also learned that screen real estate can be an issue when designing the origami map digitally. A lot of tokens had to be placed on the map to document Internet usage in the home. Unfortunately, many participants struggled with fitting the tokens in the space provided on the PowerPoint slide deck. In the paper-based format, it is very easy to accommodate for space needs. However, in the digital format, many participants did not know what to do when they ran out of space for tokens on their PowerPoint slide. Many participants naturally created additional slides, but some did not. This caused us to lose valuable data. If we were to conduct the study again, we would provide instructions on how to account for limited screen real estate or use a tool that is better suited for handling a large number of tokens.

> **LESSON**
>
> Common software can be useful for designing the digital origami map. However, when working with a wide variety of participants, be prepared as some participants may not have standard software packages or may not know how to use them. Other technical challenges may also arise.

## INABILITY TO INCLUDE EVERY MEMBER OF THE HOUSEHOLD

We assigned one or two point people who were considered the head of the household to design the origami map. We originally recruited these participants from a pool of users that completed an online survey, so we had already built rapport with them during our screening interviews. Often times they would speak on behalf of others in the family, such as describing what their children or spouse did on the Internet. For most families this was not an issue, but there were some instances where this caused us to have incomplete data. For example, there was a chance that some family members looked at websites that others may not know about or might deem inappropriate. Thus, this knowledge would not be shared with the point person in the study.

In hindsight, it would have been better to have the entire family participate in the study. Since we were having them design the origami maps on their own time, we thought it would be easier to have one person do the exercise instead of trying to coordinate with multiple family members. Getting minors to complete the exercise or having them not be a distraction during the in-home visits were also major concerns. However, it would have been worth the extra effort to include all family members in the study, especially during the interviews. While the head of household may have been able to fairly accurately report on things like what devices were in the home and where family members used them, it is unlikely that person could accurately report on the activities others did on the devices.

> **LESSON**
>
> While it may be more challenging to include multiple family members in an origami session and follow-up interview, getting data from each family member would be highly valuable to ensure that information is accurately reported.

## LESSONS FOR FUTURE STUDIES

I now reflect more broadly on the Digital Business Origami Technique to draw out additional suggestions for future studies. These relate to learning about behavioral changes and adapting research methods to digital formats.

### LEARNING ABOUT BEHAVIORAL CHANGES

A major goal of our study was finding a method that we could easily use to learn about behavioral changes in household Internet usage. The Business Origami Technique was an ideal method for the types of data we wanted to collect from our participants. There were too many activities and subtle shifts in behavior in a household to track via a survey, and the fact that we wanted to learn about usage behavior throughout a year meant that doing a diary study could have easily been too taxing on our participants.

The Business Origami Technique is recommended for any study in which capturing changes in behavior over an extended period of time is needed. This method allowed us to see at a glance what behavioral changes were occurring, such as adding new devices or increasing the frequency of certain activities. We could also easily learn about behaviors that were of particular interest to our team. On the other hand, a major disadvantage of the method is that it requires participants to recall their behaviors, which can reduce the reliability of any reported data.

Our use of the Business Origami Technique did not provide us with the ability to collect data from a large sample of users. For larger samples, a survey or usage logs would be needed. We studied only fifteen households, and it would have been too difficult to study more households for a year using this method. Similar to other qualitative research and design methods, the Business Origami Technique is not ideal to learn about behaviors that could generalize to larger populations, since sample sizes are small.

---

**LESSON**

The Business Origami Technique is an ideal method for tracking behavioral shifts in users over the course of an extended period of time. The advantages it has over other methods, such as diary studies, is that it is less taxing on the participant and is a good method for tracking unforeseen behaviors. However, be aware that findings from this method are not easily generalizable.

---

Another consideration is that monitoring behaviors with this method is always retrospective for participants. This was somewhat problematic in our study because participants sometimes had difficulty thinking through what they typically did online in a given day. Yet, the method *was* very beneficial in giving us a high-level picture of user behaviors and changes to those behaviors over long periods of time. Behaviors that need to be captured in real time would be better conducted with methods such as diary studies that prompt the participant when a particular behavior is occurring.

In reality, a likely best practice is to combine the Business Origami Technique with other methods that serve the shortcomings listed above. This is why we used surveys and field visits in combination with the Business Origami Technique. As with any method, there are advantages and disadvantages that lend the method to be used in certain situations.

> **LESSON**
>
> It is best to combine the Business Origami Technique with other data collection methods to overcome the limitations in the method.

## DIGITAL ADAPTATION WORKS WELL

Adapting the design exercise of the origami map to be digital rather than paper-based was a risk and resulted in some implementation challenges, as depicted above. In hindsight, it was the right decision for our situation. When multiple interactions are expected with the same set of participants over a long period of time, then the digital model is ideal.

In our case, a longitudinal study was necessary for tracking changes in behaviors over the course of one year. There was no way we could do this with the paper-based model. Updates had to be easily made, so the computer was much better to use than paper. Also, the need to archive the maps for an extended period of time was a good reason to do the activity digitally. Paper origami maps are easily lost or damaged, which can cause data to be incomplete in a longitudinal study.

We had also taken into consideration that our user base was 2,000 miles away from our office location. Google Fiber was installed only in Kansas City, and our team is based out of the Google headquarters in Mountain View, California. Therefore, it was not feasible for us to design the maps in person with participants on a recurring basis. In these types of situations, where proximity to users is a challenge, digitally based origami maps provide a viable alternative to the more traditional paper-based version of the method.

> **LESSON**
>
> Creating digital origami maps is ideal for longitudinal studies that require multiple visits to participants' homes and also for sessions with remote participants.

## CONCLUSION

The Business Origami Technique is a research method that we found highly valuable for the goals of our study, in which we were tasked with learning about the Internet usage of Google Fiber households for a year. It was useful in tracking an ecosystem that involved multiple members of a household, a wide range of devices, and limitless online activities. This method could be applied more generally to research that involves complex ecosystems such as the one detailed in this chapter.

As detailed in this chapter, the paper format of the origami maps did not lend itself well to conducting a longitudinal study. By making the activity digital, we were able to easily archive the origami maps and make changes to them throughout the year when we did follow-up visits. This made documenting changes and adding new tokens to the origami map easy. It also provided a quicker way of creating the initial origami map, as tokens were easily copied and pasted within the digital template.

On the downside, the digital format presented us with some unique challenges. These include explaining how to create the origami map when the moderator or researcher is not face to face with the participant and ensuring that participants can complete the activity on their own computers or devices.

In conclusion, the Business Origami Technique was the ideal method for us to learn about changes in Internet usage behavior. It gave us the details needed to understand subtle changes in participants' behaviors while also providing a lightweight way of gathering data and not overburdening our participants. We recommend this method to any researcher looking for a quick and easy way to understand complex ecosystems and behavioral changes over time.

## REFERENCES

British Columbia Government. "Business Origami." [online]. Retrieved from the British Columbia Government website: http://www2.gov.bc.ca/gov/topic.page?id=18E5E9288C2A4E3C8146E95C70350C37.

Martin, B., Hanington, B., 2012. Universal Methods of Design: 100 Way to Research Complex Problems, Develop Innovative Ideas, and Design Effective Solutions. Rockport Publishers, Beverly, MA.

McMullin, J., 2010. Business Origami [online]. Retrieved from the Citizen Experience website. http://www.citizenexperience.com/2010/04/30/business-origami/.

# The Financial Tour: Methods for Studying Sensitive Financial Questions

# 7

**Jofish Kaye**

*Yahoo Research, Sunnyvale, CA, USA*

## INTRODUCTION

Our financial lives are important and complex. How much money you have is, for better or worse, a remarkably strong predictor of many things in life: your health, the education of your children, your leisure activities, and your diet. At the same time, it can be a topic of considerable secrecy. In the United States, at least, it is nearly inconceivable to ask a friend how much money they make, or how much they have saved for retirement. It is this level of privacy that makes studying financial situations extremely difficult. At the same time, the comparatively unexplored nature of those situations makes for an intriguing area of research.

In this chapter, I discuss the techniques my colleagues and I used to study personal finances in the San Francisco Bay Area in the United States. I present the techniques we used to understand and characterize the ways these people represent and engage with their financial situation. The results of the study are well documented in our paper, "Money Talks: Tracking Personal Finances" (Kaye et al. 2014); my focus in this discussion is the interviewing process, rather than the results. I will both present a set of patterns or techniques for exploring finances and reflect on what constitutes an appropriate approach to developing a method for studying a new topic.

This project came out of discussion around a website that helps people understand their personal finances. Much of the website is concerned with providing information about stock prices, stock movements, and financial news. However, many users are concerned with their personal finances and financial education: refinancing mortgages, finding a better credit card, or finding a stable investment with a higher interest rate. It was this population that I set out to understand and characterize in this study.

In the first section, "Defining the Study," I begin with a discussion of the objectives of the study: what we wanted to accomplish and who we wanted to interview. I discuss how we recruited people and include the screener the research team used to get basic information about participants on the book's companion website. I discuss the team that came along for the interviews and the tools we used as part of the interviewing. In the second section, "Interviews," I discuss the form of the interviews themselves. We begin by gathering basic information about the household, and then have them draw a map of their finances. We discuss recent events that have a financial impact, and then talk about the tools they use to track their finances. We wrap up the section with some larger-scale questions about hypothetical situations. I then briefly discuss our practices post-interview. In the final section of the chapter, "Discussion," I look at some of the issues that arose in our paper (Kaye et al. 2014) and discuss implications for the further study of finances within the field of human-computer interaction (HCI).

## DEFINING THE STUDY

I initially framed the question we would be studying in terms of understanding people's financial identity. I put together a short presentation outlining the study based on intuition and a few conversations with interested colleagues, and then took the presentation around to different people: my colleagues in Yahoo Labs, program managers in finance and personal finance, and people in the design organization who were doing other studies in the finance domain. This helped both refine the focus for the study and build internal support. At each step, I revised the presentation to reflect the most recent feedback.

> **LESSON**
>
> Taking the opportunity to bring potential stakeholders and colleagues on board and get them interested during early stages of defining a study is easier and more productive than trying to do so afterward.

The opening slide of the presentation was a simple statement:

*Financial decisions are not just transactions, but are a key part of people's identity. Yahoo! Finance can become part of users' daily habits by supporting and engaging with this sense of identity.*

In the other slides, I made a brief case for the study as proposed. The first slide made a case for this qualitative work—a small number of people with two hours of in-depth questioning, compared to large n=1000+ participant surveys, requiring perhaps fifteen minutes of time, which is a popular way for research to be executed in corporations. The second slide was an overview of how we would execute the study, based on Technology Tours (Blythe, Monk, and Park 2002): exploring practices (the present), history (the past), and guided speculation (the future). Subsequent slides discussed the demographics, the stakeholders, and a proposed timeline.

This deck, and particularly that starting sentence, helped articulate, plan, and organize the study, and in particular helped us focus and choose the methods we discuss in this chapter. Our aim was to understand the habits people had around finance and money as a way to understand the opportunities for Yahoo! Finance within that domain. For example, as I discussed the plan with the finance product managers, we talked about the various stages of financial events that occur over the course of a lifetime. They suggested the Milton-Bradley board game *The Game of Life* as a way to think about these events, in which players move through life stages. It was a metaphor with problems, such as the linear nature and singular player, but it helped us think about the various financial life events that our demographic would encounter and have to understand and be responsible for. For example, an archetypal middle-class American might go to school and college, graduate, find their first significant job and get their first 401(k)[1], get married, buy a house, sell a house, move, have children, have medical bills, plan for retirement, inherit, plan for their death, and die. We wanted to make sure we interviewed people who would cover that spectrum.

Once we understood a bit more about what our various stakeholders were interested in, we began developing a semi-structured interview protocol. The contents of and responses to that interview protocol make up most of the rest of this chapter, but establishing that draft interview protocol was an important part of establishing what we were doing, what we wanted to get out of it, and what kinds of people we were looking for.

## PICKING PEOPLE TO INTERVIEW

The people we selected for the study had to meet certain criteria. For example, we were looking for people who were not very active traders of stocks and shares. Active traders have particular financial information needs, and the evidence suggests that those are needs that are quite well served by Yahoo's current offerings. There is no doubt room for improvement, as there is in any system, but we were looking to understand more about people who were more normal, mundane, everyday. So we picked an arbitrary cap of fifteen stock trades a year. Within that set of non-active traders, we wanted to make sure we covered a reasonable amount of diversity within the constraints of a manageable, open-ended interview study: about fifteen people.

We initially recruited users by sending a request out to a group of people who had answered a Craigslist ad looking for people to participate in research. The request asked them to fill out a survey (included on the book's companion website) and told them that, if selected, we would pay one hundred fifty dollars for a two-hour in-home interview about their financial practices. We wanted to limit the number of questions in the survey while still making sure we understood what was necessary to select appropriate people and while respecting their privacy and the unwillingness of people to provide detailed information. So, for example, we asked for their age,

---

[1] A 401(k) is a defined-contribution retirement plan popular in the United States. Workers contribute up to $17,000 a year before taxes, some of which may be matched by their employer. The funds are used to purchase a mix of stocks and shares. After the worker turns fifty-nine and a half, they can withdraw from their 401(k); if they do so before that time, they must generally pay a 10 percent penalty.

sorted into slots by decade. We asked how many children they had and how old they were. We asked for their gender (male/female/other) and their occupation. We asked if they had a mortgage, a car loan, or student debt. We asked how many times a year they traded stocks. We asked what the value of their liquid assets were (how much they could invest tomorrow). We also asked if they were retired or thinking of retiring soon, if they had a personal financial advisor, if they owned their house, and if they owned stocks or a 401(k). We gathered email addresses, phone numbers, and street addresses. We asked for their availability for each morning and afternoon over the two-week period that we had allocated for the study, which made scheduling a great deal easier. Finally, we asked them if there was anything else they'd like to tell us.

We had approximately 120 people fill out the survey. We sorted the responses into bands by age: people in their twenties, thirties, forties, fifties, and sixty-plus, and then sorted each age bracket into people with and without children. We then picked three people from each age bracket, making sure at least one did have children and one didn't have children. We then rebalanced to get a good mix of answers to other questions, with a bias toward people who we thought might have interesting financial stories to increase the diversity of our sample: people with interesting occupations (doula, for example), or who had interesting responses to our free-form questions—Anthony, sixty-eight, wrote, "I am a very handsome man" in his answer to *Is there anything else you'd like to tell us?*

---

**LESSON**

A good rule of thumb is to include, *"Is there anything else you'd like to tell us?"* as the last question in any survey. It's an opportunity for people to explain their answers, and you never know what else people will write.

---

Midway through the study we rebalanced the selection again to make it more demographically appropriate, when we noticed that we had no Latino participants in the selection—an anomaly in California, where the population is approximately one-third Latino—and rejiggered one or two selections.

---

**LESSON**

The more diverse the participants, the more diverse the information and feedback will be gathered from the study. Work with stakeholders to find out what matters to them: ages? income? nationality? There are no hard and fast rules about what *kind* of diversity one needs to have, although if there are no women in a sample—well, that's something to fix. A good heuristic: *try to not interview too many people like the researcher.*

---

We were lucky enough to have an expert on-site recruiter, Rosie Cabreros, who handled a lot of the details around recruiting and scheduling for us. And while most people aren't lucky enough to have a dedicated recruiter, one can learn a lot from talking to an experienced study recruiter about the right places to post requests for help, suitable levels of reimbursement, and study recruitment wording.

## CREW AND KIT

I brought in Mary McCuistion as a contractor. She is an experienced ethnographer with whom I revised the interview protocol and shared the fieldwork and some of the analysis. We headed out to the field, and "we", in this instance, was generally two people, me (Jofish Kaye) and Mary, although we brought along three other people at various points as ride-alongs to observe: a collaborator on our main paper (and my manager), the program manager for Personal Finance at Yahoo, and the program manager for Finance at Yahoo.

Pick ride-alongs carefully, and be sure to make expectations about their roles clear. The researcher must remain in control of the interview. Be careful that ride-alongs understand that what they're seeing is not all of "doing research": they're seeing only the interaction with the individual, not the planning that goes into the process nor the analysis afterward.

In general, there should be two interviewers. If the researcher is doing intense, long-term anthropological-style fieldwork, then he or she will be alone. But for studying domestic methods, most of the times strangers will be visited in their houses, and as a general rule, that is a good thing not to do alone. Perhaps more importantly, having two people allows them to trade off, makes sure they don't miss things, and gives them someone to discuss the interview with afterward.

The exception to the two-person rule is when a stakeholder or decision-maker is brought along for interviews, which should absolutely be done if possible: coming along helps them understand the process and the work that goes into the research. Make sure to explain to them before the interview that their role is to observe, but reassure them that you will ask questions periodically—and make sure to do so. Something can often be learned from the questions stakeholders ask, as it can help the researcher understand the stakeholders' priorities.

> **LESSON**
>
> Try to include two interviewers when possible so important data isn't missed and nuances of the interview can be discussed with someone afterward. A second person can also be helpful for personal safety reasons.

As we were studying the sensitive topic of personal finances, we believed it was important to respect the privacy of our subjects as much as possible. Because of this, we elected to only audio record our interviews, rather than video record them. We had two hand-held, dedicated-purpose voice recorders that saved recordings to SD cards, and we made a third recording with an external microphone through a laptop running Pear Note, which enabled us to take typed notes and record at the same time without too much typing noise in the recording. Photographs were taken with a

**FIGURE 7.1**

The financial items Arturo showed us from his wallet, showing in-interview anonymization.

Canon SD90, and, as much as possible, we were careful to obscure personal information using small Post-its in the photographs, rather than relying on obscuring data by blurring or blocking the images in post-processing. (See Figure 7.1.) This made clear to participants that we were taking their privacy seriously, which we believe helped them open up to us.

> **LESSON**
>
> As much as possible, avoid capturing information which might identify participants during the interview, rather than obscuring it in post-processing later.

## INTERVIEWS

In the interviews, we began by asking for introductory details and demographics, and then moved to our first tool: we asked people to draw a map and/or calendar of their finances. We asked questions about how they had learned about finances, then gave our participants the second tool: a set of index cards with financial events written on them. We asked about critical incidents—their last major investments and purchases, etc.—then looked at the tools they used, both physical and digital, to manage their finances. We finished with wrap-up questions.

We took turns leading the interview, and the person not interviewing took notes in Pear Note, commenting when appropriate. This became particularly important on days when we had two or three interviews and became exhausted. We printed out the interview protocol on paper, and the interview leader took notes on the paper, which was later scanned.

---

**LESSON**

It's a good idea to prototype questionnaire and interview protocols by trying them out on colleagues or friends before going into the field. However, the social pressure in the United States against discussing finances meant that we couldn't ask questions like, "How much do you earn?" to people we knew.

Consequently, the first actual interview may be the "pancake interview." Like the first pancake when making a batch of pancakes, be prepared to throw the first interview away, if necessary. It turned out not to be necessary for us, but keep in mind that the first interview is always allowed to be a tester or pilot.

---

## INTRODUCTION AND DEMOGRAPHICS

Our interview process had a number of distinct phases. We began by having participants sign the consent form required by our lawyers, and after that we would get explicit permission to record the session before turning on all the voice recorders.

---

**LESSON**

Always have multiple recordings. *Always* have multiple recordings. A cell-phone is an excellent low-overhead way to ensure having a second recording.

---

We introduced the study and explained our methods for anonymizing the participant's data: we would use a pseudonym, avoid identifiable images, etc. (We often decided on a pseudonym before we even entered the house, so we could say things like, "In fact, you'll be referred to as 'Annie' in all the materials.") We explicitly pointed out that there were no right or wrong answers and no ramifications for anything they said. We made it clear they could stop at any time, and if there was anything they didn't want to talk about, we were happy to skip it. We also made it clear that anything they said would not be connected to any Yahoo service they might use.

We then asked for basic information for everyone in the household: names, ages, relationship to the interviewee, profession, income, and degree of financial involvement in the household. We would get a basic understanding of how the household finances worked: did one person earn all the money? Did one person handle the finances?

## EXPLORING PRESENT PRACTICES

We gave the interviewees a few sheets of blank paper and a pen, and asked them to draw a map of their finances. Invariably, they would ask for clarification: what did we mean by a map? We'd tell them it was entirely up to them, and we would encourage them in whatever they put down. Responses varied widely, as seen in Figure 7.2: some drew pie charts, others pictures or literal maps.

We returned to these maps throughout the interviews, encouraging our interviewees to add more content as we discussed different parts of their financial lives: adding retirement accounts they had forgotten about or expenses they hadn't included in the first draft. Our choice to include the question "*Draw a map of your finances*" is influenced by cultural probes (Gaver, Dunne, and Pacenti 1999). It gave us big-picture views of their finances. At the same time, by emphasizing how people thought about their own finances, we made clear that we weren't there to test them. Everyone feels some guilt about the organization of their finances—they should be more up to date, they should be more organized—and we wanted to make sure people didn't feel we were going to criticize or correct them or tell them how they should be doing it.

---

**LESSON**

Take care to make sure interviewees don't feel judged. It isn't necessary to enthusiastically endorse what they say, but participants need to feel the interviewers are on their side, even if the interviewers would do things differently or don't approve of the interviewee's choices.

---

We encouraged people to talk aloud as they drew the maps. For example, as Charlotte drew the map in the lower left of Figure 7.2, she explained her thought process to us:

> It's always hovering there. It's angry all the time. And . . . The jobs . . . it would be kinda like stick figures that are holding an umbrella. Sometimes the umbrella is like really flimsy because the job is not so great or it doesn't pay so great. It's still helping a little bit.

> They're all coming to the center point of trying to reach my goals. (long pause) The goals would be more time with the kids . . . less jobs because I've been juggling jobs, multiple jobs for years now.

After the financial map question, we asked our participants to draw a financial calendar. We added this question after the first interview or two, when we realized that some of our interviewees' finances were highly temporal: paychecks arrived on the first and fifteenth of the month, credit card or mortgage payments were due on particular dates, regular grocery trips were made.

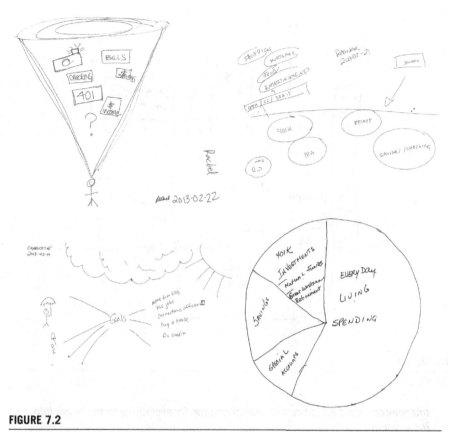

**FIGURE 7.2**

Responses to *"Draw a map of your personal finances"* from Rachel, Ragnar, Charlotte, and Jane.

---

> **LESSON**
>
> Don't be afraid to revise the interview protocol as the study goes along. Sometimes a question will arise in conversation that leads to a wealth of information.

For some of our interviewees, the calendar was a better way to represent their financial information than the map. Allan, who drew the pie chart in Figure 7.2, talked through his calendar (Figure 7.3) while both he and the interviewer pointed at it:

> *Interviewer*: You get paid on the 1st and the 15th?
> *Allan*: Yes, it's really like the 15th and the 31st or whatever, but basically . . .
> *Interviewer*: When does Tracy get paid?
> *Allan*: She is every two weeks, so it sort of varies with her, but often, I guess, we can say here, too, and then rent, we pay on the 26th just to be sure. I make a student loan payment five days after getting paid.

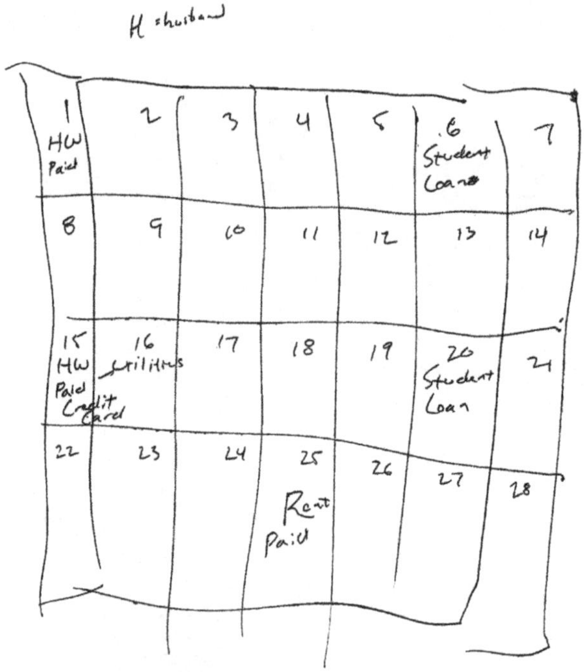

**FIGURE 7.3**

Allan's calendar.

*Interviewer*: Five days is because that gives time for everything to sort of get into the account?
*Allan*: Yes, yeah, just to be safe.
*Interviewer*: You are doing that twice a month.
*Allan*: I do that twice a month. I give my whole paycheck.
*Interviewer*: Do you know what that number is? Do you write a check every time or . . . ?
*Allan*: I do it automatically, so I don't do it, but it is $2,300 each . . .
*Interviewer*: No. Yes, but you know that number in your soul kind of thing?
*Allan*: Oh yes, yes indeed. Credit card's on the 15th.

---

**LESSON**

The general concept of asking for multiple representations of anything one is trying to understand is a useful interview technique. It's easy for both the interviewer and interviewee to get stuck on one mental model or representation. Going back and forth between multiple models gives variety and the opportunity for new insights at low cost.

We then asked about their financial education: how did they learn about managing money? This was quite an open-ended question; our interview guide for this question read:

- How do you educate yourself about finances/money management? Can you give us a specific example? Books? Magazines? TV? Websites? Friends? Family?
- Do people come to you for advice? Do you go to people for advice? Whom? How do you know what to trust? What are marks of quality in financial advice? How did you decide to do things this way?
- What did you learn from your parents about finances and money management?

That list of questions—all of which we didn't necessarily ask—gives a sense of the variety of approaches we wanted to explore. We came back to these questions—particularly, *"How do you know what to trust?"*—throughout the interview.

## FINANCIAL EVENTS

The next part of our interview was quite simple but produced some of the most impressive results in terms of stories, insights, and understandings of our interviewees. We had sixteen index cards, each of which had written on it an event with financial consequences: college, debt/bankruptcy, unexpected windfall, unexpected expense, employment, move, family change, retire, travel, birth, divorce, marriage, death, medical bills, buy/sell home, graduate. We put these out in no particular order and asked our interviewees if any of the events had had a financial impact on them recently (Figure 7.4).

Some of our interviewees went through all sixteen of the cards, telling stories about each one. Others focused quickly on an important story that was fundamental

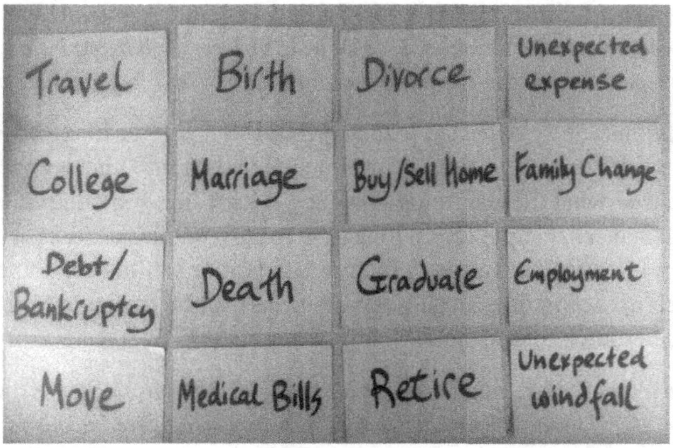

**FIGURE 7.4**

Financial event cards.

to their financial situation. This may have been the most effective part of the interview. It would have been awkward to go through each of these questions in a verbal list ("Has family change had a financial impact on you?"), and it meant that interviewees could focus on the important stories. Some participants required more prodding ("So, have any of these other events had a financial impact on you?"); others picked up the cards one by one and told us of any relevant experiences. For example, Jane immediately picked up "Unexpected Expenses":

> *Interviewer*: Is there one of these that you're experiencing right now that you feel like you're having a real financial effect from?
> *Jane*: This one. (Picks up "Unexpected Expense.")
> *Interviewer*: The "Unexpected expense." Tell me about that.
> *Jane*: My car blew up. The car has less than 20,000 miles on it and they told me that it's the transmission and I had it taken to the repair shop, they told me to rebuild the transmission, that's going to be $3,200 and we'll give you a 30 day guarantee. They said to put in a new one, that would be $4,200, and we'll give you a year guarantee.

She went on to tell us about other expenses—her roof leaking, problems with medical bills—none of which we would have asked about individually.

## CRITICAL INCIDENTS

Next, we asked about critical incidents: when they last made an expensive purchase, what tools they used to decide what and how to buy, when they last made a significant investment, and what tools they used to decide how and in what to invest. The answers to these questions gave us deeper insights into the people we interviewed. For example, one of our interviewees, Allan, told us that his most recent investment was an eight-hundred-dollar suit:

> *That was for work, and I am . . . this sounds terrible, not humble at all, but I am always the nicest-looking one in the office. The other guys wear jeans and a shirt, and I will wear the suit just because I sort of want to dress the job that I want to have and earn respect. I look young already, so I would like that as much as possible.*

That wasn't the answer we expected to that question, but phrases like, "I want to dress the job that I want to have" gave us a fundamental insight into his view of the world.

We then asked what the one thing was they'd least like someone to learn about their personal finances. People took a long time to answer this question: we could see them trying out possible answers in their heads before settling on something that they would tell us. Sometimes these answers turned out be particularly informative. For example, Veronica told us about her parking tickets:

> *I'll tell you a secret, I got a thousand dollars' worth of parking tickets . . . we got a thousand dollars' worth of parking tickets, three of them were because I parked on the sidewalk here coming home late at night after going out with my girlfriends, like, two, "I don't want to go walking around the parking lot." Those*

*are like three-hundred-dollar tickets and then another two just because I never paid them and totally forgot about them. They got totally racked up and I just kept getting parking tickets all the time. I get the parking tickets constantly; constantly I cannot stop getting parking tickets. I don't know what it is.*

Another participant, sixty-eight years old and retired, told us the thing he'd least like people to know about his finances was about an inheritance from his parents:

*Well, I think the main thing, I mean, I don't really keep it a secret, but I do find it somewhat embarrassing, is that most of the money that I got to do this was that I didn't earn it myself, I got it from my parents. That's the one thing.*

## TOOLS

We then switched interviewing tactics again and asked about the tools people used to keep track of their money and finances. We began by asking people what financial things they carried in their wallet or purse. Wallet studies—recording the objects that people carry on their person every day—have a history, both within HCI (Mainwaring, Anderson, and Chang 2005a, Mainwaring, Anderson, and Chang 2005b) and in other design work (Travis 2010; Nippert-Eng 2010; see also the Flickr tags *whatsinyourbag, whatsinyourpockets,* etc.). We asked people to take out the financial objects and lay them on the table (Figure 7.5). As they did this, we put small Post-its over the names and numbers on the cards to prepare them for being photographed.

We asked our participants to tell us about what we saw in their wallets, and that was one of the richest sources of stories in the whole project, confirming our suspicion about the value of the objects people carry with them. We found some people had multiple wallets, such as secondary wallets for keeping track of coupons, and we anonymized and photographed the contents of those as well.

**FIGURE 7.5**

Rachel's wallet, showing the labeled personal and business cards.

> **LESSON**
>
> The objects that people carry with them every day are important to them, and we believed that understanding the financial objects people carry with them might give an insight into day-to-day interactions with their financial systems.

The great advantage of the wallet study portion of the interview was that it provided an easy and understandable introduction to gathering images and stories about physical tools. It was well-delimited, and hiding private details on credit cards and the like with Post-its was a clear sign that we were taking privacy seriously. In fact, we were often taking that concern further than the interviewees themselves, which we thought was a good thing. We found that people's wallets often articulated aspects of their financial lives. Rachel, for example, found her wallet very important for separating her small business and her personal accounting (Figure 7.5). She told us:

> I was really getting them all mixed up. I had to go and I got this amazing label maker for Christmas. I have labeled them all. . . .
>
> I have—for this wallet . . . the first set of cards are related to my personal account. The second set is related to my business. The next is related to a joint account I have with my partner. I've got credit cards, I've got health stuff, I've got just loyalty cards or whatever.

We transitioned from the wallet to surveying other areas where the participants used systems or tools of one kind or another to keep track of their finances, in the manner of a technology tour (Blythe et al. 2002). First, we asked *where* they did their finances, and then we went to those locations—the kitchen table, the computer kept in the bedroom, the office—and then asked for a tour of objects related to their finances.

We had a lucky break with this study: we were doing this study in February, and in the United States, tax returns for the previous year were due in April. This meant that between January and April, almost anyone with a job or a bank account receives a pile of paper statements, and until that pile is complete, it is difficult or impossible to complete a tax return. This meant that we knew there were likely some tax documents somewhere around the house, and asking people to show us where they were keeping those documents was an excellent way to open a discussion of how they kept financial documents.

> **LESSON**
>
> Look for serendipitous opportunities in terms of the timing of the study and other contextual factors. This may enhance the data the researcher is able to collect.

We photographed the locations—file drawers, shoe boxes, plastic crates—after suitable anonymization through Post-its or strategic rearranging of documents. We saw several examples of physical tools people had developed to track their money: a simple paper spreadsheet kept in a spiral-ring notebook to track finances, a stack of index cards to track investments in municipal bonds. These were also recorded and discussed.

We completed the inventory by looking at the digital tools people used to understand their financial life. Sometimes these were custom solutions; for example, we saw one elaborate spreadsheet (Figure 7.6) that was used as a dumping ground for a large amount of heterogeneous data such as frequent flier numbers, insurance information, passwords and usernames, as well as credit card numbers, bank account details, and other financial details.

Much more common was the frequent use of bank websites to check balances and recent transactions. We asked if participants ever used a website like mint.com or quicken.com to keep track of their finances. Somewhat surprisingly, not a single person in our fifteen-person Bay Area sample did so, although two people had used mint.com before giving it up. We asked people who regularly logged into their bank accounts to check their balances to show us how they did so (Figure 7.7) and, after anonymizing private information, took pictures of the screen.

Anthony, whose bank account is shown in Figure 7.7, used this opportunity to further elaborate on his financial strategy.

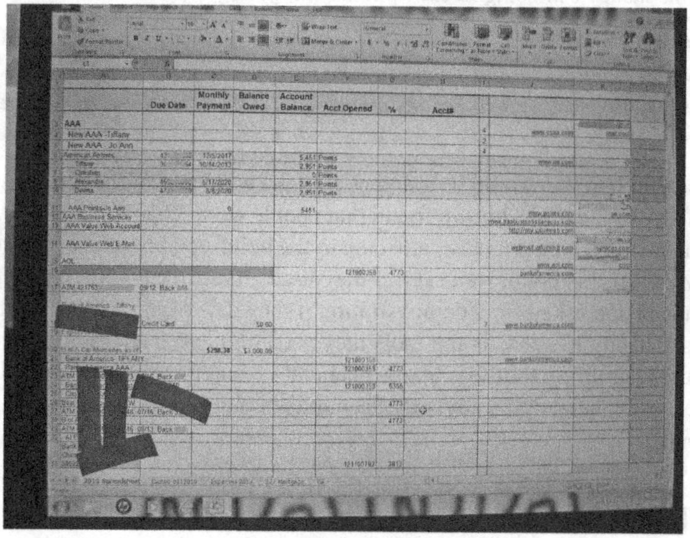

**FIGURE 7.6**

Jane's spreadsheet of heterogeneous information. Note Post-its for anonymization on site and later digital image manipulation for further anonymization.

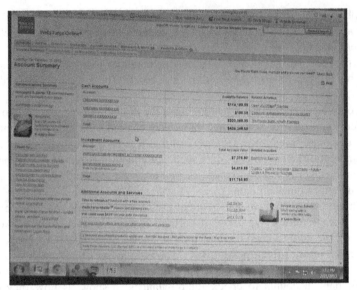

**FIGURE 7.7**

Anthony was happy to log in and show us his balances.

*Because the way I look at it again is nobody pays any interest and so I like to make a lot of liquidity. I would rather do that than put it into a lot of risky stuff. And that's the money I'm going to start putting into foreign investments.*

*I just like . . . first of all, I have enough cash that I don't really need to grow my money that much and I don't want to take much risk. If you don't want to take any risk, you're not going to get any money, so it doesn't really matter where you put it.*

We thought that this would be a potentially awkward part of the interview due to the sensitivity of the topic, but we found that people were remarkably happy to show us this information, something we attribute to the build-up of trust over the course of the interview. At this point, we asked if they used a tablet or mobile phone for anything financial and asked for a demonstration if they did. Again, people were almost surprisingly happy to show us the tools they used on these devices. The final question in our wrap-up section was about financial resources they used outside of the home such as financial or tax advisors, accountants, safety deposit boxes, and investment groups.

## INTERVIEW WRAP-UP

We referred to the final section of the interview as the wrap-up portion. We usually began this section by asking any outstanding questions that had arisen in earlier sections, and by checking in with the other interviewer or the ride-along to see if they had any questions. We had a series of questions we referred to as the "genie" questions: what would people do if a genie gave them a sum of money? (These questions were influenced by questions in the interview guide included in Stocks, Diaz, and Halleröd 2007.) We began by asking about $20,000—a substantial amount of money, but not an amount that would produce major life changes.

> *Interviewer*: If a genie came and landed on your doorstep and gave you $20,000, what would you do with it right now?
> *Charlotte*: I would put it in the bank and go to work (laughs). I would sit back and go, "okay." No, I would probably take a couple of weeks to decide what to do with it. One of the things that I would probably do is pay off two credit cards.
> *Interviewer*: Which two?
> *Charlotte*: Just to open them up. The two bigger ones that are open, not the ones that are closed. I would not pay those off because it's not going to do me any good. I would pay off, I'll tell you right now. I would pay off one of my Capital Ones and my Apple Bank. That would open up $3000. The credit would start improving and then I would go from there. I would not pay off my truck, but I would probably put a chunk down on it. I'd probably go half because I only owe about $7500 on it now. I'd probably pay off half of it.

We then asked the same question with an amount equal to the total household income they had told us in the first few minutes of the interview. (We had discussed asking what they would do with ten million dollars, but we thought we wouldn't learn a great deal for this study from variations on "stop working and live off the interest.") We then changed the question: what would you do if you had a sudden, unexpected expense of $20,000? We wanted to understand how porous the boundaries were between different pots of money. Zoe, for example, would get the money from her mother:

> *Mary*: What about touching the pension or the 401(k) or your $50,000?
> *Zoe*: No. No. If I had to, I guess I could borrow twenty from my Mom and then just pay her like a loan. It's an option.

We asked "What would you do if you had a sudden, unexpected expense of your total monthly income?", for which we got somewhat more interesting answers from the people for whom $20,000 was a manageable expense.

We asked what three wishes the participants would request about financial management tools, again in the manner of the technology tour (Blythe et al. 2002 ). In retrospect, we didn't learn a lot from the answers to the three wishes questions, but they do provide a sense of completeness.

Our final two questions were the two with which I try to end every interview. The first is to ask, "What else should we have asked?" This can produce great results, as it shows the things that we hadn't realized people thought were important.

The second is to ask, "Is there anything else you'd like to ask us?" This is something that both emphasizes the importance of their participation in the interview and also gives an opportunity for further engagement.

> **LESSON**
>
> Conclude interviews by posing questions that allow participants to talk about things the interviewer may not realize are relevant or interesting.

Finally, we gave the participants a one-hundred-fifty-dollar gift card to thank them for their time, had them sign a sheet confirming receipt of the gift card, and turned off the recorders.

## DEBRIEFING THE INTERVIEW

We tried to debrief—to discuss the interview we had just had—as soon as possible. As we drove to the next interview or back to the office, we discussed what we had just seen, and whoever wasn't driving took notes. In addition to general discussion, we identified five things we thought were particularly salient about the interview, which made later summarization simpler.

In the debrief, talk about the things the interviewers learned and the ways they matched what was expected. Sometimes, interviews go wrong: both interviewers may feel uncomfortable with the findings of an interview or things just won't quite click. Don't be afraid to leave this data out of the analysis and move on. It's hard to explain when the plug should be pulled, but even when the researchers have used expert screeners, data from an interview may still need to be removed from the study data.

> **LESSON**
>
> Debrief as soon as possible after a study session, with someone explicitly tasked to take notes. Talk about what was learned, what went well, and what didn't go well. This technique helps make sure nothing is missed.

### RECORD-KEEPING

To facilitate keeping track of the data, all of the documents related to a single interview were kept in a folder on a Google Drive and labeled with the date and an alias of the interviewee that related to his or her real name. For example, an interview on February 22 with someone whose real name was Kristina might be in a folder called 2013-02-22 Lucy, starting with the next letter of the alphabet. Other researchers use other techniques: be consistent and think through the options.

Using an alias is a significantly superior practice to identifying participants as P1, P2, etc., as using an alias makes remembering and keeping track easier, something that is always a problem with any significant number of interviewees. Using the same first letter as the real name helps keep track of anonymity at minimal cost; we also tried to choose names from the same cultural or ethnic background as the interviewee. Be aware that this is potentially at a cost of anonymity. Think hard about using this method if there is a concern that it could be a problem.

---

**LESSON**

Be smart when creating aliases to describe participants, as being able to easily identify who is who without compromising anonymity is important.

---

Audio recordings were placed into the folder along with any photographs taken, and both were renamed, for example, klara1.jpg, klara2.jpg, and klara.mp3. One voice recorder functioned strictly as a backup, so we didn't put a second recording in the folder. Notes, maps, calendars, and other documents were scanned and placed in the same folder. Recordings were sent to rev.com for transcription, and when transcripts returned, we went through the file and changed all names and any identifying information before saving to the folder.

## A BRIEF NOTE ON ANALYSIS

The process of analyzing and extracting knowledge and understanding from interviews is worthy of a chapter unto itself, but the process is not specific to the financial domain or to studying domestic life, and so I will not go into detail here. In our CHI paper (Kaye et al. 2014)—where we also describe our results from this process—we described the analysis step like this:

> We took raw transcripts of interviews, and multiple authors tagged and highlighted potential themes in each transcript. We extracted those themes, represented as approximately 500+ post-its, supported by sketches and printed and annotated photographs. We then performed a process of iterative aggregation, permutation and summarization to extract a list of 14 meta-themes and opportunities for design, which we focused and summarized as we wrote iterations of the paper. Throughout the process, we repeatedly returned to the raw data in the form of the transcripts, field notes, photographs and audio recordings.

Two practices helped this process that seem worthy of mention. First, we had all of the photographs that we took printed: a relatively trivial expense, but it allowed us to flip through images and form passing recollections—wallets, boxes, files—as well as making the invisible work of interviewing visible to others in the company (Suchman 1995). Second, we assembled summary sheets for each participant (Figure 7.8). These allowed us to compare information across participants during discussions ("How many married people did we have again?") and helped us keep track of which participant was which. They also contributed, again, to the endeavor of making visible our interviewing and work as they became artifacts displayed around our workspace in the course of discussion.

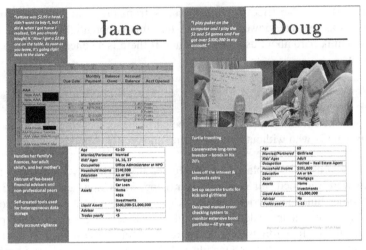

**FIGURE 7.8**

Summary pages for two participants. Design by Mary McCuistion.

---

**LESSON**

Print any images from the study sessions to act as conversation pieces. They will help to easily recall the stories of the participants. It also helps to create "summary sheets" that describe each participant.

---

# DISCUSSION

The aim of this chapter was to show one particular path that we developed to navigate the potentially awkward but fascinating topic of people's personal finances. By sharing the nitty-gritty detail, we hope this can serve as a model for future work for people to build from, change, and improve. I began with the idea of doing a "technology tour for finances" and ended up with the method seen here. In the course of the development of this study, and particularly with the interview guide, I was grateful for the work that came before this, which gave me insights into how people have thought about and discussed these issues. In particular, I really appreciated the interview protocol as an appendix in Stocks et al. 2007, which encouraged me to include the interview guide on this book's companion website.

One aspect that I wanted to emphasize in this discussion was the importance of not just respecting the privacy of our interviewees, but also explicitly *being seen* to respect their privacy. At several points throughout the interview, we made it clear that we were taking particular steps to safeguard their privacy: telling them the alias we would use to refer to them in publication, eschewing video, being thorough in anonymizing photographs with Post-its, making it clear (particularly for the tours of wallets and physical spaces) that we were interested only in financial information, and not other personal information that was visible in the locations we examined.

There may not be any such thing as a perfect method for understanding any domain, but this method seems to have produced valuable results that have helped us understand a great deal about personal finances and how people understand them. Currently, the study of financial practices within the domain of human-computer interaction is a very limited topic of study. My hope is that this will become a rich and fruitful domain of research, both producing value to HCI as a field and improving the tools people use to understand and plan their finances every day.

## ACKNOWLEDGMENTS

While I wrote and take responsibility for this chapter, the project was a joint effort by many people. Particular credit goes to my co-interviewer, the talented Mary McCuistion; my co-authors, David A. Shamma and Rebecca Gulotta; very useful feedback from Jon Sweet and Emily Jipson; recruiting support from Rosie Cabreros; and support, discussion, and feedback from many other colleagues. This chapter received extensive reviewing and support from David A. Shamma; thank you.

## REFERENCES

Blythe, M., Monk, A., Park, J., 2002. Technology Biographies: Field Study Techniques for Home Use Product Development. In: Proceedings of the Extended Abstracts on Human Factors in Computing Systems. (CHI EA). ACM Press, New York, NY.

Gaver, B., Dunne, T., Pacenti, E., 1999. Design: Cultural Probes. interactions 6 (1), 21–29.

Kaye, J., Gulotta, R., McCuistion, M., Shamma, D.A., 2014. Money Talks: Tracking Personal Finances. In: Proceedings of the SIGCHI Conference on Human Factors in Computing Systems (CHI). ACM Press, New York, NY.

Mainwaring, S.D., Anderson, K., Chang, M.F., 2005a. Living for the Global City: Mobile Kits, Urban Interfaces, and Ubicomp. In: Proceedings of 7th International Conference, Ubiquitous Computing (UbiComp 2005). Springer-Verlag, Berlin Heidelberg.

Mainwaring, S.D., Anderson, K., Chang, M.F., 2005b. What's in Your Wallet? Implications for Global E-Wallet Design. In: Proceedings of Extended Abstracts on Human Factors in Computing Systems. (CHI EA). ACM Press, New York, NY.

Nippert-Eng, C., 2010. Islands of Privacy. University of Chicago Press.

Stocks, J., Díaz, C., Halleröd, B., 2007. Modern Couples Sharing Money, Sharing Life. Palgrave MacMillan, London.

Suchman, L., 1995. Making Work Visible. Communications of the ACM, New York, NY. 38 (9), 56–61.

Travis, J., 2010. Personified [Online]. Available at. blurb.com.

# Technology Design and Evaluation

# Autobiographical Design in the Home

**Carman Neustaedter\*, Tejinder K. Judge[§], Phoebe Sengers[¶]**

*School of Interactive Arts and Technology, Simon Fraser University, Surrey, BC, Canada\*;*
*Google Inc., Mountain View, CA, USA[§]; Cornell University, Ithaca, NY, USA[¶]*

## INTRODUCTION

User-centered design approaches for human-computer interaction (HCI) teach us to understand our users and their routines and needs, to iteratively design with these aspects in mind, and then to evaluate the design's usability and impact on everyday routines, behaviors, and practices (Nielsen 1993; Dix et al. 2003). The value of such an approach is clear, yet studying and designing for domestic life presents special challenges for executing it. Family life is complex, home environments are more and more dynamic, and technology use is increasingly integrated into this complexity (O'Brien and Rodden 1997). As detailed in Chapter 1, with the ubiquity and proliferation of digital devices, it is increasingly difficult to design technologies, understand how they are used in real settings, and evaluate new systems to understand their true effects (Greenberg and Buxton 2008; Rogers 2011). We believe that the dynamics, embeddedness, mobility, and complexity of the home and domestic life exacerbate these problems.

One approach we have found valuable for the design and evaluation of domestic technologies is autobiographical design: "design research drawn from extensive, genuine use by those creating or building the system" (Neustaedter and Sengers 2008, 2012a, 2012b). With autobiographical design, researchers engage in many rapid design-evaluation cycles, drawing on their own experiences to understand, develop, and fine-tune systems. Drawing on Neustaedter and Sengers (2012a, 2012b), who explore the generalized practice of autobiographical design, this chapter focuses specifically on the home context, exploring autobiographical design as a method for designing for domestic life and evaluating domestic technologies. The goal is to provide readers with an understanding of the benefits and pitfalls of the method such that it can be used effectively for research and design activities.

Naturally, there are a variety of approaches that one could use to address the challenges of studying and designing for domestic life. This includes ethnography and ethnomethodology (O'Brien et al. 1997); new methods for requirements, or "inspiration" elicitation (Gaver, Dunne, and Pacenti 1999); new styles of prototypes, or "technology probes," to elicit reactions from family members (Hutchinson et al. 2003); techniques to conduct field trials in the so-called "wild" (Rogers 2011; Brown, Reeves, and Sherwood 2011), where researchers participate to varying degrees; methods focused on empathic design (Wright and McCarthy 2008); and ways to design for specific user types as a source of innovation (von Hippel 1986; Cooper 1999; Djajadiningrat, Gaver, and Fres 2000; Håkansson, Ljungblad, and Holmquist 2003). Autobiographical design is similar to and builds on these approaches: like ethnography, it seeks to make sense of the complexities of everyday life; like technology probes, it explores users' appropriations of a new technology (Hutchinson et al. 2003); like "in-the-wild" approaches, it utilizes field trials (Rogers 2011; Brown et al. 2011); like empathic design, it draws out empathic understandings; and like specific user types, it leverages one kind of user as a source for inspiration to design for many. *Unlike* these approaches, it synthesizes field trials and analysis of user experience with design iterations, while foregrounding the standpoint of the designer-researcher.

We are not arguing that autobiographical design is *the* approach to use. It is but one method in the toolkit of a researcher or designer. This chapter teases out the ways in which autobiographical design provides insights and benefits that may be different from other methods. Like any method, it also has its drawbacks, and we will discuss these as well.

We start with background details on autobiographical design, including its origin and a discussion of other systems that have used it as part of their design processes. Then we explore how autobiographical design was used in a specific situation to design and evaluate a video communications system for families. We identify how autobiographical design was used in this research project, what worked well, and what was challenging. We also discuss how we overcame difficulties with the method. Lastly, we discuss takeaway lessons for those who want to employ autobiographical design as part of research or design activities for family life or home settings.

## AUTOBIOGRAPHICAL DESIGN

User-centered design approaches teach researchers and designers to include end users in their design efforts throughout the design process. These approaches encourage system builders to move beyond their own limited preconceptions of use by gathering empirical evidence of users' desires, practices, and activities, including developing understanding of user tasks, routines, and needs in the initial design stages (Nielsen 1993; Dix et al. 2003). It also involves receiving feedback on design ideas through the creation of prototypes and interfaces, as well as during evaluations of a more refined prototype or design (Nielsen 1993; Dix et al. 2003). Feedback from iterative design can help adapt systems to fit better with people's actual needs and emerging practices rather than relying on designers' thoughts of what those needs and practices might be.

But what happens when researchers and designers themselves are legitimate end users of a system? In these cases, one could argue that using one's own design and learning from this experience is at least helpful, and perhaps critical, for understanding how a design will be used in practice. "Eat your own dog food" methods have been used in industry for many years, in which designers and developers use their own products to find bugs and to understand and build on the experience of using the software (Anon. 2010; Vick 2011). Beyond this pragmatic approach to improving software, there is also a long but, to some degree, hidden history of some computer scientists and HCI researchers using their designs as they are creating them in order to generate deeper insights into the design, to develop new design conceptualizations, and to understand their designs' broader usage implications and meaning in the lives of users.

For example, in the 1980s, early computer scientists often designed for themselves as a *reflexive user*, where they would imagine what a future user might be like and try to use a system with this mindset (Bardini and Horvath 1995). One of the creators of PARC's Alto computer describes this as a way to overcome "bootstrapping" issues, or problems associated with the initial setup costs of using a system:

> *A strategy for carrying out work in experimental computer science was also adopted at this time. It was based on the idea that demonstrations of "toy" systems are insufficient to determine the worth of a system design. Instead, it is necessary to build real systems, and to use them in daily work to assess the validity of the underlying ideas and to understand the consequences of those ideas. When the designers and implementers are themselves the users, as was the case at PARC, and when the system is of general utility, such as an electronic mail system or a text editor, there is a powerful bootstrapping effect. (Thacker 1988, 269)*

We also see this idea carried forward through the early days of the field of Computer Supported Cooperative Work (CSCW), where researchers commonly used their own systems as part of their design work. Most of the reported usage of the original media space by PARC, for example, was researchers' own accounts of the functioning of the system and the reactions from designers and other users in their own office (Bly, Harrison, and Irwin 1993). Subsequent publications about media spaces from the University of Toronto (Mantei et al. 1991) and EuroPARC (Dourish et al. 1996) also focused on the experiences of the designers and researchers themselves.

Despite the field of HCI typically being opposed to the idea of self-usage, it has also been reported to be part of the design process of other systems. For example, in 1996, Tom Erickson described the design and use of Proteus, a digital notebook that he created for himself and used over the course of five years while at Apple (Erickson 1996). More recently, Neustaedter and Sengers (2012a, 2012b) uncovered a host of other systems that were designed for and tested at least in part through a researcher's or design team's own usage, although this self-usage was often not reported in publications. These systems included personal information management tools (Whittaker et al. 2002), personal memory systems (Peesapati et al. 2010), media spaces (Gaver 2006; Kim, Gutwin, and Subramanian 2007; Voida et al.

2008), computer-mediated communication tools (Bradner, Kellogg, and Erickson 1999; Harrison, Minneman, and Marinacci 1999; Whittaker et al. 2002; Boehner, Sengers, and Warner 2008), navigation systems (Priedhorsky 2010), and programming toolkits (Greenberg and Fitchett 2001; deAlwis, Gutwin, and Greenberg 2009).

In all of these cases, researchers and designers went beyond simply "dogfooding" to using their experiences to deeply explore the nuances of their systems and designs. Neustaedter and Sengers call this "autobiographical design": design research drawn from extensive, genuine use by those creating or building the system. At the most basic level, autobiographical design involves a person or design team creating a system, using it while it is being designed and built, and using experiences with the system to modify it in the manner of iterative design. Usage can continue to occur and span months or even years. Autobiographical design can be done as part of activities within a design team, or it can be done by an individual. Neustaedter and Sengers argue, based on these cases, that autobiographical design is not simply an improvisational "do-it-yourself," but derives its benefit from rigorous application of the five attributes discussed below (Neustaedter and Sengers, 2012a, 2012b):

1. **Genuine Needs:** Autobiographical design should only be done in cases where the researcher has a real need for the system. Genuine understanding derives from usage experience when system builders have an inherent need to use the system for real rather than contrived purposes. This contrasts with other forms of design research where the researcher may be designing for users whose practices they are unfamiliar with and therefore need to study as part of the design process. In this case, the external users (hopefully) have a genuine need for the system, but the researchers may not.

2. **Real Systems:** Autobiographical design requires a real functional system because the design is actually being used by researchers for real purposes. In order to generate true usage, it is not enough to have a prototype that simply shows the user interface or one that does not contain core functionality. Instead, the design must *actually* work for the intended purpose such that the researcher can see the effect of the functionality on his or her own life. In some situations, this can be challenging to do if the design requires a complex infrastructure underlying the user interface.

3. **Fast Tinkering:** Autobiographical design provides a means for designers to tinker with their design creations. They can start with an initial idea, try it out, and quickly see if it will work in the way they thought, or if additional iterations are needed. They can also change the scope of the design by adding new features or removing old ones. Because the researchers are also designing and building the system, knowledge of what works well and what doesn't can immediately translate into changes to the system. This means adjustments to the system can happen quickly, without the need for a time-intensive (and costly) user study with external participants.

4. **Record Keeping and Data Collection:** Autobiographical design should incorporate rigorous record keeping and data collection, just like any other

research method in HCI. This is important to allow researchers to compare their *expected usage* of the system with their *actual usage* and eliminate some of the biases that may occur because the researcher is also the user.

5. **Long-Term Usage:** While most evaluation studies with external participants evaluate usage in time frames on the order of hours to weeks, autobiographical design lends itself to uncovering an understanding from long-term usage on the order of months to years, since researchers have a double commitment to the system based both on genuine need and on their interest in the design itself. The informality of self-usage (as opposed to protocols that need to be approved by an ethics review board) also makes long-term usage more practical. The length of engagement afforded by autobiographical design allows for a deeper and more holistic understanding than is typically achieved in user studies. That said, autobiographical design could also be valuable for shorter term usage, especially to help researchers understand whether a design idea or product concept might be worthwhile to pursue.

When using autobiographical design, one must realize that there are some forms of knowledge it can provide and others that it cannot (Neustaedter and Sengers 2012a, 2012b). First, and perhaps somewhat obviously, autobiographical design does not lead to generalizability. It is not necessarily the case that the experiences of the researcher will be the same as those of other users. Instead, autobiographical design allows researchers to see the "big effects" of the technology, often rapidly. It provides a deep, experiential understanding, because the researcher is intimately involved in the usage of the technology, and the use of the system is interwoven throughout much of the researcher's life. This makes the implications of the technology more real, and this sense of real effect can lead to reflection on ethical considerations. Sometimes, outsider perspectives are also useful and could come from additional studies with external participants (Neustaedter and Sengers 2012a, 2012b). Yet in many cases, the results of such studies may simply validate the results found with the researcher's own usage (Neustaedter and Sengers 2012a, 2012b).

Autobiographical design can be useful in a variety of contexts and work situations. In this chapter, we explore its potential as an effective research method for studying and designing technologies for the home and domestic life and what challenges or limitations researchers could face in doing so. We do this by describing the autobiographical design of the Family Window—a system designed and evaluated by Judge, Neustaedter, and Kurtz (2010), which includes both an autobiographical component and a field study with external participants.

## THE AUTOBIOGRAPHICAL DESIGN OF THE FAMILY WINDOW

The Family Window project was started at Kodak Research Labs by the chapter's first author, Carman Neustaedter, as a way to explore new uses for video communication in the home. It built on Carman's prior work studying video communications in the workplace (e.g., Neustaedter and Greenberg 2003) and his desire to create technologies for his own family to use to connect with their geographically distributed family members—in particular, the paternal grandparents of Carman's children. With this initial backdrop and motivation, other collaborators were added to the project, including Tejinder Judge (the second author of this chapter), Andrew Kurtz, and Elena Fedorovskaya, all researchers in HCI or related fields. The Family Window was designed through an autobiographical design process with Carman's family, described in Neustaedter (2013), and also formally evaluated by Tejinder with additional families, described in Judge et al. (2010). A video that shows the final design of the system can be found in Neustaedter et al. (2010).

In its most basic form, the Family Window provided an always-on video connection—without an audio connection—between two families' homes, running on a tablet PC that acted as a prototype digital frame. Figure 8.1 shows the Family Window in Carman's home: the black tablet PC that runs the software is sitting on a bar adjacent to the kitchen, and a detachable USB camera is shown facing a dining room area. Figure 8.2 shows the Family Window running in the home of Carman's parents, on a desk near family photos.

Figure 8.3 shows a connection between Tejinder and Carman while testing out the Family Window's functionality. The local user's video is shown in the bottom left corner of the screen and the remote user's video fills the main portion of the interface. Users can start and stop the video recording by touching their own video in the bottom left. In this way, the Family Window provided a "window" or view into the other family's home. Users could also leave messages for each other on top of the video using a stylus or their finger. Additional writing controls were located at the top right corner of the display. A timeline at the top of the display showed when people were around their Family Window based on motion in front of the display's webcam.

**FIGURE 8.1**

The Family Window in Carman's kitchen, facing toward the dining room table.

**FIGURE 8.2**

The Family Window in the home of Carman's parents, on a desk near family photos.

**FIGURE 8.3**

The Family Window user interface connecting two locations with always-on video.

With these features in mind, people could use the Family Window as a passive awareness display. They could walk by it, glance at the video feed and see what was happening at the remote home. They might see people around, they might see an empty room, or they could even see other things that might interest them, such as pets. Regardless, the goal was that this awareness information would help people feel closer to one another over distance simply because they were "present" in the remote home and could see what the remote family members were up to, or if they were around. This could, in turn, provide availability awareness—knowing when someone was at home and not engaged in another activity, suggesting a good time to phone the remote home. Family members could also actively interact with one another using the Family Window; they could write messages back and forth on the screen, or they could use the phone to talk to the remote family member while also seeing them on video.

In the following sections, we describe how the five tenets of autobiographical design applied in the design of the Family Window. We follow this with a discussion of a more generalized set of lessons on how autobiographical design can be used in the context of designing for and studying domestic life. Throughout the following sections we included quotes from family members who were using the Family Window. We have also interspersed quotes from Carman that were captured in an interview conducted by Phoebe Sengers, the third author of this chapter. To reflect the first-person nature of autobiographical design, the remainder of the sections are written in the first person from Carman's perspective.

## TENET 1: GENUINE NEEDS

The first tenet of autobiographical design is that the designer must have a real and genuine need for the design. When studying and designing a system for an entire family, or multiple family members, it is important that all of those involved (or at least most) have a genuine need for the system. Without this, there is a chance that the technology will not be used "for real" and that the family's experiences with the system will not be rich or typical.

The Family Window project emerged out of the real experiences and needs I faced in my own life. After completing my PhD, I moved from Calgary, Canada, to Rochester, New York, USA, a distance of approximately 3500 km. The move meant that my family members and I were now separated from our extended family by approximately 3500 to 4000 km. At this time, we had a two-year-old son and a newborn daughter. Thus, the move to Rochester meant that the children's grandparents would now be several flights away from seeing their grandchildren. After moving, we felt a great deal of isolation from our family, as is the case for many people who experience a long-distance move. The Family Window was a way to try to address this and also to connect my children to their grandparents. Clearly, there was a genuine need for us to connect with the remote grandparents. This need extended beyond just me to include Kayla (my wife; her name is changed for anonymity) and my children.

Turning to the grandparents, their needs for the Family Window varied. I had anticipated that both Grandma and Grandpa would have a genuine need for the Family Window. Yet from the initial creation of the design, while the genuine need of the Family Window for Grandma was strong, it became clear that Grandpa had little real need for the Family Window. I had anticipated that Grandma would most often use the Family Window because she was the grandparent who most frequently talked to the family on the phone and stayed in touch. Grandpa was not seen as a direct user of the system because he was unlikely to actually interact with it. However, it was still anticipated that he would be a primary user because he would be susceptible to being caught on camera by the Family Window and might interact with my family members. I expected this would create interesting data from him on being watched but it turned out Grandpa was very rarely seen on camera. The Family Window's location in a den of the grandparents' home meant that Grandpa was hardly ever on camera, as it was in a space that, mostly, only Grandma occupied. Overall, this reveals that one may easily misjudge particular family members' genuine needs of the system. This meant that the study of the Family Window design and usage drastically changed from a study of grandparents, grandchildren, and adult children to a study of a grandmother's connection with her children and grandchildren.

> **LESSON**
>
> Family members' genuine needs for a system may be different from what one expects. Be cognizant about this and ensure that genuine needs for the system do, in fact, exist in the family.

## TENET 2: REAL SYSTEM

Autobiographical design requires a real system to work, because the design is actually being used by researchers for real purposes. Clearly, for two households to connect and share video that was always on, such a system had to actually work. First, at the most basic level, I had to create the system to support continuous video links. This required a large amount of infrastructure programming. Existing commercial software, such as Skype, did not provide the functionality that was deemed to be important for advanced concepts that I wanted to include, such as access to individual video frames for manipulation. For this reason, I had to write my own software and rely on programming toolkits. It also meant that the most important aspect of the design was getting the core functionality working: the continuous video connection. Figure 8.4 shows the initial bare-bones system, which only supported a video link.

Even after weeks of programming efforts prior to starting to use the Family Window, and continuous updates throughout several months of my family's year-long usage of the system, the Family Window was still prone to crashing. Sometimes,

**FIGURE 8.4**

The initial design of the Family Window containing very minimal features.

video would be plagued with so much latency that it would appear to freeze for minutes at a time. Other times, it would simply not run. I had to program feedback mechanisms into the system so that family members would know that the system was still operating as it should; a frozen video of an empty living room could easily be mistaken for live video of an empty living room. The following comment from Grandma shows that the system wasn't working for two days, but she assumed her remote family members simply weren't near their Family Window:

> *When the family window was down for a couple of days, I really missed it. I did not realize that it was not working, I figured bad timing to see them because of the time and distance factor. I would rush home from work to check if I could see my family. I would check first thing in morning and continuously all evening. Then was disappointed when I never saw them, I was really happy when it was working again. It was so good to see my family. (Email excerpt from Grandma to Carman)*

Because the technology was distributed, software crashing became a very difficult thing to diagnose and repair. The primary remote user was Grandma, and she was not particularly tech-savvy. This meant that I had to have phone conversations at least once every week to either try to fix the Family Window or walk her through the steps to restart it.

---

**LESSON**

Be prepared to offer technical support for other family members and quickly fix problems with the system.

My family's usage also revealed that the Family Window project was not just about the single device we were testing. *The Family Window was part of a larger ecology of technology in the home, which also had to work.* This included, most prominently, the Internet connection of both households and wireless Internet access. If the Family Window stopped working, it could be a result of the system itself, the Internet, or the WiFi access point. This played into the over-the-phone diagnoses of the Family Window when it would crash. It also was a key factor when initially setting up the Family Window. Grandma had to have modifications done to the setup of her wireless router to allow the Family Window to transmit data through specific Internet ports. Thus, overall, we see the realization that new domestic technologies are part of a much larger ecosystem of devices and infrastructures that must also work as needed.

---

**LESSON**

New domestic technologies are part of a larger ecosystem of devices and infrastructures that must all work together.

---

## TENET 3: FAST TINKERING

Autobiographical design provides a means for designers to tinker with their design creations. They can start with an initial idea, try it out, and quickly see if it will work in the way they thought or if additional iterations are needed. We did just that with the Family Window. As mentioned, the basic design initially contained just a video connection, but the features grew as the perceived needs of my family presented themselves. Tinkering with the design lasted approximately five months, until adding new features no longer seemed relevant. We used Family Window for another seven months after that point.

> So initially, I came to them with a prototype so it was already initially built, but a very basic system with no advanced features. So it definitely didn't start out from sketches or anything. Yeah. And at that point it was basically just a system that connected to two locations with a video. You can turn the video on and off, and essentially the idea was to leave it going all the time. (Excerpt of interview with Carman)

One of the first additions to the Family Window was a "knocking" feature. Both Kayla and Grandma told me that they wanted a way to tell the person at the other end of the Family Window to come near the device because one had something to show the other. This feature was simple to add and took little time. Following this, it became clear that family members wanted to know when another person was around the Family Window; often, just an empty room at the remote home was seen, and it was almost a surprise to see someone on camera. Grandma, Kayla, and I wanted a better awareness of presence in front of the display. This was a complicated addition and took me several weeks to implement, as it required recording a history of motion in front of the display as well as a timeline display of it. Following this, the family members also discovered that it would be nice to leave messages for each other, and so I added this feature in. However, once again the technical challenges of implementing the new features took a couple of weeks to complete. Tejinder and I also had to think through the possible ways of providing messaging capabilities: text entry, like an instant messaging client, or something more personal, like handwritten messages. The list of additions continued and, over time, included privacy blinds, time-shifted video recording and playback, an optional audio link, etc. Some features became integral parts of the design, such as the messages and knock functionality, and others were more secondary in nature. Some were barely ever used, including time-shifted video and the privacy blinds.

> We changed it mostly for the first, I want to say, like, five months. It took about five months before I think it sort of got to a steady state where we basically realized it was as sort of good as we could get it, and then after that we just used it as was. And so we iterated, I guess, whenever a need arose, and we realized, Oh, jeez. It needs this feature. Then we would update the system, so updates, how they happened, like every other week, every three weeks or something. There's no sort of schedule. Just whenever it happened that we saw something. (Excerpt of interview with Carman)

Within this near-constant tinkering and design thinking, several lessons emerged. First, the addition and usage of features was not just a result of what I thought would work well or be needed. It was much more nuanced, where feature suggestions would come from Grandma, Kayla, or myself, or a mixture of us. If feature ideas came from only one or two people, discussions happened with the other family members to get people's reactions to the ideas before they were acted upon. I tried to gain some sense of consensus before adding the features, given the anticipated work in implementing them. This was often one on one between me and either Kayla or Grandma. New design features were also added as a result of my children being involved. Because the children were very young, I had to use my observations to understand what worked best for them.

Second, as likely could be seen, the addition of features was not always simple. It took time to implement some features, and sometimes people wanted them sooner than they could be produced. The design updates to the Family Window was "fast" tinkering in the sense that I did not need to run a user study to understand what features were needed, but it was slow tinkering from the other users' points of view in actually creating some of the features for real. Beyond my own skills, the technical understanding of programming was minimal, so the complexity of additional features was not always understood by Kayla and Grandma. The Family Window was also not the only project that I was working on, and so updates to it needed to be intermixed among the many other things I was doing. That said, because the Family Window was affecting my life so drastically—it was now the primary communication tool being used with Grandma—updates to it were very important and became a priority. This also meant that much of *both* my personal time and work time revolved around a single technology—the Family Window.

---

**LESSON**

Additional features may need to be added to the system, and suggestions could come from family members and not just the researcher. Be aware that new features will take time to implement, and not everyone may understand why that takes so long.

---

Third, new features to the Family Window also meant updates, both on my family's display and on Grandma's remote display. Updating my own system was relatively straightforward and involved copying a single file to the device and then running a setup program. However, updating Grandma's client was more challenging because of her limited technical abilities. As one could imagine, the file had to be sent to Grandma, copied from the device it was received on (e.g., in email) to the Family Window tablet, and then set up using an installation package. While this seems simple, there were many failings at various points in this process that caused hassles, delays, and, certainly, frustration. Again, this made it challenging to tinker as quickly as one might like. Yet it highlights the reality that, even though designers can incorporate new ideas into a design very quickly with autobiographical design as compared to projects involving other user study methods, the realities of working in a real household with people of varying technical abilities must be taken into account. The researcher must be a designer, programmer, *and* also a technical support person.

---

**LESSON**

Installing updates or troubleshooting issues in remote homes is often not straightforward or easy. Be prepared to spend extra time helping remote homes with technical issues.

---

## TENET 4: RECORD KEEPING AND DATA COLLECTION

Autobiographical design should incorporate rigorous record keeping and data collection, just like any other research method in HCI. In the design of the Family Window, we used a combination of email and a specially set-up blog to keep track of design thoughts and reactions to the system. The blog was used in addition to email, with the idea that there would be a place for *all family members* to see the posts of others and build on the comments people made. The blog (Figure 8.5) was private between my family members, but also included Tejinder, who was a member of the research team. Tejinder was given access to the private blog so that she could learn about usage patterns, understand the practices of the family, suggest new features, and also compare our usage to findings from her external field deployment. Here we found it especially valuable to have an unbiased outsider (who was not a part of the family) available to analyze our usage.

Overall, the use of data collection tools revealed several challenges. First, and most fundamental, it was difficult to get people to record their thoughts about the Family Window because it took time, energy, and reflection. The majority of the observations in the blog were recorded by me alone. I observed many of the things that I thought my family members were experiencing, but I wanted them to write their thoughts down in their own words to alleviate any biases that I might introduce by writing things down myself. This would help avoid lead participants from dominating the data (Brown et al. 2011). However, family members wanted to use the technology, not to write about it. This extra work was not something they were accustomed to and certainly not something

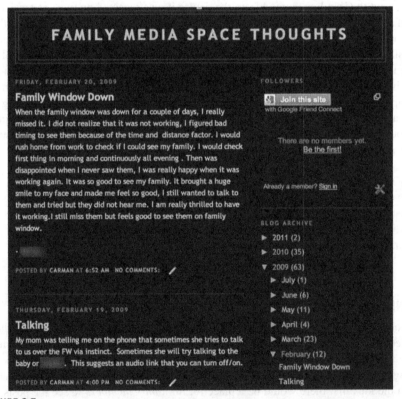

**FIGURE 8.5**

A private blog set up to record the family's thoughts on the family window.

they had to do with other technologies they used. Like most external users, they were also not trained to be reflective about their usage and needs around technology.

> **LESSON**
>
> Getting family members to record their thoughts about the system may be difficult, especially since it is something extra they have to do in addition to using the technology. Be aware that family members may also not be able to articulate their experiences with the technology, since they are not trained researchers.

Second, it was far easier for family members to just tell me their thoughts when they had them, rather than write them down. This happened frequently in informal conversations. It was also much easier for Kayla and Grandma to send me an email with their thoughts than it was to blog about them. This was despite the fact that posting to the blog only required one to send an email to a specific blog-enabled email address. The act of sending emails to me mapped more easily to their existing routines because they were already used to sending emails to me. It was also easy for them to embed their thoughts about the Family Window into emails that included comments about other things, such as the day's activities, the children, etc. Of course, the challenge with this is that the emails were really visible only to me and not the other family members who might be able to comment on the observations of the Family Window.

Third, perhaps the most important piece of data was one that was difficult to record. These were the deep, experiential understandings I had on how the technology was affecting my family members and how I was becoming emotionally attached to the technology. Some of this information was easy to articulate, yet there were also observations that were harder to put down into words. For example, strong emotional feelings of how the Family Window affected Grandma's sense of closeness to her remote family members or the simple joy in Kayla's voice when she saw Grandma on the display were difficult to comment on in a meaningful way that would exhibit the deep emotions and sense of connection. Data collection is certainly important for autobiographical design; however, when one is having a deeply personal experience with a technology, it can be challenging to record it, even for the designer/researcher.

> **LESSON**
>
> Over time, family members may have deeply personal experiences with the technology. The researcher needs to creatively choose how family members are able to articulate and report their thoughts on the system.

## TENET 5: LONG-TERM USAGE

Autobiographical design lends itself to uncovering an understanding from long-term usage of a technology, on the order of months to years. The researcher is often heavily tied to the design because it is being used for real purposes, and so it is less difficult to continue using the design over time. The Family Window was used for approximately one year, from January 2009, shortly after the birth of my daughter, to January 2010. What one cannot anticipate is the myriad of things that will happen during this time period—which the design itself must weather—and also when the technology's use might end.

The autobiographical design of the Family Window involved a range of both mundane situations and somewhat extraordinary situations during its use. First, it involved the everyday comings and goings and activities of the family, including cooking, eating meals, watching television, conversing, etc. Second, it also included some unexpected events that one could not have necessarily predicted or designed for ahead of time. The birth of my daughter caused an influx of visitors to our home. This included a three-week visit by Kayla's mother to visit with the baby and help attend to her right after birth. This introduced a different design situation than what I had previously thought would occur and, unexpectedly, now connected both grandmas through the system. This introduced new privacy challenges that had to be managed. The arrival of my daughter also meant more friends came to the house to see the baby and either be accidentally caught on camera or told about it. This would often lead to follow-on conversations about the role of video in communication and its effects on privacy. Thus, the reality is that, while one may expect a design to be used for certain situations with certain people, with autobiographical design in the home, one may easily get something different. Such a lesson is also more broadly applicable to the design of domestic technologies in general.

A natural question is, if the experience was so enlightening and valuable, why did we stop using the Family Window? The reason was twofold. First, after a full year, we had a solid understanding of how the technology was being used. The pragmatics of research are often such that when we have learned what we want from a situation, we are often compelled to move on. This was the feeling I had, and I wanted to explore new instances of always-on video in the home that would require the re-appropriation of the hardware (tablet PCs) that I had been using for the Family Window. Thus, it would mean altering the design configuration and exploring a new system with different features.

The second reason was somewhat more tragic. In mid-January 2010, my mother was hospitalized for a somewhat routine surgery. In recovery, however, the situation turned from routine to very unfortunate when Grandma had several heart attacks in the hospital and was on the brink of death. She ended up staying in the hospital for approximately six weeks, during which time her doctors did not know if she would make it. As one can imagine, this caused our use of the Family Window to stop completely. Grandma managed to recover and return home, yet the incident caused larger life changes to occur, and my family and I had a strong desire to live much closer to our distant family. In May of 2010, I changed jobs, and we moved back to Western Canada. Since this move, the need for an always-on video connection diminished somewhat, since we could see each other every few months in person. The clear lesson is that autobiographical design must intertwine itself within the real workings of life. These can be unexpected, even tragic, and one must weather the storm.

> **LESSON**
>
> A system may not be used in the way one expects it to be. Be prepared for unexpected uses, and embrace them. Autobiographical design intertwines itself within real life; be ready for it.

## LEARNINGS

The autobiographical design of the Family Window uncovered a deep, nuanced understanding of technology usage for my family. The Family Window was found to be an important awareness tool for both households, where we could gain an easy understanding of what others were up to and have a sense of their presence; it provided awareness of availability, which helped us know when to phone the other home; and it allowed us to interact directly through the system in new and personal ways through handwritten messages (Judge et al. 2010; Judge, Neustaedter, and Harrison 2012; Neustaedter 2013). Certainly these findings were specific to my family, as autobiographical design does not aim to generalize to other users or situations. However, a field study with four additional households conducted by Tejinder showed that other families largely used the Family Window in the same way as my family, and the lessons learned were often the same (Judge et al. 2010). Thus, the external study acted as a "security blanket," a validation of what we had already learned and knew from our own usage. It allowed us to verify that we were actually seeing things correctly. This is not to say that one must always conduct additional studies beyond learning from one's own experiences. Nor are we saying that a person should only ever use autobiographical design alone. The choice of research method (including the use of multiple methods) should depend on the system and the researcher's goals, including the focus of research questions, the depth of understanding desired, and the preferred generalizability of one's findings.

## THE BIG AND LITTLE EFFECTS

What was most fundamental about the learnings from the autobiographical design was both the big and the little effects that it had on the family. Because I was using the Family Window with my family, I could see first-hand the ways in which it was changing our routine. This included the subtle changes, such as how often we talked to Grandma on the phone, or how often someone in the house commented on Grandma. These types of things may easily go unnoticed or unmentioned by someone participating in a typical field study, as they could easily be unremarkable (Tolmie et al. 2002). It also included the somewhat obvious things that a person wouldn't need an expensive and laborious field study to uncover: the importance of the location of the technology, and the role of relationships (Neustaedter 2013).

---

**LESSON**

Autobiographical design can allow one to see both the big and the little effects of the technology on one's domestic life.

---

We also found unexpected usage patterns from our own use of the system; as researchers, we know the expected usage of a technology and can easily spot differences with this in usage. This enables us to understand what is interesting in the design. Study participants often are not able to do this because they do not necessarily have a broader technological or design understanding. This suggests that autobiographical design might be better at identifying unanticipated design uses compared to studies with external users.

> *I think I had a much richer understand of how it would be used because I was actually using it. I think if I stuck it in somebody's home, there'd be a lot of details I would miss out because I think the methodologies there don't give you the rigor that you see when you're actually using something on your own. . . . Well, so I mean if I stuck it in somebody's home, they would tell me sort of the high-level things that they saw when they used it, but they'd miss out, I think, on a lot of the details because they may not think it was important to actually tell me about that, but by using it myself, I saw every single little detail of its usage, and so as a researcher I think I got a much broader perspective of it, how it was used. . . . So I guess I saw the sheer number of times we would look at the display, for example. Basically, our pattern of what we do when we walked into our kitchen, for example, completely changed. Once we started using the system, every time we walked into the kitchen we would glance at the display to see if we could see my mom there, and so as you see it myself, I could see the sheer number of glances that we would use; whereas if it was another family, I would have no idea how many times they just glanced at the display, and they probably couldn't articulate that to me either, and there'd probably be no tool in existence that could log all of that and tell me how often they were looking at. (Excerpt of interview with Carman)*

## THE EMOTIONAL IMPACT

We were also able to understand the deep emotional impact that the design had on our lives. This included many subtle things that would be hard for participants in a traditional study to notice (or talk about): the additional smiles in the home, the tone of one's voice in phone calls, kids' expressions when they see someone over video, the quarrels over the technology, etc. These things may simply be too subtle for external field study participants to talk about. They may also simply not want to mention them, or may just give generic answers, for example, "We liked the Family Window." On the other hand, we felt strong emotions when we used the Family Window. For example, the following quotes clearly show a strong emotional reaction to the Family Window from Grandma. Read through them and you will see the sense of experiential understanding. Then read them again as though this was your mother telling you how the system you designed affected her. Imagine the tears on her face as you may have seen them before in the past. Imagine the joy you gain from simply having her feel happy.

> Also it is so good to see you on Family Window. It is so awesome when you show me [your daughter]. It brings a smile to my face, sometimes tears to my eyes. She is so beautiful and I wish I could see her and hold her for real. But I am happy to see her almost daily on the Window. Then you adjust the camera so I can see [my grandson] that is so special. I appreciate that. He looks so happy and full of energy. I keep wondering if he still asks WHY? I feel that you and I got closer with my visit and now I get to see you daily. We get to signal a phone call is needed or wanted and follow through with that. You wave, you smile, you show me the kids and we both move on with our day or evening. Tonight Carman showed me the popcorn bowl and I knew you were watching tv, relaxing as a family. That made me feel good. (Email from Grandma to Carman)

> Sometimes I feel sad when I see that person it doesn't matter whether it is my grandchild, my son, or my daughter in law. I feel like Oh I just miss that person so much! I wish I could be right there with them. Then I stop and tell myself you are so lucky you can see them on the window. It seems to make me emotional when I see them before bed time. I do not know why, I just usually get tears. I think sometimes it really makes me realize the time difference also and the fact that you are so far apart. It is like you are so happy to see them wish you could hug them good night. I would not give up this opportunity to see them and say good night in this way. (Email from Grandma to Carman)

As can be seen, autobiographical design made the emotional implications of the design very clear because we experienced them firsthand. It would likely be very difficult to get or understand such an emotional reaction from objective third-party methods containing external users. Emotions are a very important part of domestic life, and autobiographical design allowed us to tap into them in a deep and experiential way.

**LESSON**

Autobiographical design can allow one to see the deep emotional impact that a design has on one's domestic life.

## THE REAL IMPACT OF THE TECHNOLOGY

The autobiographical design of the Family Window also made the implications of the technology very real for my family. Because the Family Window was meant to explore an always-on video connection, we faced the real challenge that our privacy could be at risk. For example, Kayla's in-laws might see her in situations that she was not comfortable with, like walking around the house in pajamas, not being "fixed up" for the day, etc. To adopt and use the system for real, the threat to privacy needed to be perceived as being less than the benefit of the system to Kayla and our children. It clearly was, but Kayla was hesitant when she first started using the Family Window. This was tempered by her trust in me that I knew what I was doing. I had to anticipate the expected usage of the Family Window based on my design and research experiences to trust that this was a safe path forward. Also, understanding the likely benefits of the Family Window was not instantaneous. I had to discuss the design with Kayla several times over the course of a few weeks before it was built and used. "Buying in" to the design and its use takes time, even before the system is even being used. Discussion with Grandma revealed that she was willing to use the system because her son had made it, but she didn't understand how it would benefit her at the onset of its use.

> *I had to try to carefully balance, I guess, the relationship needs. Like I had to think a lot about, well, you know, what's my wife going to think about this or what's my mom going to think about seeing her daughter-in-law, and so I had to manage sort of the personal relationships, but I probably wouldn't have thought about that as much if it was an external family. (Excerpt of interview with Carman)*

Our usage of the Family Window had very real impacts at the end as a result of Grandma's hospitalization. In an instant, the technology was gone. The Family Window was unused. And Grandma was no longer visible over distance. My family couldn't easily travel to see her, and we longed for a video window into her life again so we could see how she was doing, and, possibly, even see her for a final time. Fortunately, her situation turned around, but for a few dramatic weeks, the importance of *seeing* a remote loved one over distance became a deep, desired emotion for my family.

---

**LESSON**

Autobiographical design makes the implications of the technology very real to both the researcher and his or her family members.

---

## CONCLUSION

This chapter has explored autobiographical design from the perspective of using it as a design research method for creating and evaluating systems for domestic life. In particular, it has explored the autobiographical design of the Family Window as a case study. We have articulated the various nuances of how the Family Window was designed and what challenges were faced. Stepping back from this, we see two additional overarching lessons that are broadly applicable to those who may want to use autobiographical design as a research method for studying and designing for domestic life.

First, designing something for one's own domestic life is an explicit gesture that the researcher is fine with mixing work and personal life. At this juncture, he or she is saying that doing work from home is fine, as is integrating family members into work and having the routines, practices, and needs of one's family at the mercy of the design work. The same is said for one's family members. They are essentially saying that they are fine mixing the researcher's work activities with their domestic life. Some people do not like such blurring of contexts together, and doing so can easily disrupt domestic life. This is certainly something that people should think about before deciding to use autobiographical design in the home. When using autobiographical design in the workplace as part of a team, team members would all presumably have a similar investment in the system. Yet in the home, it is likely the case that not all family members will have the same investment in the system and its design process. This uneven commitment will potentially be reflected in the amount of feedback people are willing to give and the attention they are willing to invest in the system, and could potentially lead to domestic conflict if the design's demands conflict with family members' felt investments.

Second, and related, by designing for a researcher's own domestic life, he or she is placing it in harm's way of the system. The implications of the technology are made very real. What happens if the technology breaks? What if it disrupts the home routine in a negative way? This could easily affect family relationships and create drastic negative consequences, which are of a different sort than one might experience at work. Because the technology is new and, likely, frail, there is a good chance it does cause disruption, at least initially. This must be recognized and the researcher must be okay with it. There is also a chance that initial disruption is fine, and it isn't until the design idea is tinkered with that the researcher gets it right. But if one isn't willing to continue tinkering because of disruptions to domestic life, then a great idea could easily be quashed that was simply not yet ready for real use.

---

**LESSON**

Using autobiographical design in the home means both the researcher and his or her family are fine with mixing work and personal life. Approach this dynamic with caution, as it has the potential to put the researcher and the family's routines in harm's way.

---

Certainly there are many more lessons that one could uncover as they relate to using autobiographical design for designing and studying domestic life. We have likely only scratched the surface. Our goal is to illustrate that autobiographical design is an important design method that can be included in a researcher or designer's tool belt of methods for use when it is appropriate. In this case, we hope that our presentation of the underlying details of the Family Window's autobiographical design has helped lay a foundation for thinking more broadly, and reflectively, about designing for one's own family and domestic life.

## ACKNOWLEDGMENTS

We are grateful to Andrew Kurtz, Elena Fedorovskaya, Rodney Miller, Steve Harrison, and Andrew Blose for their intellectual contributions to the Family Window research project.

## REFERENCES

Anon, Sept. 2011. Chowing Down on Dogfood [online]. http://buzz.blogger.com/2006/10/chowing-down-on-dogfood.html.

Bardini, T., Horvath, A., Summer, 1995. The Social Construction of the Personal Computer User. J. Commun. 45 (3).

Bly, S., Harrison, S., Irwin, S., 1993. Media Spaces: Bringing Together a Video, Audio and Computing Environment. Comm. ACM 36 (1). ACM Press, New York, NY.

Boehner, K., Sengers, P., Warner, S., 2008. Interfaces with the Ineffable: Meeting Aesthetic Experience on Its Own Terms. ToCHI 15 (3). ACM Press, New York, NY.

Bradner, E., Kellogg, W.A., Erickson, T., 1999. The Adoption and Use of 'BABBLE': A Field Study of Chat in the Workplace. Proc. ECSCW. Kluwer Academic Publishers.

Brown, B., Reeves, S., Sherwood, S., 2011. Into the Wild: Challenge and Opportunities for Field Trial Methods. In: Proceedings of SIGCHI Conference on Human Factors in Computing Systems (CHI). ACM Press, New York, NY.

Cooper, A., 1999. The Inmates Are Running the Asylum. Macmillan Computer Publishing.

deAlwis, B., Gutwin, C., Greenberg, S., 2009. GT/SD: Performance and Simplicity in a Groupware Toolkit. In: Proceedings of the ACM Symposium on Engineering Interactive Computing Systems (SIGCHI). ACM Press, New York, NY.

Djajadiningrat, J.P., Gaver, W., Fres, J.W., 2000. Interaction Relabelling and Extreme Characters. In: Proceedings of the conference on Designing interactive systems (DIS). ACM Press, New York, NY.

Dix, A., Finlay, J., Abowd, G., Beale, R., 2003. Human-Computer Interaction. Prentice Hall, Upper Saddle River, NJ.

Dourish, P., Adler, A., Bellotti, V., Henderson, A., 1996. Your Place or Mine? Learning from Long-Term Use of Audio-Video Communication. J. CSCW 5 (1). Kluwer Academic Publishers.

Erickson, T., 1996. The Design and Long-Term Use of a Personal Electronic Notebook. In: Proceedings of the Conference on Human Factors in Computing Systems (SIGCHI). ACM Press, New York, NY.

Gaver, W., 2006. The Video Window: My Life with a Ludic System. Pers. Ubiq. Comput. 10 (2–3).

Gaver, W., Dunne, T., Pacenti, E., 1999. Cultural Probes. interactions 6 (1), 21–29.

Greenberg, S., Buxton, B., 2008. Usability Evaluation Considered Harmful (Some of the Time). In: Proceedings of the SIGCHI Conference on Human Factors in Computing Systems (CHI). ACM Press, New York, NY.

Greenberg, S., Fitchett, C., 2001. Phidgets: Easy Development of Physical Interfaces through Physical Widgets. In: Proceedings of the ACM symposium on User interface software and technology (UIST). ACM Press, New York, NY.

Håkansson, M., Ljungblad, S., Holmquist, L.E., 2003. Capturing the Invisible: Designing Context Aware Photography. Proceedings of the conference on Designing for user experiences (DUX). ACM Press, New York, NY.

Harrison, S., Minneman, S., Marinacci, J., 1999. Draw Stream Station or the AVCs of Video Cocktail Napkins. Proceedings of IEEE International Conference on Multimedia Computing and Systems. IEEE.

Hutchinson, H., Mackay, W., Westerlund, B., Bederson, B., Druin, A., Plaisant, C., Beauduin, M., Conversy, S., Evans, H., Hansen, H., Roussel, N., Eiderback, B., Lindquist, S., Sundbad, Y., 2003. Technology Probes: Inspiring Design for and with Families. Proceedings of the Conference on Human Factors in Computing Systems (SIGCHI). ACM Press, New York, NY, pp. 17−24.

Judge, T.K., Neustaedter, C., Kurtz, A.F., 2010. The Family Window: The Design & Evaluation of a Domestic Media Space. Proceedings of the Conference on Human Factors in Computing Systems (SIGCHI). ACM Press, New York, NY.

Judge, T.K., Neustaedter, C., Harrison, S., 2012. Inter-Family Messaging with Domestic Media Spaces. In: Neustaedter, C., Harrison, S., Sellen, A. (Eds.), Connecting Families, The Impact of New Communication Technologies on Domestic Life. Springer.

Kim, H., Gutwin, C., Subramanian, S., 2007. The Magic Window: Lessons from a Year in the Life of a Co-Present Media Space. Proceedings of the International ACM conference on Supporting group work. ACM Press, New York, NY.

Mantei, M., Baecker, R., Sellen, A., Buxton, W., Milligan, T., Wellman, B., 1991. Experiences in the Use of a Media Space. Proceedings of the Conference on Human Factors in Computing Systems (SIGCHI). ACM Press, New York, NY.

Neustaedter, C., 2013. My Life with Always-On Video. Electron. J. Commun. COIS.

Neustaedter, C., Greenberg, S., 2003. The Design of a Context-Aware Home Media Space for Balancing Privacy and Awareness. Proceedings of the Fifth International Conference on Ubiquitous Computing (UbiComp 2003).

Neustaedter, C., Judge, T., Kurtz, A., Fedorovskaya, E., 2010. The Family Window: Connecting Families over Distance with a Domestic Media Space. Video Proceedings of the Conference on Computer Supported Cooperative Work (CSCW 2010). ACM Press, New York, NY.

Neustaedter, C., Sengers, P., 2012a. Autobiographical Design in HCI Research: Designing and Learning through Use-It-Yourself. Proceedings of the Designing Interactive Systems Conference (DIS). ACM Press, New York, NY.

Neustaedter, C., Sengers, P., 2012b. Autobiographical Design: What You Can Learn from Designing for Yourself. interactions 19 (6), 28−33. Nov. 2012.

Nielsen, J., 1993. Usability Engineering. Morgan Kaufmann, Burlington, MA.

O'Brien, J., Rodden, T., 1997. Interactive Systems in Domestic Environments. Proceedings of the Conference on Designing Interactive Systems (DIS). ACM Press, New York, NY.

Peesapati, S.T., Schwanda, V., Schultz, J., Lepage, M., Jeong, S., Cosley, D., 2010. Pensieve: Supporting Everyday Reminiscence. Proceedings of the Conference on Human Factors in Computing Systems (SIGCHI). ACM Press, New York, NY.

Priedhorsky, R., 2010. The Value of Geographic Wikis. PhD Dissertation. University of Minnesota.

Rogers, Y., 2011. Interaction Design Gone Wild: Striving for Wild Theory. interactions 18 (4), 58–62.

Thacker, C.P., 1988. Personal Distributed Computing: The Alto and Ethernet Hardware. In: Goldberg, A. (Ed.), A History of Personal Workstations. ACM Press, New York, NY, pp. 267–289.

Tolmie, P., Pycock, J., Diggins, T., MacLean, A., Karsenty, A., 2002. Unremarkable Computing. In: Proc. CHI. ACM Press, New York, NY.

Vick, P., 2010. Dogfooding and Microsoft [online]. http://www.panopticoncentral.net/archive/2004/12/10/2828.aspx. August 2010.

Voida, A., Voida, S., Greenberg, S., He, H.A., 2008. Asymmetry in Media Spaces. Proc. CSCW.

von Hippel, E., 1986. Lead Users: A Source of Novel Product Concepts. Manag. Sci. 32 (7).

Whittaker, S., Hirschberg, J., Amento, B., Stark, L., Bacchiani, M., Isenhour, P., Stead, L., Zamchick, G., Rosenberg, A., 2002. SCANMail: A Voicemail Interface that Makes Speech Browsable, Readable and Searchable. Proceedings of the Conference on Human Factors in Computing Systems (SIGCHI). ACM Press, New York, NY.

Wright, P., McCarthy, J., 2008. Empathy and Experience in HCI. Proceedings of the Conference on Human Factors in Computing Systems (SIGCHI). ACM Press, New York, NY, pp. 637–646.

# In-Home Deployments

**A.J. Brush\*, Brian Meyers\*, James Scott**[§]

*Microsoft Research, Redmond, WA, USA\*; Microsoft Research, Cambridge, UK*[§]

## INTRODUCTION

In-home deployment is a critically important method for studying technologies for domestic life, as it is only when these technologies are inserted into the reality of daily home life that many of their properties become fully apparent. An in-home deployment study can also be referred to as a field study, or *in-situ* study, where the "field" is someone's home. In our view, the main benefit of an in-home deployment compared to other commonly used evaluation methods, such as laboratory studies or interviews, is *realism*. A deployment study takes place where people actually live, and the data that is gathered is from their normal lives. This chapter focuses on studies where each home in a study is an independent deployment site, while Chapter 10 provides more details on field trials with multiple connected homes (e.g., children and grandparents sharing an always-on video connection).

The two most common types of in-home deployments are studies of current behavior and prototype deployments. Current behavior studies seek to understand what household members currently do, for example, how often they are home together or how much energy they use. This may require deployments of non-interactive devices, such as for logging purposes. On the other hand, the goal of a prototype deployment is to study people's reactions to and use of a prototype, as well as how the prototype influences their behavior. While current behavior studies sometimes lack some of the challenges of prototype deployments—for example, the occupants may not be required to interact with a new technology—they have similar complexity in the time and effort of deploying to homes and ensuring that data collected is valid.

This chapter will help in the planning and successful execution of in-home deployment by sharing insights drawn from our combined experiences running many different studies in the home and by using a recent, fairly complicated study, the PreHeat prototype deployment (Scott et al. 2011), as a concrete example. PreHeat is a prototype thermostat that automatically controls home heating using occupancy sensing and prediction. We deployed and studied the system in five homes over the course of several months. Prototype system development and debugging, planning the study, and running the study took approximately one year. During this time, we faced challenges that included accurately sensing home and room

159

occupancy, building a robust heating system that failed infrequently and recovered quickly if it did fail, and designing the study to fairly compare multiple long-running conditions. In this chapter, we reflect on those issues and provide take-home lessons from our experience.

## IN-HOME DEPLOYMENTS

First, we discuss in general when in-home deployments are appropriate, how to anticipate the effort required when doing a study in the home, and how to deal with the challenges of in-home deployments. We provide guidelines and strategies relevant to all types of in-home deployments. We then focus more closely on challenges presented by our deployment of the PreHeat prototype and what lessons we gathered from that experience.

### CAREFULLY CONSIDER THE VALUE OF AN IN-HOME DEPLOYMENT

Deployment studies are appropriate for observing current behavior over time or needing to place novel technology into a home environment to see how participants interact with it during their normal lives. The trade-off is that there is much less control over what people do during the in-home deployment study.

While in-home deployments result in rich data and can lead to very robust findings, caution should be used when deciding to pursue one. In-home deployments are challenging for a number of reasons. First, conducting them is time consuming. Typically, a home must be visited multiple times, including at the beginning of the study, end of the study, and sometimes during the middle of the study (e.g., if a prototype needs to be repaired). Second, the technology deployed must be robust enough to survive both the intended use and any unintended uses that will almost certainly arise during the study period. Lastly, there is little control over how participants use the technology during an in-home deployment. One might well find that one's technology is used more for some unrelated purpose rather than the topic of the study, or not used at all.

With these challenges in mind, we encourage researchers considering an in-home deployment to reflect carefully whether another method might be more appropriate or have a better cost/benefit trade-off. For example, laboratory studies are more appropriate for any research questions in which people must perform specific tasks, and a single in-home interview at several different households may provide enough data to understand current behavior (e.g., Brush and Inkpen 2007). More information on a wide range of study methods can be found in HCI textbooks, including Interaction Design (Rogers, Sharp, and Preece 2011) and Human-Computer Interaction (Dix et al. 2004). Information on field studies in particular can be found in the "Ubiquitous Computing Field Studies" chapter in Ubiquitous Computing Fundamentals (Brush 2010).

That said, we reiterate that in-home studies offer unparalleled *realism* and insight into the use of technology in real contexts. Therefore, while we recommend careful consideration of the challenges that accompany in-home deployments, there are often studies that just cannot be performed any other way with the same fidelity. In many cases, a full in-home deployment may be most appropriate only after conducting a number of other pilot investigations, such as surveys or lab studies, which help to refine the system to be deployed, the study methodology, and the hypotheses or areas of interest to be explored during the study.

---

**LESSON**

Look carefully at the full costs involved in an in-home deployment, and consider using other study methodologies (e.g., lab studies, logging studies, surveys), either as alternatives or precursors to an in-home deployment.

---

## TIMEFRAME FOR AN IN-HOME DEPLOYMENT

In-home deployments typically last anywhere from a couple of weeks to several months, depending on the level of interaction the household members have with the deployed system. For example, a study of current behavior by silently logging energy data is invisible to residents and can likely go on for as long as one desires. At the opposite extreme, a study that requires participants to track what they ate or what time they went to bed might experience issues with participant fatigue. Often, instead of thinking in terms of days, it is more useful to consider the number of data points that can be collected. A study of a new alarm clock might only be able to collect a single data point a day, and thus, in order to collect enough data to have confidence in the evaluation, one might need multiple months of use.

Hnat et al. uses the analogy of a battery to think about how participant effort required during a deployment study interacts with the length of the study (Hnat et al. 2011). Essentially, participants have a certain amount of "energy" available to participate in a study. That energy can be spent in a short amount of time by asking them for a high-level of participation or spent over a longer period by requiring less effort from the participants. Gratuities, or payments to the participants, can also be used to adjust the amount of effort participants are willing to expend in a study. For example, if participants must self-report, they can be paid for each self-report or given a reward for reaching a minimum level of reports. However, if the study aims to report on the naturalistic usage levels for a prototype system, then a different gratuity solution is needed to avoid having the payment bias the results.

Finally, it is important to note that a research project will last much longer than the length of time the in-home deployment study is conducted. This is not only because of the preparation time, but also because it is valuable to pilot a study before deploying it into participant homes. Every study we conduct has an initial pilot in our own homes and often one or two friends or family members. The pilot study does not have to last as long as the real in-home deployment, but the researcher should pilot every part of the study, especially if he or she has different conditions. A pilot also helps to verify that the researcher knows exactly what will happen at each visit to the home (make a script and a checklist) and that all the necessary equipment and tools are acquired to successfully deploy a prototype or conduct a study of current behavior. Once the researcher deploys into someone's home, it can be difficult to schedule time to go back, so do everything possible to get it right the first time. We recommend always having extra extension cords, surge protectors, a small toolkit, and a camera. We photograph the space both before and after our deployment, even if we do not intend to use the photos for anything more than reminding us about each setup.

> **LESSON**
>
> Plan timelines for in-home studies that include time for study overhead, such as pilot deployments, setup and debugging time, deployment overheads, and teardown time. Bear in mind "participant fatigue" in the level of interaction demanded of participants during the study.

## DATA PRIVACY CONCERNS

The data collected during an in-home deployment will vary depending on the research question. One important general consideration is how to handle privacy concerns. Think carefully ahead of time about how to analyze the data, and test this during the pilot phase. Ensure that all the data needed is being gathered and at the appropriate granularity for the analysis required. However, it is also important to avoid doing too much data logging, since the additional data can make it harder to focus on the data needed, and with additional data comes increased privacy concerns.

Because in-home deployments collect data from people as they live their lives, the deployments can often capture data in sensitive spaces. Sometimes these concerns are very clear, for example, audio recording in a bedroom (Kay et al. 2012) or always-on cameras in household public spaces, such as kitchens (Pousman et al. 2008). In other studies, the sensitivity can be less obvious. In the PreHeat deployment, we collected occupancy information that could reveal times when the home is unattended, wake/sleep times, when and for how long bathrooms are used, and so on. It is very important to have a plan around what data will be collected, who will have access to it, how it will be anonymized, and how long to keep it. This plan should be shared with the participant households so they fully understand what is being collecting and how it will be used. In most settings, an institutional review board (IRB) will require the researcher to address these questions.

While collecting data in a privacy-sensitive manner may take some creative thinking, there are many options available. One option we have used successfully was to offer participants an additional gratuity if they opted in to that aspect of the study we considered sensitive. In our Speech@Home study (Brush et al. 2011) we wanted to collect five hours of audio data to understand typical noise level in kitchens. We put a "record now" button on our prototype and offered participants an additional gratuity item if they recorded the extra audio data. Other studies have offered the option to review and delete data locally before it goes to the research team. The Lullaby sleep-capture system deployed on bedside tables used multiple cameras and a microphone. It offered three types of privacy controls, the ability to turn off recording, selective deletion of recorded data, and the ability to delete the last hour of recorded data (Kay et al. 2012). While such controls may skew the data captured, such a skew may be unavoidable in order to address privacy concerns.

---

### LESSON

Gathering specific data in participants' homes is difficult without also unintentionally capturing additional data through accidental logging or by inference from intentionally gathered data. Take a strong and holistic privacy approach to protect private data, for example, by allowing participants to vet their data.

---

## COST TRADEOFFS

When conducting deployment-based research, there are many tradeoffs to make involving the cost of the deployment. These costs are not just the monetary costs of the equipment or gratuities, but also include the costs in preparation time before the deployment, in management time during the deployment, and the risk of things going wrong that might necessitate re-running deployments.

When purchasing equipment for home deployments of either type (studies of current behavior or prototype deployments), we recommend significantly over-specifying the equipment and valuing robustness, both in the physical hardware and in the software engineering. The home introduces unknowns to any system, whether it be power outages, flaky networking, occupants that move sensors, and so on. The simple fact that the system will be running constantly, instead of being restarted each day (as it might have been during the development phase), can introduce software and hardware problems, such as memory leaks or "disk full" errors. The equipment not only has to run the actual deployment system, but it also needs spare capacity to cope with the overhead of being part of a research system. These overheads include logging for subsequent analysis, both in the device itself and through a cloud service (preferably) for offsite backup; remote access and control so the system can be monitored and fixed without site visits when possible; and debugging and development tools so the system can be modified in place without relying on external software or hardware. It should also be flexible enough that if, after a pilot deployment, the focus of the study shifts toward some interesting and novel use, the equipment can cope with that change in focus and be repurposed to support a new study.

Another cost tradeoff is deciding whether to use off-the-shelf hardware or build custom hardware. There are several reasons for using off-the-shelf systems when possible. Compared to designing, implementing, and manufacturing custom hardware, off-the-shelf hardware is easier and faster to acquire. Additionally, off-the-shelf hardware is often cheaper than custom hardware due to economies of scale, even just considering the bill-of-materials cost, let alone the development time. This option also allows flexibility in the number of devices to be deployed. Often, adding a new off-the-shelf device requires only a little time and small delivery fees, while trying to build one custom device can require reordering multiple base components, setting up the assembly space, and finding time to build and test the new device. Finally, using off-the-shelf hardware frees the project team from either hiring or learning skills such as soldering, PCB design, and industrial design.

However, off-the-shelf systems are limiting; they may do certain things very well but permit only limited reprogrammability or configurability, and, often, research systems may wish to go beyond that envelope by the very nature of the work. Off-the-shelf systems may not have sufficient robustness or logging capabilities required for research analysis. Frequently, device functionality is limited by a desire from the manufacturer to keep the costs down. Even with these drawbacks, given the time required to develop and debug custom hardware, we recommend using off-the-shelf hardware whenever possible and developing custom hardware only when necessary or if the device itself is part of the research focus.

Finally, a cost tradeoff exists between time before the study and time during the study. Consider a project that uses experience-sampling surveys to assess participants' opinions about a deployed prototype. This could be accomplished by either automating the process using a custom software program written and deployed by the research team, or manually emailing a questionnaire to participants each week/day/hour as appropriate. Depending on the size of the study and the complexity of building out a new tool, either may be appropriate. Carefully and realistically evaluating the time requirements of each option will help select the best approach. Sending a preformed email message to ten people each day for two weeks is certainly easier than authoring a custom application that has to run reliably on their hardware for two weeks. On the other hand, if the number of participants were a hundred and the timescale were months, it would perhaps be well worthwhile to write the custom application.

Sometimes, time can be traded for money, for example, by using Amazon's Mechanical Turk to process data, or by choosing a more expensive hardware/software system that does what is wanted "out of the box" rather than using a cheaper system that requires significant tweaking and modifying before deployment.

**LESSON**

In-home studies offer many ways to ask the same basic research question, with cost tradeoffs in terms of money, time before the study, and time during the study. Carefully consider which is best, and value robustness and flexibility for the equipment deployed, as the home environment will cause unforeseen issues.

## VISITING THE HOME

Our final suggested consideration for all in-home studies concerns the frequency and timing of site visits. Scheduling times to visit homes can be difficult, especially if the study design requires talking with multiple family members. Be prepared to be available in the evenings and on weekends. We have found that offering to bring a pizza or other dinner items can be a valuable icebreaker and allows for a meeting during the dinner hour. Always send a reminder email, or make a reminder call, a day or so ahead, or risk showing up and finding the home empty (not a fun experience). Ideally, minimize the number of times required to visit the home, for example, by visiting only at the beginning and end of the study. If additional data collection is required during the middle of the study, try to do it through email or phone calls.

For safety reasons, it is important to avoid visiting an unknown participant's home by oneself. Particularly on the first visit, always bring at least one other person. While we have never had a safety incident, there have been a few visits where it felt more comfortable to have multiple people visiting together. In addition, since one person will be focused on interacting with the members of the household, having a second person will help ensure that required steps are not forgotten. Also, they can take additional notes as needed.

In very rare cases, it may be possible to conduct an in-home deployment without visiting the home. This is worth considering because it becomes possible to work with families that are outside of the researcher's immediate geographic region. For the SPARCS study (Brush, Inkpen, and Tee 2008), we deployed a photo- and calendar-sharing prototype to pairs of families (e.g., grandparents and kids) to run on their home computers. We sent the software by email and then did phone support with families to get it installed. The prevalence of video-calling programs such as Skype makes it easier to consider studies where technology is sent to participants, and then they are interviewed remotely. (For more on this approach, refer to Chapter 2 on conducting remote interviews with participants.) However, in most cases, the researcher will need to go to the house to deploy the system and possibly also visit after the study to gather data on how the system was used (e.g., photographs or interviews) and/or to tear down the deployed system.

> **LESSON**
>
> Treat home visits with care. Be well prepared in order to maximize the utility of each visit (e.g., pilot the visit and send reminders), expect scheduling to be difficult, and do not go alone if the participants are strangers.

## PREHEAT STUDY AND METHOD

We now focus on our case study, the in-home deployment of our PreHeat home heating system. We cover the goals of our deployment, why we conducted an in-home deployment, and what data we collected and analyzed. Using occupancy sensing and a novel prediction algorithm, PreHeat strives to reduce the energy consumption of a household's heating system without compromising the thermal comfort of household members. PreHeat heats a space when it is occupied and also builds a predictive model so that even when a space is not currently occupied it may be proactively heated in advance of the next predicted occupancy. This allows PreHeat to react dynamically to the occupancy patterns in a household on a given day.

The two key metrics in evaluating whether PreHeat performs better than commonly used methods for heating homes are the amount of energy used to heat the home and the MissTime (time in which an occupied space is not within $1°C$ of the predefined temperature setpoint). MissTime is used as an indicator of thermal comfort. We wanted to compare the PreHeat algorithm against two other conditions: using a heating schedule (Schedule) or leaving the thermostat set at a single temperature (AlwaysOn).

One approach to quantifying energy used and MissTime for the three conditions (PreHeat, Schedule, and AlwaysOn) would have been to use a simulator (such as EnergyPlus), an approach some previous research has adopted (Gupta, Intille, and Larson 2009; Lu et al. 2010; Mozer, Vidmar, and Dodier 1997). However, we had concerns about how accurate a simulation would be and whether the simulation would capture the intricacies of a real-world deployment, and in any case, we needed to deploy sensors in real homes to get the fine-grained occupancy data (at the room scale) for the PreHeat algorithm. This led us to consider a full prototype deployment.

Several factors enabled us to make the decision to go ahead with this deployment. We had conducted several lower-overhead studies deploying GPS receivers (Krumm and Brush 2011) and temperature sensors (Scott et al. 2010), so we were confident that our deployment would have good results. We could limit the overhead of deployment by using our own homes and those of close collaborators, which also simplified, though by no means eliminated, privacy concerns. Based on our work on the Microsoft .NET Gadgeteer rapid prototyping platform, we had the expertise to use custom hardware, which gave us full control of the system behavior right down to the hardware level. Feeling comfortable that we could fix issues that arose "in the wild," we decided to go ahead with performing actual control of home heating systems to evaluate PreHeat. We believed this offered a clearly superior evaluation technique to other options.

We conducted our deployment of PreHeat in five family homes: three were our own homes and two were homes of colleagues working in our research lab. These homes were also spread across two countries, with three homes in Seattle, Washington, USA, and two in Cambridge, UK. We chose these homes based on a number of considerations. First, because the study involved replacing a critical piece of infrastructure—the home's heating system—we wanted to ensure that there was at least one computer expert in each house who could work with the system in case of emergency. Second, because the homes were our own and our colleagues', we could visit the homes more freely to debug and fix the systems as necessary, and the participants were more open to living with an experimental system because they trusted us to fix any problems quickly. Finally, we selected homes where participants left the house for significant parts of the day, so there was the potential for energy savings by identifying those time periods. Because our evaluation took place in our own homes and those of close colleagues, we explicitly restricted ourselves to collecting quantitative data and excluded any qualitative data to avoid the potential that we might be biased toward our own system. Chapter 8, "Autobiographical Design in the Home," describes advantages, disadvantages, and things to consider when using one's own home as a deployment site.

We evaluated two other homes of colleagues who expressed an interest in being part of the study as potential deployment sites, but excluded them. We excluded one UK home because we could not easily augment the gas meter to be electronically readable (so we would not have been able to gather energy use data easily), and one US home because the home was occupied nearly all of the time and therefore offered few opportunities to reduce heating time.

Our study had three phases. In our Debug phase, which lasted around seven days in each house, we replaced the home's heating system with our custom system, initially using the Schedule condition, which was most similar to the occupants' previous thermostats. In the three US homes, we controlled whole-house forced air heating systems by deploying a custom thermostat (Figure 9.1) and a home heating server that ran the heating algorithms, sent commands to the thermostat, and logged data. For sensing when occupants were home, we used active RFID (radio frequency

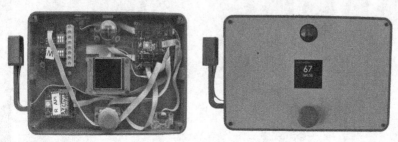

**FIGURE 9.1**

.NET Gadgeteer hardware for US thermostat.

**FIGURE 9.2**

To sense when participants were home we placed small, active RFID tags on their key chains and attached an RFID reader to our home heating server.

identification) tags that occupants put on their key chains (Figure 9.2) and a reader attached to the home heating server. In the two UK homes, we additionally augmented hot water radiators and underfloor heating to exercise per-room control. In these homes, we sensed per-room occupancy using passive infrared motion sensors (Figure 9.3). The installation was particularly complex in the UK houses

**FIGURE 9.3**

Room units deployed all over a house in the UK.

because each room had to be separately instrumented. This required installing and configuring around fifteen different hardware elements per house, and, for some elements, rewiring 240V electrical circuits. Naturally, a system of this complexity did not work flawlessly the first time, and we needed several return visits to refine the prototype. Starting with our own houses first reduced the overhead of making system changes. The Debug phase also gave households a chance to adjust the temperature setpoints if desired, and to fine-tune the heating schedule to allow the Schedule condition to match their actual occupancy pattern as much as possible. This also mitigated any potential novelty effect common with new technology.

Phase 1, the first data collection phase, lasted fourteen days, and our system alternated daily between using AlwaysOn and Scheduled algorithms to heat the homes. During this phase, the system collected fourteen days of occupancy data that was then used by the PreHeat's prediction algorithm in the next phase. The final and main phase of the study, Phase 2, alternated between Scheduled heating of the home and PreHeat's predictive heating algorithm. This phase lasted at least forty-eight days in every house. Using data from Phase 1, we estimated what the energy use of AlwaysOn would have been during Phase 2 to make a final three-way comparison.

In comparing the performance of the three heating algorithms, PreHeat, AlwaysOn, and Scheduled, there were two main confounds to overcome: weather and house occupancy variability. To cope with variable weather (most importantly, the variation in outside temperature both day to day and as winter became spring), we alternated which algorithm was running on a day-by-day basis. To try to account for and balance out potential schedule differences that might unfold in each house, we ran the study for many weeks. Taking Phases 1 and 2 in total, deployments ranged from sixty-two to eighty-four days.

Our results showed that PreHeat enabled occupants to make more efficient use of home heating (i.e., achieve a better tradeoff of energy used versus MissTime incurred), particularly in UK houses with per-room control, where energy savings of 8 to 18 percent were achieved over Scheduled, and 27 to 35 percent over AlwaysOn, while still reducing MissTime by 38 to 60 percent.

## CHALLENGES AND LESSONS LEARNED

We now describe the main challenges we had to overcome when conducting the Pre-Heat study and the lessons we learned from dealing with them.

## IMPLEMENTING THE MINIMUM VIABLE PROTOTYPE

For a system that controlled a vital part of a real house's infrastructure, we had to build out the system's features and user interface (UI) so that it largely matched the capabilities of occupants' existing heating systems. In the UK, for example, this meant including hot water control and scheduling as well as heating control, and supporting per-room temperature setpoints. In the United States, we had to deal with controlling the circulation fan as well as furnace control. However, while these are non-negotiable features, we were also aware of many other features (e.g., remote control of heating) that would have been nice to have, but were not strictly necessary for our particular study. To strike a balance on what to implement, we found a useful analogy in the advice popularized by The Lean Startup Movement (Ries 2011), that start-up companies must focus on implementing the Minimum Viable Product (MVP) and eliminate all extra features so they can ship their first product rapidly. In this vein, we tried to carefully identify and implement the minimum viable prototype of a heating and occupancy sensing system. This helped make possible the development effort to build the prototype in a reasonable period with the resources we had.

We identified some features that were required as part of a minimum viable prototype, for example, the ability to manually override the setpoint temperature with a simple action on each device. However, we decided that other existing features of heating systems could be acceptably implemented by participating households sending an email to us, the researchers, rather than as a functioning UI in the prototype. For example, changing the temperature setpoints and activating vacation mode were accomplished by us manually editing the settings files when participating households emailed us asking for these changes in the system. Remotely editing the configuration files was much simpler than implementing an end-user-facing control UI.

Piloting in our own homes and during the debug phase was critical for identifying whether we had missed any required features and correcting problems. For example, we had not initially included mechanisms to dim the screens of the UK devices at night, but as soon as we deployed them, we received feedback that glowing screens were disturbing at sleep time, and we added an automatic dimming feature.

---

### LESSON

Think carefully about what set of features make up the minimum viable prototype and where development time and effort can be saved. Only automate features that would otherwise involve excessive researcher time or occupant inconvenience to update manually.

---

## DEPLOYING A SAFETY CRITICAL SYSTEM

In our deployment, we controlled the heating of the home, a safety-critical system, particularly in the winter months. We were very concerned about making sure that the system worked robustly and, if any problems occurred, there were fallbacks in place at every level, from the prototype hardware device up through the software layer. Our guiding principle was to always "fail safe" and keep the house at a comfortable temperature if a problem occurred.

For example, if a device controlling the heating ever lost communication with the computer responsible for issuing the heating commands, the device defaulted to the occupants' preferred setpoint so that the house would stay warm even though a failure occurred. Another example is that all of the various hardware and software elements in the system were built with "watchdog" timers, that is, systems that monitor whether an element is operating correctly and will restart or reset it if not. This was true of our home heating server software (where a separate program constantly monitored whether the heating program was running and restarted it if not), home heating server hardware (the PC BIOS was set to automatically turn back on if there was a power cut), the firmware in our embedded devices (which rebooted and reset the hardware if the system was not functioning correctly), and of the communications between them (our network protocols included heartbeat signals and acknowledgments of every command so that the home server could monitor the status of the embedded devices at frequent intervals).

Such care is rarely necessary for in-lab studies or demonstration prototypes, which have to operate for a few minutes or hours only. For real-life deployments, this care offers a valuable safety net for rare or hard-to-anticipate errors; for example, electrical noise from the furnace occasionally caused one of our embedded device processors to hang and require rebooting.

To cope with cases where these automatic safeguards could not recover the system, we implemented an alerting mechanism, specifically, "emergency" state notification emails that were sent every thirty minutes whenever the system was not fully operational. In addition, we logged the times the system was in an "error" state so we could account for that during our data analysis phase.

By using watchdogs, heartbeats, acknowledgments, and alerts, we achieved a 99.8 percent uptime during the study, and our system "failed safe" at other times. For nearly all problems, the system recovered automatically and never reached the threshold where an email alert was sent that required manual attention. Most failures ended up being due to contention in the 2.4GHz radio band, in which our system was competing with WiFi devices; however, these were temporary, and the system recovered automatically. In case all this work sounds like overkill, remember that we were replacing a critical system for which one normally expects to have a 100 percent uptime.

---

**LESSON**

An in-home deployment requires the system to run extremely robustly, or there is the risk of having participants respond more to the quality problems rather than the system being evaluated. Think about techniques for automatic recovery from unpredicted errors, "fail-safe" behavior, and automatic alerts should unrecoverable failures occur.

---

## SENSING IN THE REAL WORLD IS TRICKY

In the PreHeat study, we needed to sense the following real-world variables: the temperature of the space, the occupancy of the space, whether or not the heating system was turned on in each space, and how much natural gas was being used. Since we were in control of switching the heating system on and off, we could record that information directly. That left the natural gas reading, the temperature, and the occupancy variables that needed to be sensed in real time.

To sense gas usage, we used different methods in the United States and UK because of having to adapt to differences in local infrastructure. In the United States, the local utility company made gas meter data available from its smart meters. In the UK, we augmented the gas meters with off-the-shelf devices from RFXCOM that detected the meter's numeric digits rotation, and hence gave us gas readings.

We discovered that sensing the temperature was not as easy as it might appear. When validating the temperature sensor's readings from our prototype device against an accurate lab thermometer in our early device designs, we found that heat generated by the processor in the device was measurably affecting the temperature readings. Therefore, we ended up trying several case designs, finally settling on one that had the temperature sensor on a separate curved arm to maximize thermal isolation (see Figure 9.1).

To sense space occupancy, we bought several off-the-shelf systems and did test deployments to evaluate them relative to our needs. Our first attempt was to use the household WiFi router as a way to detect when smart phones entered or exited the house. Testing this approach in one of our homes revealed that this approach did not have sufficient granularity (often the phones would not connect to the WiFi for up thirty minutes after arriving), nor was it reliable (the phones frequently went to sleep and appeared to have left the house). Next, we tested putting off-the-shelf motion sensors in each room. While these devices were inexpensive, they were often unreliable when run continuously for several days; for example, a radio packet loss would cause us to lose a "departure" event, and so a large time period would be misclassified. We finally located an active RFID tagging solution that was a reliable way of doing house-wide occupancy detection. Tagging did come with a cost to our participants, as they were required to carry the tag itself on their key rings; however, we felt that requirement could be managed. Figure 9.2 shows the tags we used. New options for tagging have been developed since our study, and if we were re-running the study today, we would likely use Bluetooth Low Energy (BLE) tags, which can be lower power and smaller than the Active RFID system we used.

While Active RFID tagging solved the issue of household-level occupancy, in the UK, deployments were still needed for per-room occupancy. This was accomplished by having our custom prototype control unit for each space contain a motion sensor. By using careful placement of the units and tuning the parameters, we found that we could get the accuracy we needed in our test houses.

In each case, we needed to run multiple trials against known ground truth in order to get a reliable and accurate system. In the case of the occupancy, we had to deploy the systems in our houses and manually record our movements to compare against the sensor data and verify that the system was working as expected.

> **LESSON**
>
> Sensing in the real world is difficult, and more than one sensing solution may be needed if there are differences in the households. Be sure to validate the sensed data to ensure the sensors are accurate, and plan for multiple iterations of prototyping in case the first solution is not robust.

## ENSURING VALIDITY OF THE COLLECTED DATA

A study is all about collecting data, and thus the most important thing a researcher can do is ensure that the data collected is both accurate and preserved in case of system failure or downtime. We stored local log files so that any network connectivity loss or unexpected power events would not result in lost data. All data was eventually uploaded to an SQL database, and that database was backed up each day, both to the cloud and to a local solid-state USB drive. Thankfully, we did not experience any serious hardware issues, and our backups were not required, but several times, power failures or other events occurred that had the potential to have caused data corruption.

The care we took in system development allowed us to respond quickly to failures (e.g., devices unplugged) and avoid losing days from the study. Moving beyond system robustness, we also had to ensure that we were collecting valid data throughout the study. In particular, we were concerned about ensuring the validity of the home occupancy data. Both occupancy-sensing methods we used had the potential for problems. The active RFID tags on people's key chains, which tracked whether they were home or not, had a relatively limited range, requiring participants to put their keys within the range of the reader attached to the home heating server. The passive IR sensors used for room-level occupancy in the UK had trouble at night, when people moved much less while they were sleeping, and also had trouble covering some of the larger rooms.

To carefully monitor the occupancy data being collected and quickly spot any potential problems, we wrote a program that each morning emailed a visualization of the previous day's occupancy data for each household. Figure 9.4 shows an example of the information sent daily, including the success of data backups, the heating schedule that was followed in the house, and occupancy data, including motion sensor (US houses had a single motion sensor in the thermostat) and RFID data. At least one project team member inspected each visualization every morning and followed up as necessary with household members for clarification while the events were still fresh in their minds. In addition, we ran consistency checks examining the recorded data in the United States for situations when the RFID tag disappeared and reappeared frequently—which were typically RFID radio range problems—and in the UK, comparing the RFID data to the room-level motion data to highlight time when the house was occupied but the motion sensors were not

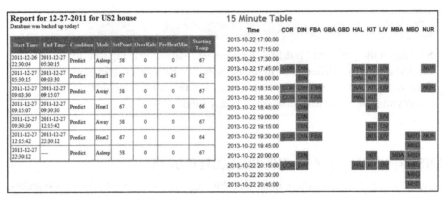

**FIGURE 9.4**

We set up the system to send emails each morning (illustrative excerpts above) showing what happened in the house the previous day. These assured us that data was being backed up and allowed us to look for any issues in the heating control periods and occupancy data.

active. During the study, we encountered both "social" issues, for example, where someone forgot their keys, and "technical" ones, such as RFID radio range problems. Using these cross-checks, we manually identified fifty-seven errors in the sensed occupancy data that could affect the analysis. To ensure our results (e.g., the MissTime calculation) were accurate, we created a "ground truth" occupancy table for use during the data analysis.

---

**LESSON**

Remote monitoring allows the researcher to keep a close eye on the data being collected so he or she can have confidence in its validity and address any issues quickly, for example, by asking participants while their memory is fresh. Log everything, in case it is useful, in backed-up storage, and if possible, log complementary data sources that can be used to cross-validate each other. It may be necessary to manually correct some data errors to maximize the validity of the analysis.

---

## CUSTOM HARDWARE REQUIRED

In order to build out the PreHeat system, we first looked for off-the-shelf hardware and software systems to accomplish what we wanted, but we ended up building some custom hardware and software in cases where the available off-the-shelf systems was inadequate for one reason or another. In addition to developing the custom software for the heating control algorithms, which was the main focus of the research, we identified three areas where we needed to source and purchase hardware for the house and started looking for off-the-shelf solutions. First, we needed a device to run the heating control software. Second, we needed full control over the heating system. Third, we needed to sense the temperatures, occupancy, and gas readings as described in the previous subsection.

For the home heating server, we elected to use an off-the-shelf small form factor PC. While this was more a powerful and expensive device than required to run a heating system, it allowed us to run the development tools on the devices themselves, facilitating in-situ debugging, and making remote control simpler (e.g., via remote desktop).

For controlling the heating system, our investigation discovered that there were no off-the-shelf devices that provided the fine-grained control (for each of our diverse heating systems) and logging that our system would need in order to test our algorithm. While we did find off-the-shelf radio-controlled thermostatic radiator valves (TRVs) that could perform per-room heating control in the UK, we realized we needed to build custom radio transmitter units to control them. Thus, we ended up designing three types of custom devices. In the UK, we had a device in each room that performed occupancy and temperature sensing and local TRV control, and provided our custom UI. We also had an additional type of device that simply actuated the boiler through 240V relays. In the United States, we built a device replacing the wall thermostat, which performed temperature sensing, supplied a custom UI, and actuated the furnace.

We did not start from scratch to build these custom devices, but instead based our prototypes on Microsoft .NET Gadgeteer (Villar et al. 2012), a modular prototyping toolkit. While we had to design a few custom hardware elements (e.g., the transmitter that communicated with the thermostatic radiator valve actuators), most of the hardware was standard .NET Gadgeteer modules. This saved us a lot of time over building fully custom hardware from scratch. Being a modular toolkit, there was also a lot of overlap between the hardware in the two types of UK unit and the US unit—indeed, they actually run the same software that detected the unit type on the fly by detecting the presence of various hardware modules. The inside of a US thermostat unit is shown in Figure 9.1, illustrating the modular hardware. We used a 3D printer and laser cutter to manufacture custom device cases.

---

**LESSON**

Use off-the-shelf hardware and software where possible. If custom hardware is needed, rapid prototyping toolkits can reduce the total workload and enable faster design iterations.

---

## CONSISTENCY ACROSS STUDY CONDITIONS

We conducted a study with three heating conditions (AlwaysOn, Scheduled, Pre-Heat) that were each used on different days depending on which phase of the study the house was in. To ensure household members behaved in the most consistent manner, for example, doing a heating override if they were cold, we did not want people's interactions with the system to change when the heating condition changed. Such consistent behavior is important to ensure the validity of the results. We therefore took several steps to ensure that the user experience across the study conditions was as uniform as possible.

First, we developed a UI and system configuration that hid the existence of different conditions. Specifically, while the device display informed a user of the current setpoint of the system, it did not specify the mode of operation, nor why the current heating setpoint was chosen. Second, if the participant decided to override the current temperature they had the choice of doing so "until the next sleep" (the time that the system went to the nighttime set point) or "until the next wake" (the morning time when the system went to the daytime set point). Since these two times were the same in every condition, the participant had no feedback on which condition was being evaluated at that time. Finally, our day-by-day alteration of the study condition, primarily done to mitigate the effect of weather, also hid the current condition from participants better than having each condition be a large contiguous block of time.

> **LESSON**
>
> Think about how to implement study conditions so they present participants with a coherent experience across conditions as much as possible, to avoid measuring participants' reactions to irrelevant differences.

## THE END OF THE STUDY

At the end of our study, we allowed households to keep the system if they wished because they could maintain it themselves. Three houses opted to continue running PreHeat. We also shared the output of the study with the participants. We advise doing the same whenever possible, as many people participate in deployments because they are interested in research and the findings may be more valuable to them than any other gratuity.

One US house appreciated the reactive heating on the weekends, which kept the house warm when they were home. Eventually the husband wanted the system removed when he was going to host his office party because of a power cord that was unattractively taped across the ceiling to power the thermostat. (Attractiveness of the deployed system does matter, but was not part of our minimum viable prototype.)

In the two UK houses, the system continues to run today, more than four years after the original study. It requires occasional maintenance (e.g., the disk on the home PCs fill up because of log backups), and some features that were excluded from the minimum viable prototype were subsequently implemented for long-term use, such as a "master off" for summer. Additionally, we showed the lead occupant how to change the setpoint in the configuration files to replace the "email us" interface we had used during the study.

---

**LESSON**

Make a plan about how the study will end, and either allow people to continue using the prototype or smoothly return their homes to the pre-study state.

---

## CONCLUDING REMARKS

In-home deployments result in rich data that would be impossible to get from any other evaluation method. While all researchers should carefully consider when an in-home study is most appropriate, once the decision is made to move forward with an in-home deployment, there are many steps one can take to ensure that deployment is successful. The best chance of collecting good data is had by carefully considering the functionality necessary for a minimum viable prototype, evaluating a range of technical choices—including both off-the-shelf and custom hardware— and allowing plenty of time to debug and pilot the study. Remote monitoring will alert the researcher to any potential problems and provide time to correct them, while making plans for how to handle privacy concerns and how to end the study will help avoid any surprises.

Our experience deploying PreHeat and other in-home studies and, in particular, the amount of custom engineering work these studies required, was part of the motivation to develop and open source both the .NET Gadgeteer (Villar et al. 2012) and the Lab of Things platforms (Brush et al. 2013). We hope these platforms will allow future studies to reuse and build upon past engineering efforts.

.NET Gadgeteer (http://netmf.com/gadgeteer/) is an open source modular prototyping platform that supports solderless assembly of devices through modular hardware and standard cables, enables software development and debugging using managed C# code and Visual Studio, and facilitates device case design through standard mounting fixtures on each module. Between the various manufacturers making .NET Gadgeteer-compatible hardware, there are currently more than one hundred types of .NET Gadgeteer modules available for purchase.

The Lab of Things SDK (http://lab-of-things.com/) strives to reduce the amount of development necessary to conduct a home study and, more generally, grow a community of people conducting studies that contribute to shared infrastructure. We hope that by working together we can ease the burden for everyone and enable in-home deployments at much larger scales than typically occur—hundreds of homes rather than tens—and with greater geographic diversity.

We hope these two toolkits are beneficial to researchers working in the home, and that the more general lessons we learned and shared in this chapter provide useful guidance for home deployment studies.

# REFERENCES

Brush, A.J., Inkpen, K., Tee, K., 2008. SPARCS: Exploring Sharing Suggestions to Enhance Family Connectedness. Conference on Computer supported cooperative work (CSCW 2008). ACM Press, New York, NY.

Brush, A.J., Filippov, E., Huang, D., Jung, J., Mahajan, R., Martinez, F., Mazhar, K., Phanishayee, A., Samuel, A., Scott, J., Singh, R.P., 2013. Lab of Things: A Platform for Conducting Studies with Connected Devices in Multiple Homes. UbiComp (Adjunct Publication), 35–38.

Brush, A.J., 2010. Ubiquitous Computing Field Studies. In: Krumm, J.C. (Ed.), Ubiquitous Computing Fundamentals. Chapman and Hall/CRC.

Brush, A.J., Inkpen, K., 2007. Yours, Mine and Ours? Sharing and Use of Technology in Domestic Environments. In: Proceedings of the 9th International Conference, Ubiquitous Computing (UbiComp 2007).

Brush, A.J., Inkpen, K., Johns, P., Meyers, B., 2011. Speech@Home: An Exploratory Study. In: Proceedings of the Extended Abstracts on Human Factors in Computing Systems (CHI). ACM Press, New York, NY.

Dix, A., Finlay, J., Abowd, G., Beale, R., 2004. Human-Computer Interaction, 3rd ed. Pearson Prentice Hall, Upper Saddle River, NJ.

Gupta, M., Intille, S.S., Larson, K., 2009. Adding GPS-Control to Traditional Thermostats: An Exploration of Potential Energy Savings and Design Challenges. In: Proceedings of the Pervasive. Cambridge, MA.

Hnat, T., Srinivasan, V., Lu, J., Sookoor, T., Dawson, R., Stankovic, J., Whitehouse, K., 2011. The Hitchhiker's Guide to Successful Residential Sensing Deployments. In: Proceedings of the 9th ACM Conference on Embedded Networked Sensor Systems. Nov. 2–4, 2011. ACM Press, New York, NY.

Kay, M., Choe, E.K., Shepherd, J., Greenstein, B., Consolvo, S., Watson, N.F., Kientz, J.A., 2012. Lullaby: A Capture & Access System for Understanding the Sleep Environment. In: Proceedings of the 14th ACM International Conference on Ubiquitous Computing (Ubicomp '12). ACM Press, New York, NY.

Krumm, J., Brush, A.J., June 2011. Learning Time-Based Presence Probabilities. In: Pervasive. Springer Verlag, Berlin, Heidelberg.

Lu, J., Sookoor, T., Srinivasan, V., Gao, G., Holben, B., Stankovic, J., Field, E., Whitehouse, K., 2010. The Smart Thermostat: Using Occupancy Sensors to Save Energy in Homes. Proceedings of the 8th ACM Conference on Embedded Networked Sensor Systems (SenSys, '10). ACM Press, New York, NY.

Mozer, M.C., Vidmar, L., Dodier, R.M., 1997. The Neurothermostat: PreHeat Optimal Control of Residential Heating Systems. In: Advances in Neural Information Processing Systems 9. MIT Press, Cambridge, MA, pp. 953–959.

Pousman, Z., Romero, M., Smith, A., Mateas, M., 2008. Living with Tableau Machine: A Longitudinal Investigation of a Curious Domestic Intelligence. In: Proceedings of the 10th International Conference on Ubiquitous Computing (UbiComp 08). ACM Press, New York, NY.

Ries, E., 2011. The Lean Startup: How Today's Entrepreneurs Use Continuous Innovation to Create Radically Successful Businesses [online]. Crown Business, Lean Startup. http://theleanstartup.com/.

Rogers, Y., Sharp, H., Preece, J., 2011. Interaction Design: Beyond Human-Computer Interaction. John Wiley & Sons.

Scott, J., Brush, A.J., Krumm, J., Meyers, B., Hazas, M., Hodges, S., Villar, N., Sept, 2011. PreHeat: Controlling Home Heating Using Occupancy Prediction. In: Proceedings of the UbiComp. ACM Press, New York, NY.

Scott, J., Krumm, J., Meyers, B., Brush, A.J., Kapoor, A., May 2010. Home Heating Using GPS-Based Arrival Prediction. In: Proceedings of Pervasive 2010 Workshop on Energy Awareness and Conservation through Pervasive Applications. Microsoft Research.

Villar, N., Scott, J., Hodges, S., Hammil, K., Miller, C., June 2012. .NET Gadgeteer: A Platform for Custom Devices. In: Proceedings of Pervasive 2012, Lecture Notes in Computer Science.

# Field Trials with Multiple Connected Households

# 10

**Tejinder K. Judge\*, Carman Neustaedter[§]**

*Google Inc., Mountain View, CA, USA\*; School of Interactive Arts and Technology,*
*Simon Fraser University, BC, Canada [§]*

## INTRODUCTION

Field trials are a method for studying the use of technologies by real end users in their naturalistic setting (Brown, Reeves, and Sherwood 2011). The goal of a field trial is to evaluate a system in either a formative or summative manner in which investigations typically go beyond exploring usability issues, such as task performance time, to understanding and exploring the deeper issues that end users face when using a technology amidst their everyday lives. Thus, field trials explore real usage practices along with the ways in which users assimilate technology into their everyday routines and context. Field trials can also generate information about the value of the technology in the lives of users. Given the real-world context of field trials, they are often thought of as a useful method for gathering longitudinal data about the usage of a system, in particular after any novelty effects have worn off (Nielsen 2004). Over the years, field trials have been referred to with a variety of names, including field deployments, field evaluations, field studies, in-situ studies, and "in-the-wild" studies.

In this chapter, we discuss the ways in which we have utilized field trials as part of our research on the design of video-based family communication systems. We have deployed a number of different systems for family use in the home and, in each case, learned valuable lessons about how to conduct field trials. This chapter focuses in particular on the case where collaborative technologies are deployed in domestic settings where they provide connections *between multiple* distance-separated homes. Thus, it is not a matter of testing out or trying a technology in a single home; instead, the usage of the technology spans several homes, where each is tightly coupled and interwoven with the practices that emerge in other homes. Field trials are challenging in and of themselves; however, we have found that when field trials move beyond just a single home to connect multiple homes with new prototype technologies, the challenges increase dramatically.

This chapter unfolds as follows. First, we provide background knowledge about field trials in which we describe the basics of the method along with pointers to examples of field trials within the Human-Computer Interaction (HCI) literature. Second, we focus on our own experiences of conducting field trials by describing a system called Family Portals that we designed, developed, and deployed in families' homes (Judge et al. 2011). Family Portals is an always-on multi-family video media space that provides a continuous video connection between three different homes. Third, we outline the various lessons that we learned about conducting field trials through our own experience of deploying Family Portals. Lastly, we step back and reflect on the ways in which we think multi-location field trials can and should be conducted in domestic settings.

## FIELD TRIALS IN HCI

Field trials involve the evaluation of a system that either is already in place within a setting or is given to users who are asked to use the system as a part of their everyday activities in their own environment (e.g., work or home). Field trials allow researchers to understand how similar technologies might be used if they were released commercially (Brown et al. 2011). Field trials can also lead to an understanding of user behavior and usage patterns that can be used to iterate on the design of a system or to develop design guidelines and recommendations for future similar systems.

In field trials, users are typically asked to use a system for a given time period as part of their daily routine while researchers collect data on this usage. A field trial can range from a few days to a few months or even years, depending on the nature of the research, the commitment of the users to using the system, and the frailty of the prototype being evaluated. Data from field trials are collected using a variety of methods including system logs, user interviews, observations, and self-report diaries. Prototypes tested in field trials can be fully functional versions of a final product or they can be early explorations that may have little to do with a final product (Korn and Bodker 2012).

Over the past two decades, field trials have become an increasingly common method for conducting research in HCI. In the first half of the 1990s, HCI research interests shifted from focusing on task performance in laboratory experiments to evaluating user interactions with technology and their understanding of the system (Olson and Teasley 1996; Barkhuus and Rode 2007). This is because traditional evaluation methods and metrics such as task completion times "... fail to capture the complexities and richness of the real world in which the applications are placed" (Rogers et al. 2007; Greenberg and Buxton 2008). Early field trials were investigations of prototypes that were used longitudinally in research lab settings. Examples of these include Portholes at EuroPARC (Dourish and Bly 1992), the Active Badge system at AT&T Laboratories (Harper, Lamming, and Newman 1992), and the media space at PARC (Bly, Harrison, and Irwin 1993). Although these early field trials were conducted by researchers in their own workplaces, their reflections from long term usage were valuable in "... forming an understanding of what happens when these technologies became more widespread" (Brown et al. 2011).

We have also seen an expansion over the years from the design and study of computing technologies solely for the workplace to increased interest in computing technologies designed for the home and domestic environments. This includes commercial products such as video chat technologies (e.g., Skype, Google+ Hangouts), home entertainment systems (e.g., Apple TV, Chromecast), and technologies that promote health and wellness (e.g., Wii Fit). A similar shift has also emerged in HCI research where, starting in the late 1990s, there has been increasing interest in studying technology design for families. This naturally involves studying the way technology is used *in situ* because it is often very difficult to replicate domestic life and domestic environments in a laboratory setting. Such real-world testing and evaluation is not easy and, because of this, some researchers have created "living labs," such as MITs PlaceLab (Intille et al. 2006) and Georgia Tech's Aware Home (Kidd et al. 1999), to simulate home settings for design and evaluation research. By controlling the environment, researchers hope to reduce the uncertainty found "in the wild" while retaining many aspects of a field trial. Although field trials in a living lab can provide both quantitative and qualitative data, they tend to lack ecological validity (Creswell 2003) because study participants are asked to live in a new environment and may or may not be able to recreate their typical routines and lifestyles.

Given the limitations of laboratory-based evaluation and living labs, field trials that occur in real users' homes remain a popular method for evaluating domestic technologies and understanding their usage. In fact, we have seen many examples of the use of field trials in domestic computing research over the years. For the purposes of this chapter, these generally fall into two categories: field trials in single home units and field trials of technologies that connect people across multiple homes.

The first type, single-home or single-family field trials, involves individuals in a family using a system with other co-located family members. For example, Neustaedter and Brush (2006) evaluated a digital family calendar called LINC in the homes of four different families to understand their use of the technology over a period of four weeks (Neustaedter and Brush 2006; Neustaedter, Brush, and Greenberg 2007). Family members within single households used the calendar as a group, but interaction did not span multiple homes. Other single-home field trials include the evaluation of Family Archive, a multi-touch tabletop system that acted as a technology probe to learn about families' photo archiving practices (Kirk et al. 2010), and Froehlich et al.'s (2012) field trial of novel eco-feedback displays that enable families to learn about their water consumption. Chapter 9 provides more detail on planning and conducting single-home field trials

The second type of field trial is a multi-home or multi-family field trial. In this situation, people in multiple homes use the same system where it connects household members across locations. The simplest form involves dyads, where two households connect through the use of the system. An early example is the Casablanca project, in which multiple prototypes and early concepts, such as the Commute-Board and MessageBoard, were initially evaluated by researchers in their own homes, followed by field trials with actual users (Hindus et al. 2001). In these cases, the technologies were used to transmit information such as messages between households. Another example comes from Digital Family Portraits (Mynatt et al.

2001; Rowan and Mynatt 2005), a prototype technology in the form of a photo frame that shares awareness information between an older adult's home and her adult child's home. Digital Family Portraits was deployed between two homes for a period of one year to understand longitudinal usage. Findings from the field trial led to refinements in the design and an understanding of how the device was used to support awareness between families (Rowan and Mynatt 2005). Other examples include dyadic field trials of SPARCS, a system for sharing photos between two households (Brush, Inkpen, and Tee 2008), and our own Family Window, an always-on video media space used for connecting two distance-separated households (Judge, Neustaedter, and Kurtz 2010).

The above examples all focus on connecting two households; however, multi-home field trials can also involve more than two homes. For example, field trials of videoProbe connected a triad of households through the use a photo sharing system (Conversy et al. 2003), while Wayve connected small networks of families and friends (quartet, triad, dyads, and single households) using a messaging device (Lindley, Harper, and Sellen 2010). Although the difference between a field trial with two connected homes and a field trial with three or more connected homes seems like a trivial increase in locations, the difference is actually quite complex.

First, with three or more households, researchers must deal with more users and more dynamic relationships within and between the households, all of which could affect usage and adoption of the system. For example, in a field trial with two homes that have four members per household, there are eight users in total and twenty-eight unique relationships within and between households (i.e., six unique relationships per household and sixteen unique relationships between households). These relationships include husband-wife, father-child, child-sibling, and child-aunt, among others. In contrast, in a field trial with three homes that have four members per household, there are twelve users and sixty-six relationships within and between households. This is a much more complicated scenario for researchers to understand and study. Our own experiences, as well as that of others, have demonstrated that more homes and more family members connected to each other between homes creates additional technical challenges and complexities, as compared to studying a system in only one home location (Hindus et al. 2001; Plaisant et al. 2006; Judge et al. 2011). This is not to say that single-home field trials are not complicated in their own way, yet they are certainly different from a multi-home situation.

Next, we dive more deeply into exploring multi-home field trials by reflecting on our own field trial of the Family Portals system (Judge et al. 2011).

## THE DESIGN OF FAMILY PORTALS

The Family Portals (FP) project was part of a larger series of explorations on the design of communication systems for families (Judge 2011). The overarching goal of these explorations was to understand how we could design video communication systems for families by changing the design paradigm from one involving "calling" family members (akin to commercial video chat systems available at the time) to one involving connecting homes with persistent video feeds. We did this by exploring the idea of "always-on" video in the home. Here the intention was that a family could leave a video feed running all the time between their home and that of remote family members. People in both households could glance every now and then at their "always-on video device" (e.g., a digital picture frame or tablet showing the video link) to see what people at the remote home were up to. They could also move from this awareness to interaction by communicating through features in the system or using other technologies, such as the phone, to augment the video feed.

We started by studying the ways in which people used existing commercial video chat systems (e.g., Skype, Apple FaceTime, Google+ Hangouts). This showed us that some families left video chat systems running for extended periods of time in order to share everyday life with a remote home (Judge and Neustaedter 2010). This was particularly prominent in families with children. Building on this idea, we created an always-on video system called the Family Window to connect two homes with a persistent video link (Judge et al. 2010). Chapter 8 describes our autobiographical design and evaluation of the Family Window. Following this, we conducted a field trial of the Family Window and found it was quite successful at connecting family members over distance: non-collocated family members valued the ability to see one another, and privacy concerns were minimal (Judge et al. 2010). Next, we decided to extend our design idea to explore how a triad of homes might connect with always-on video; here we wanted to try to "push the limit" to see when the idea of always-on video might break down or if it could continue to be extended to connect even more households in a positive way. This led us to the design of Family Portals, described in its entirety by Judge et al. (2011) and Judge (2011).

Next, we provide a brief description of the design of Family Portals to illustrate its features and to provide readers with an understanding of some of the design considerations in the system.

As mentioned, Family Portals (FP) was an always-on multi-family media space that connected three households together through a persistent video link. We called this media space "Family Portals" because it contained "portals," or views into distant families' homes (Figure 10.1). FP was prototyped on a touch and pen sensitive tablet PC with an external webcam to simulate the idea of it being a dedicated information appliance as opposed to a computer used for multiple tasks. The dedicated mobile device meant that FP could be easily moved throughout a family's home, depending on where household members wanted to share their activities from with a remote home. The user interface was divided between two types of portals: Targeted Portals for seeing individual homes and interacting with them on a one-to-one basis, and a Shared Portal for interacting with both families at the same time. We describe these next.

**FIGURE 10.1**

The Family Portals system showing shared video connections between three homes.

## TARGETED PORTALS

The left side of the screen in Figure 10.1 shows two Targeted Portals (top and bottom), one for each family that a local user is connected to. The Targeted Portals were intended to allow families to interact and share information with *one* of the two remote families in a dyadic manner. The main portion of each Targeted Portal showed video from the remote family's home, which could be obscured, if the remote family desired, by adjusting "privacy blinds," as shown in Figure 10.2. The bottom left corner of each Targeted Portal showed a feedback view of what that particular remote home saw of the local user's home; again, blinds could be adjusted, depending on one's privacy needs.

**FIGURE 10.2**

Privacy blinds "pulled" halfway down at night in one home.

Within each portal, users had options for interacting with the remote family. An audio feed was not provided because of potential privacy concerns and the possibility of audio being too intrusive and distracting. Instead, families could write handwritten messages on top of the video feed, if they wanted to. They could also click a "knock" button to attract the attention of the family members at the remote location; the expectation was that family members would then approach their display.

We expected that families might want to focus their attention on one remote family at a time, for example, if the third family was not home. In this case, users could toggle between *Full Screen* and *Split Screen* views by clicking a button to the left of the portal. In Full Screen mode, the portal expanded to cover the entire screen, as shown in Figure 10.3. The third family's video was minimized and displayed at the bottom right corner of the screen.

**FIGURE 10.3**

A full screen view showing how a local home could focus on seeing one of the two remote homes.

## SHARED PORTAL

The right side of the user interface was the Shared Portal (Figure 10.1, right). It provided shared interactions intended for the entire triad to see. Dourish et al. (1992) called this type of interaction *broadcast*, where all users of the system have access to all information. The main portion of the Shared Portal displayed a whiteboard, where users could write messages for *both* remote families to see. A multi-family knocking feature let a local family knock on both remote families' portals simultaneously.

## THE EVALUATION OF FAMILY PORTALS

Following the design and implementation of FP, we wanted to learn how families would use the system in their daily lives, what communication and awareness practices would emerge, and what privacy concerns they would face. A field trial was the best method to explore these questions and to get ecologically valid usage data from real users who were using the system in their homes.

In the following section, we describe how we handled participant recruitment and deployment of the system, as well as the data collection and analysis. In the subsequent section, we talk about the issues and challenges that emerged during our study and how we overcame them.

## PARTICIPANTS AND RECRUITMENT

When recruiting participants, we have found that a good approach is to have a multi-stage screening process. This may be time-consuming, but it ensures that the participants who are recruited match the needs of the study. For instance, in our study, we created an initial advertisement that broadly stated the requirements, timeframe, and compensation for the study and asked interested people to contact us by email. We posted this to local mailing lists (e.g., university students, internal company email lists, an email list of participants from previous studies we had conducted) and websites such as Facebook, Twitter, and Craigslist. When people contacted us expressing their interest, we sent them an email that asked screening questions about specifics such as what type of Internet connection they had and what their current practices were in relation to our research questions (e.g., how often do you use video chat?). We also asked potential participants if they had family or friends that they would like to connect with using a futuristic video system. (We were vague to avoid biasing respondents.)

This multi-stage recruiting process allowed us to generate a shortlist of potential participants for the study. We then followed up with people who met the demographics we were aiming for (e.g., families with children) to ask them if they and all members of their family were *interested and wanted* to participate. We found it especially important to ensure that all participating families were available to participate for the duration of the study and that none of the families were going be away from their home for an extended period. Since our study occurred during the summer months, when families tend to go on vacation with their kids, this was especially important to determine.

> **LESSON**
>
> Use a multi-stage recruiting process (e.g. advertisement, screener, and phone call) to narrow down a large respondent pool to a short list of suitable participants.

We selected six families (two triads) from the United States who we thought would provide interesting and diverse relationship dynamics. We believed it was important to pick participants who had a *real need* that could be fulfilled by using the system. For example, in this study, we recruited participants who were already communicating with remote households but wanted to *communicate more* and participants who were not communicating very often with remote households and wanted to change this pattern. If participants have a real need or can see the benefit of using a system, they will be more likely to adopt the system instead of just thinking of it as "something they have to use for the study." Tolmie and Crabtree (2008) found that conducting field trials with users who do not treat the prototype or system as an integral part of their home lives leads to data that may not accurately describe usage patterns or feedback about the system. Hence, determining participants' needs and sharing the value proposition of the system should lead to buy-in and higher user engagement with the system.

---

**LESSON**

Recruit participants who have a *real need* for the system and could benefit from using it as part of their everyday lives.

---

Our participant households were composed of young families, blended families, a divorcee, and retirees. We decided to select six families—two triads—because we thought that one triad would not be enough to understand usage patterns, as we would not have other families to compare the triad's experiences with. We thought that having three triads would be extremely difficult for a team of two researchers to manage (weekly visits with each home, ensuring that the system was constantly connecting all families within a triad, etc.). On the other hand, two triads seemed like a suitable number from which to gather rich qualitative data.

Next, we describe our participant families. Relationships are described from the point of view of the *seed family*, who responded to the advertisement for the study. A seed family is connected to two *remote families*.

**Triad 1:** The seed family (top of Figure 10.4) consisted of two parents and a three-year-old son. They used FP to connect with the wife's mother and stepfather and her maternal grandparents. In total, there were seven family members in this triad with diverse relationships and various communication needs. Figure 10.4 shows the families in Triad 1.

**Triad 2:** The seed family (top of Figure 10.5) consisted of two parents and a three-year-old son. They were connected to the wife's mother and her older sister and family. There were nine family members in this triad with diverse relationships and various communication needs. Figure 10.5 shows the families in Triad 2.

## INITIAL INTERVIEW AND SYSTEM SETUP

The first stage of the study involved visiting each family's home and interviewing them about their existing communication practices with their extended family and, more specifically, about the families they were going to connect to using FP. One family lived outside our driving distance and was interviewed using Skype.

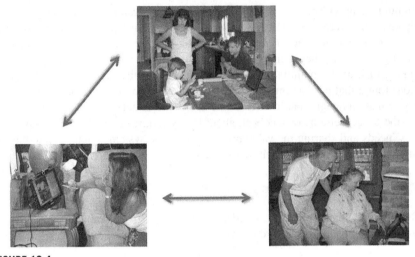

**FIGURE 10.4**

Participants in Triad 1 and location of Family Portals in their homes.

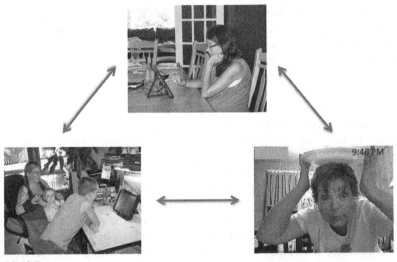

**FIGURE 10.5**

Participants in Triad 2 and location of Family Portals in their homes.

Chapter 2 provides more information about conducting interviews with remote participants.

We notified the local families beforehand that, since we were visiting on a week-night, when they might already be very busy, we would bring pizza and have a light dinner with the family. This helped us get to know the family in an informal manner before starting the interview. After the interview, families were walked through the initial setup of FP on their home wireless Internet connection and asked to select a location for FP. The initial interview lasted one to two hours, and setup took an additional hour.

Because of the pragmatics of the situation, we had only one researcher attend our initial interviews and setup of the prototype in participants' homes. Unfortunately, we learned the hard way that it would have been better to have two or three members of the research team present during the initial interview and setup. Since this is the initial face-to-face visit with a participant family, having more than one researcher present is essential in ensuring the researchers' safety in an unknown environment. And with at least two team members, one person can focus on interviewing and the other on note taking. Having a dedicated note-taker will allow the interviewer to focus on the conversation and develop rapport with the participants.

We encourage field teams to include at least one person who is familiar with the prototype or software during the initial home visit. This person should be able to debug and troubleshoot issues that come up during setup and installation. This will also allow the interviewer to focus on interviewing the users without having to worry about installation issues.

---

**LESSON**

Field teams should comprise two or three people with separate roles such as interviewer, note-taker, and software expert.

---

## DEPLOYMENT AND INTERVIEWS

Getting the system up and running in participants' homes is a huge milestone in a field trial. However, the research team cannot sit back and relax once this occurs. We would argue that the actual deployment period can be the most challenging part of a multi-home field trial because one needs to ensure the system is running normally for all households and be available if a situation goes awry. After the initial interview and system setup, we found following up with participants via email or phone calls at predetermined intervals was critical to ensure that they were using the system and that the system was working as intended. We found that we frequently had to play the role of technical support; prototype systems are often frail and plagued with errors and issues, and FP was no exception.

All six families had FP in their homes for a period of eight weeks. We visited families throughout the deployment and conducted weekly, semi-structured, contextual interviews with them during this time. The one distant family was interviewed weekly using Skype. Questions focused on families' usage of FP, changes in communication, connectedness, and awareness of remote families, and privacy concerns. Adults were interviewed individually when possible, and children were interviewed with parents present. We interviewed adults in the family individually to learn about changes in the family dynamics and the effects of being connected through always-on video with not just one but two other families. Each family was given a diary to log self-reports between interviews. In addition to this, we sent emails and phoned participants between interviews to check for technical difficulties and to troubleshoot problems.

We removed FP from the families' homes at the end of eight weeks, after we conducted end-of-deployment interviews. We conducted post-deployment interviews two weeks later. Questions for the post-deployment interview focused on changes in communication, connectedness, and awareness of remote families' lives in the previous two weeks compared to the eight weeks when the families used FP in their homes.

Although FP was placed in families' homes for eight weeks, they were only able to use the system for an average of five weeks. Despite rigorous testing before deployment, numerous technical issues related to connectivity arose. Nonetheless, we found that five weeks of use was sufficient for participants to overcome novelty factors, develop patterns of usage, and incorporate the system into their daily lives. We discuss these technical challenges in more detail in the next section and share tips for overcoming them.

## DATA COLLECTION AND ANALYSIS

Given that field trials are unpredictable, we have found it is very important to utilize multiple data collection methods. This is especially helpful if one method does not gather enough data. For example, solely relying on usage data from system logs may not be sufficient, as the system might be down for a few days, families may have issues with their Internet connection, or a family member might accidently drop and damage the system. Having multiple data collection methods will also lead to richer data and more engaging user stories, allow for comparing responses from different participants, and fill gaps in the data through triangulation (Creswell 2003).

We collected data using multiple methods, including interviews, diaries, observations, and client-side system logs. All interviews were audio recorded, and handwritten notes were taken to aid analysis. We also observed families interacting with FP either before or after some of our interviews. In total, we acquired data from approximately 108 hours of interviews and observations across all six families. The interviews were the primary sources of data, as participants would often forget to fill out the self-report diaries. This is a common problem in diary studies, which makes relying on diaries as a primary source of usage data difficult. Our system also logged the usage of features (e.g., blinds, full screen) throughout the study. Having multiple sources of data gave us the opportunity to gather as much information as possible during the field trial.

Use multiple data collection methods to ensure there is enough data to analyze after the field trial.

During the analysis phase, we used open coding (Corbin and Strauss 2008) to analyze the interviews, observation notes, and diary entries. We generated codes that reflected a variety of usage patterns, which are described in their entirety in Judge et al. (2011) and Judge (2011).

In the following sections, we describe the challenges we faced and lessons we learned through our field trials of FP.

## PROTOTYPE FRAILTY AND PILOT TESTING

Perhaps the largest challenge we faced in our study of FP related to the frailty of our prototype. Field trials are typically conducted with research prototypes instead of high-quality finished products. This is because the design is still being refined and has not gone through a commercialization process. A prototype is by definition unfinished, which means it can be buggy and prone to having technical issues. FP was no exception, despite rigorous testing prior to the study.

We designed and developed FP in a work environment at Kodak Research Labs. This meant that most of the initial testing of FP was done in the lab on a local intranet (internal to Kodak) with a bandwidth higher than what is achievable in users' homes.

Given that most prototypes are conceptualized and created in a lab environment, it is easiest to test the system in the same lab environment. However, a lab environment setup is very different from users' homes, and it is easy to be unaware of technical challenges that may occur in the field without conducting pilot tests away from the lab. For instance, most academic and industry labs have high-speed Internet access and a firewall. This setup does not necessarily translate to those in the homes of users. Homes may easily have lower Internet bandwidth that can vary depending on the time of day or number of devices utilizing it. Family members are responsible for ensuring their Internet connection and devices within the home are working, which contrasts with work settings, in which there are often trained technical staff who monitor and fix issues related to Internet connections, computer software and hardware. Because of this, we decided to pilot test FP outside of the lab to find additional problems and bugs that we could fix before the field study. However, this raised several issues.

## FAMILY PORTALS SYSTEM ARCHITECTURE

First, we had issues related to the underlying system architecture we used for the system. FP had been designed to use a client-server architecture. This meant we launched specially-designed server software on a computer and each FP system acted as a client and connected to it. The server software then acted as a central distribution point for data sent between each client. For example, video from any client would be sent from the client to the server. Upon receipt, the server software would then retransmit the video data to the other clients. There are certainly other ways to design a networked system like FP, for example, by using a peer-to-peer architecture. Yet we wanted to ensure that any of the three households using the system could have the ability to turn their video on or off such that they could join or leave the media space on their own accord. This would create a "persistent place" that any client could connect to. In our view, a client-server architecture lent itself most naturally to this situation.

However, this created problems as soon as we tried to pilot test FP outside of the lab prior to the field trials. We ran our server software on a server computer connected to Kodak's internal network, which had an external IP address that one could use to see it from the "outside world." Yet it was still behind the Kodak firewall and, as such, any clients running from outside Kodak's internal network could not reach it to connect to it. Given that we were testing a multi-home system, all three instances of the system had to connect to the same server to establish a persistent connection. Because Kodak had privacy and security concerns about corporate data, it was not possible for us to create the ideal server setup within a reasonable timeframe. To circumvent this, we moved our server to the home of one of the researchers to be uninhibited from networking restrictions typical with most companies. This worked reasonably well, though it did mean that we were restricted in terms of Internet bandwidth, which is typically less for home Internet connections compared to corporate connections.

## SIMULATING A THREE-WAY CONNECTION FOR TESTING

Second, we found it difficult to simulate a three-location connection for pilot tests prior to the study. We wanted to test the system in a setup that was similar to the real setup we would use in the field study: three homes connecting together, with our server software running in a fourth location. Connecting one location to the server was easy because we could have one project team member run a client on a home network and another run the server on his home network. However, moving beyond this to a true multi-family situation was challenging. We tried testing with three employees, each at their own home; however, this involved recruiting additional colleagues beyond our core design team, and organizing and coordinating became challenging.

In the end, we were not able to fully simulate the real setup that we were going to use in our field trials. Yet we believed that we had uncovered many of the issues we would face in our study and that our pilot testing was good enough to ensure few issues would occur during our field trials. We were, unfortunately, wrong, and this meant we spent many painstaking hours during the first three weeks of the field trial fixing problems and issues that arose based on the real-world setup of the system in the families' homes. The lesson is that testing a system in a real situation is extremely valuable; however, the reality is that, with multiple connected households, adequately carrying out such pilot testing can be challenging.

> **LESSON**
>
> Test and retest the system setup and installation in environments outside of the research lab that are similar to the real-world setting in which the field trial will take place.

## INSTALLING THE SYSTEM IN MULTIPLE CONNECTED HOUSEHOLDS

After our pilot testing was completed, we conducted our initial visits with families and set up FP in their homes. This revealed several interesting challenges (and lessons) that increased the length of our initial home visits beyond our initial expectations of a couple of hours. These challenges also created more technical hurdles than we expected.

### HIGH-SPEED AND RELIABLE INTERNET CONNECTIONS

We quickly realized that FP would not be an isolated system during its testing. It would become part of a larger ecosystem of devices and infrastructure in participants' homes. As researchers, we might think that we are installing a new piece of technology that will be separate from other devices in the home. However, the reality is that new technology often has to fit within an existing ecosystem of devices and technology set up in the home. In our case, it was of utmost importance to get the prototype connected to wireless routers and Internet connections in participants' homes. We had to play the role of technical support specialists to get the prototype up and running while troubleshooting network connectivity issues.

For a multi-home deployment, we found it was important that all homes had an Internet connection with high bandwidth, because if the Internet connection was slow at one home, it affected the experience at the other homes. This is quite different from a single-home deployment, where, if the Internet connection is down or slow in one home, it does not affect any other participants in the study. In single-home deployments, the system can be programmed to work in an offline mode, which synchronizes data with a server once the Internet connection is back up. In our case, such a setup was not possible because video had to transmit in real time between home locations. We had naïvely forgotten to ask about Internet bandwidth in our screening questionnaire. And often, the actual home Internet bandwidth is lower that the bandwidth that the provider advertises.

In retrospect, we also found it was important to know, prior to our initial home visit, whether participants' homes had a wireless router, which would allow participants to place FP in a location of their choosing. Ideally, we did not want the device to be restricted to one location or tied to the nearest wired Ethernet port. At the time of the study, wireless routers were commonplace, and we had anticipated that all of our participants' homes would naturally have it. Again we learned that our assumptions were wrong, and, unfortunately, we had not included this question in our screening questionnaire. In one instance, we drove an hour and a half on a Sunday evening to get to a participant's home to set up FP, only to find that they did not have a wireless router. We then had no choice but to drive around an unfamiliar town at 7:30 pm looking for an open store where we could buy a wireless router for the participant's home.

> **LESSON**
>
> Before the field visit, identify the equipment and technological setup that the participants' homes need to have. Do not assume that all homes have high bandwidth Internet access and other pertinent hardware (e.g., wireless routers).

We learned that, even if participants have the necessary hardware such as a wireless router, they need to know any setup information for it or have this information available during the initial study visit. In our case, several participants did not remember their wireless router password, and we did not ask them to find this information before we arrived. This caused delays in setting up the FP prototype while family members searched for their instruction manuals and tried out various passwords. It also meant that, in some instances, we had to reset their router so that the password would reset as well. If this happens, the researcher might also be asked to help the family reconnect their existing devices to the wireless network, as we were. Be prepared to receive frantic phone calls when, later, they try to connect other devices to the home Internet connection and are unable to do so.

From our experience conducting field trials, we knew that each home typically has a tech-savvy family member who deals with things like connecting devices to the Internet. It is a good idea to identify this person ahead of time and have him or her present during the home visit to aid in connecting devices and altering a family's home Internet infrastructure.

While the above challenges mostly relate to Internet connections and wireless routers, which will naturally improve over time and become standard devices in most homes, the lessons certainly apply to any type of hardware or connectivity that a prototype system relies on. In our case, it was a wireless router, and in other cases, it may be a new piece of hardware of the future that some families have and others do not.

## SETTING UP THE PROTOTYPE IN A REMOTE LOCATION

In our study, we worked with families who lived in remote locations. Given that we were studying how families connected with each other over distance, it was natural that our triads were spread across multiple states within the United States. This made it impractical to travel to each location to set up the prototype in person. We were lucky in that only one participant family lived farther away than driving distance; we were located in Rochester, New York, and they were located in Florida, about 1,500 miles away. As such, we mailed them the prototype system in advance and scheduled a time to use Skype to walk them through the setup. Fortunately, the prototype was not damaged during the shipment, which is certainly a concern when shipping computer hardware.

When we conducted our virtual initial visit with the participant family in Florida, we experienced similar setup issues as we had with the families we had set up in person. This related to being unable to connect the FP's tablet to the home's Internet connection. The problem was the same as in other homes, yet now we needed to manage it over a Skype connection and have the family members solve the problem, as opposed to us solving it. In this case, using a Skype connection was extremely helpful because we could ask the participants to turn the FP tablet to face their laptop webcam so we could read error messages that appeared and guide them. It was also helpful to have a similar tablet PC device next to us that we could look at to determine troubleshooting options. Eventually, we were able to successfully set up this remote family with FP; however, we learned that walking remote families through the installation of our prototype took at least twice as much time as it did with a local family. This has implications for scheduling the initial home visit to ensure there is enough time to adequately work with the family to set up the prototype. It also means letting the family know that the initial visit may take a substantial time commitment on their part.

---

**LESSON**

Installing and setting up a prototype in a remote home takes longer than setting it up in person in local homes.

---

## CONNECTING ACROSS LOCATIONS

We found that, because we were connecting across multiple locations, our installation and setup of FP was iterative. That is, connections would happen in stages as we set up each family. The first family who was set up would not be able to see anybody else on the system until we set up the second family. Once the second family was set up, they would only see the first family. It would not be until the third family was set up that all three families could see each other. Overall, this meant that we had to check in with families multiple times after their initial setup procedure to ensure they could see their remote families, who were being iteratively set up with the system.

To avoid issues with this iterative setup process, we tried to be strategic, such that we made sure the most tech-savvy family was the first that was connected. This way they could help other families when they were getting set up and connected. This approach also made it much easier for us to explain the functionality of the prototype to the second and third families, because they could see live video feeds coming from the other homes. We ensured that one or both of the remote families were available when we installed the prototype in a local family's home. By doing this, we gave the participants an opportunity to learn about and test the functionality of the prototype in our presence. Added benefits of doing this were that we were able to observe the initial interaction between families and note initial impressions and feedback. This was valuable data, as it gave us a baseline to compare against in the following weeks of usage.

> **LESSON**
>
> Consider setting up the system in the home of the most tech-savvy family, followed by the less tech-savvy families. This will help the less tech-savvy families easily understand the system when it is installed in their homes.

## OWNERSHIP AND USAGE OF THE SYSTEM

We recognized in our field trials that it was very important to ensure that participants felt a sense of ownership over the prototype that we were giving them. We found that this was an important factor in the adoption and usage of the prototype and also led to rich data from our participants. Giving participants ownership will prevent them from just thinking of the system as "stuff" in their home that has low value (Tolmie and Crabtree 2008).

We encouraged participants to feel a sense of ownership of the system in two ways that worked out well. This was evident by the way participants talked about the system as being theirs, as well as how they moved it around in the home on their own accord and decided how they would use it.

### PICKING OTHER FAMILIES TO CONNECT TO

During our recruitment, we had asked our seed families to pick two other families they wanted to connect to using the system. By doing so, we gave them ownership over the system and its use and provided them with a sense of agency as part of the study process. That is to say, they themselves were in charge of whom they would use the system with and how they would use it. We relied on the seed families to socialize the idea of FP to their extended families as part of the recruitment process, rather than us telling the other families about the system and its features. By allowing seed families to pick other families they wanted to connect to, we learned about their current communication practices with the other families and how they would like to use the system to improve or change their communication practices and, at times, even their relationships. Overall, this meant that, after we identified seed families, we were able to easily get an additional two families in each triad to participate in the field trial.

## DECIDING ON THE PLACEMENT OF THE SYSTEM

We gave participants ownership over the system by allowing them to choose where to place it in their homes. Ownership, as it relates to device placement, manifested itself in two ways with the families. First, we found that some families had a default placement for the system that did not change much from the initial placement of the device. The device was then moved around the home based on where family members were gathered or where they were doing activities that they wanted to share with the remote families (e.g., kitchen, porch). For instance, Figure 10.6 shows that a remote family temporarily placed their FP on their porch to share their garden, and another family temporarily placed FP in their family room to share a child's play time with remote families.

Second, we found that some families frequently moved FP for the first week until they found a placement they were comfortable with. After this point, these families did not move the FP around their homes, and the remote families saw only one constant view. The primary reason for doing this was privacy. For instance, one of the sisters in Triad 2 was not comfortable sharing all of the activities in her home with her older sister's family and her mother, so she placed the FP on her dining table facing a wall and only turned it around to face the family room when she was communicating with the remote families (Figure 10.7). This led to many complaints from the remote families that they were only seeing her wall.

Together, these findings illustrate the importance of supporting a diversity of placement options such that most families will be able to gain a sense of ownership based on device placement and usage.

**FIGURE 10.6**

Family Portals was moved around the home based on where family members were gathered. On the left, the remote family placed their Family Portals on their porch, and on the right, the local family placed Family Portals in the family room to share a child's play time.

**FIGURE 10.7**

Family Portals in the younger sister's home was placed on the dining table facing a wall.

> **LESSON**
>
> Give participants ownership over the system by allowing them to pick whom they use it with and where it is placed in their homes.

## MANAGING THE COMPLEXITY OF RELATIONSHIP DYNAMICS WITHIN AND BETWEEN FAMILIES

Having discussed technical challenges and lessons learned from deploying a multi-home system, we now discuss another challenge in multi-home field deployments: managing and navigating the relationship dynamics within and between families.

### VARYING LEVELS OF COMMUNICATION NEEDS WITH EXTENDED FAMILY

Although all families agreed to participate in our study, there were varying degrees of need to communicate with remote families and varying levels of buy-in from family members. The primary, or most active, users of FP in each triad were the women. In Triad 1, this was the daughter, mother, and grandmother (Figure 10.4). In Triad 2, it was the younger sister, older sister, and their mother (Figure 10.5). This is consistent with the findings from Hindus et al. (2001), which show women are generally the "household communicators." It is important to note that one woman in each triad answered the advertisement for the study and determined who they would like to be connected to using FP. It is no surprise that they all chose to connect to their own families instead of their in-laws.

As we expected, there were certain individuals who did not like or were apathetic to always-on video being broadcast from their home. These users did not necessarily voice their concerns or their lack of need for the system at the beginning of the study, but their lack of use and, sometimes, even disdain for the system became more apparent as the study progressed. Findings from our initial field study of the Family Window showed that privacy concerns and lack of interest in the system were not issues in dyads where families shared a close relationship (Judge et al. 2010). However, this was not the case in triads, as there are more families and more individuals per triad. For instance, we found that the husband and the live-in boyfriend in Triad 2 avoided FP because they did not want to be seen by their in-laws all the time.

We also found that the grandfather in Triad 1 did not use FP because he was intimidated by the technology. After technical problems with the system (because of set up issues), he was afraid to use FP because he was concerned he "might break it." He did, however, occasionally look over his wife's shoulder while she interacted with the remote families.

---

**LESSON**

Not all family members are going to want to use a prototype or system that is placed in their homes. Be cognizant about this during the study and try to learn about the reasons behind the lack of usage.

---

The challenge here was developing rapport with the participants so they were comfortable enough to share such private and, at times, even embarrassing information (e.g., not wanting to communicate with his mother-in-law) with the research team, who were essentially strangers.

## DEVELOPING RAPPORT AND TRUST WITH PARTICIPANTS TO LEARN ABOUT RELATIONSHIPS DYNAMICS AND USAGE PATTERNS

As we expected, learning about the primary users' successful adoption of FP was easy enough, but our findings would have been incomplete without learning about privacy concerns and other reasons for lack of adoption. We found that the way around this issue was to establish trust and rapport with the participants early on in the study. We did this by conducting separate interviews for each adult in a family and by repeatedly assuring them that the information they shared would not be shared with other families in the triad.

For instance, the older sister in Triad 2 shared with us that she was not happy that her mother was in a relationship with someone she did not approve of. Also, she quickly discovered that when her mother's boyfriend was visiting, her mother would turn off the FP camera or turn it to a different direction. Here, it was important for us to be mindful that this was private information and could potentially lead to conflict in the family if it were shared with the mother. However, it was important for us to learn more about this phenomenon from the mother's point of view.

To do this, we casually mentioned to the mother that her eldest daughter said there was no video feed from her mother's home a few times in the previous week. This led to the mother telling us about her boyfriend's visits, her daughter not approving of him, and hence, her need for some privacy from the always-on video. By approaching the issue this way, we *triangulated* (Creswell 2003) the data given to us by the eldest daughter with responses from her mother. Knowing both sides of the story enabled us to create a rich narrative that described the occurrence. We found triangulation to be an important interviewing and data analysis strategy to learn about FP usage. We also learned that ensuring privacy and confidentiality was important, especially when personal and often contradictory information was shared about other family members.

Another way to create rapport with the participants and make them comfortable during interviews was to have the same interviewer throughout the study. By doing so, we thought that participants would not have to start over with a different interviewer in each session.

---

**LESSON**

Developing rapport and trust with participants is important in order to learn about their usage and potential concerns with the system. It is also ethical to protect the privacy and confidentiality of the information shared by participants and to avoid sharing it with other family members.

---

## CONDUCTING INTERVIEWS INDIVIDUALLY

When possible, we conducted individual interviews with the adults in each family. It was the only way we could find out what participants *really thought* about the system and about connecting with remote families via always-on video. For instance, these interviews allowed us to learn how a son-in-law felt about being connected to his mother-in-law and sister-in-law's home through the always-on video system. It would have been difficult to learn about his privacy concerns and discomfort if he had been interviewed with his wife, who was happy about being connected to her mother and sister.

However, we quickly learned that individual interviews were not easy to do because of families' routines and work schedules. For instance, the live-in boyfriend of one of the sisters in Triad 2 worked night shifts and was often asleep during the day when we visited their home. Because of the difference in work schedules between adults in the families, we changed weekly interview times so that we could alternate interviewing the two adults in the family. This was not ideal, but it was the only option for some families. In other families, especially families with young children, we interviewed one parent while the other was looking after the children in a different room and then had them switch places. This strategy, when it was possible, worked very well, as we were able to interview one adult without interruptions from the children.

---

**LESSON**

When possible, interview participants individually to learn about their usage of the system and potential privacy concerns.

---

We also found that we had to be flexible and open to interruptions during the interviews especially if there was only one adult present in the home with children. For instance, the eldest sister in Triad 2 had a one-year-old daughter, who frequently interrupted our interviews by crying. Sometimes this participant had to be interviewed in the kitchen while she was preparing dinner and helping her kids with their homework. The lesson here is to be flexible and respectful of things that might be going on the participants' homes, and be prepared for multiple interruptions and short attention spans from participants. These are some of the challenges of working with families, which are also reflected in other chapters in this book.

## BEING RESPECTFUL AND REFLECTIVE OF YOUR ROLE IN PARTICIPANTS' LIVES

Because our study lasted eight weeks and we visited families weekly, we became privy to their daily routines as well as their ups and downs. For instance, one of the families in Triad 1 started treating the interviewer, a young graduate student at that time, as one of their grandchildren and would spend half the interview talking about their younger days and sharing health concerns and information about doctor visits. Being mindful of this is important, as participants may start treating members of the research team as part of their family, especially for longitudinal studies. This phenomenon is common in ethnographic studies, where a researcher becomes a part of the community he or she is studying (Spradley 1980). When this happened, we had to stay unbiased and not be emotionally attached to the participants. This was easier said than done, because we felt very welcome in some participants' homes, and we were even invited to their family get-togethers. As only one member of our research team was in the field interviewing users and collecting data, one of our methods to overcome potential bias in the data collection was to do *peer debriefing* (Creswell 2003). After each interview, the interviewer debriefed with members of the research team to share findings, identify potential holes in the data, and overcome any biases in the data analysis.

---

**LESSON**

Be aware and respectful of your role in participants' lives especially for a longitudinal study. Take necessary measures such as *peer debriefing* to ensure there is no bias in the data collection and analysis.

---

## DISCUSSION AND CONCLUSIONS

This chapter describes the use of multi-home field trials as a method to evaluate and understand the usage of domestic technologies. We used Family Portals (Judge et al. 2011), an always-on video media space that connected three homes, as a case study to illustrate lessons and challenges in conducting a multi-home field trial. Although a multi-home field trial seems similar to a single-home field trial, this chapter highlights two primary differences between multi-home and single-home field trials: an increase in technological challenges and an increase in the diversity of relationships between participants in the study.

First, we found that a multi-home field trial is more complex and technologically challenging to set up compared to a single-family field trial. Since most prototypes are developed in a lab setting, it is important to pilot test them in a setting that is similar to participants' homes before the field trial. However, we found that accurately simulating a three-home connection with a server that was behind a firewall was difficult. The lesson is that pilot testing a system in the real situation is extremely valuable; however, in practice, adequately carrying out such pilot testing with multiple connected households can be challenging. We also found it important to know ahead of time about the reliability of participants' home Internet connections and to be prepared to play a technical support role during the study. An important lesson here is realizing that one is not installing a standalone system or prototype in a participant's home. Instead, the system is a part of a larger ecosystem of devices and technological setup.

Second, we found that there are many diverse and dynamic relationships within and between homes in a multi-home field trial, and researchers must be aware of these dynamics. One lesson is to be aware of potential conflict or discomfort that may arise from the longitudinal use of a system. To learn about this, interview family members individually and triangulate data. We found that developing rapport and trust with users early on in the study is important. This will help users feel comfortable to share information about their lives, which may be affected by using the system. In addition, as researchers, it is ethical to protect the information that is shared with us and to make sure information shared by one family is not revealed to another family, as this could potentially lead to conflict between families.

In conclusion, although multi-home field trials are challenging to set up and conduct, we believe that, if one is mindful of the lessons presented in this chapter, these types of field trials can be successfully conducted to evaluate the use of domestic systems. Although our field trial focused on connecting three households, we anticipate that the lessons we uncovered are applicable to studies of systems that include even more than three connected homes. Naturally, the complexity would increase beyond this as the number of homes increases.

## ACKNOWLEDGMENTS

This research was generously funded by Kodak Research Labs. We thank our collaborators at Kodak Research Labs and Virginia Tech for valuable feedback on this work. They include, but are not limited to, Andrew Blose, Rodney Miller, Andrew Kurtz, Elena Fedorovskaya, Steve

Harrison, Manuel Perez, Dennis Kafura, Deborah Tatar, and Andrea Kavanaugh. We also thank all the families involved in the field trial for welcoming us into their homes and sharing their experiences with Family Portals.

# REFERENCES

Barkhuus, L., Rode, J.A., 2007. From Mice to Men — 24 Years of Evaluation in CHI. In: Proceedings of the SIGCHI Conference on Human Factors in Computing Systems. ACM Press, New York, NY.

Bly, S., Harrison, S., Irwin, S., 1993. Media Spaces: Bringing People Together in a Video, Audio, and Computing Environment. Commun. ACM Press, 36 (1), 28—46.

Brown, B., Reeves, S., Sherwood, S., 2011. Into the Wild: Challenges and Opportunities for Field Trial Methods. In: Proceedings of the SIGCHI Conference on Human Factors in Computing Systems. ACM Press, New York, NY.

Brush, A.J., Inkpen, K., Tee, K., 2008. SPARCS: Exploring Sharing Suggestions to Enhance Family Connectedness. In: Proceedings of the 2008 ACM conference on Computer supported cooperative work. ACM Press, New York, NY.

Conversy, S., Mackay, W., Beaudouin-Lafon, M., Roussel, N., 2003. Videoprobe: Sharing Pictures of Everyday Life. In: Proceedings of the 15th French-speaking conference on human-computer interaction on 15eme Conference Francophone sur l'Interaction Homme-Machine (IHM). ACM Press, New York, NY.

Corbin, J., Strauss, A. (Eds.), 2008. Basics of qualitative research: Techniques and procedures for developing grounded theory. Sage.

Creswell, J., 2003. Research Design: Qualitative, Quantitative, and Mixed Methods Approaches. Sage Publications.

Dourish, P., Bly, S., 1992. Portholes: Supporting Awareness in a Distributed Work Group. In: Proceedings of the SIGCHI Conference on Human Factors in Computing Systems (CHI). ACM Press, New York, NY.

Froehlich, J., Findlater, L., Ostergren, M., Ramanathan, S., Peterson, J., Wragg, I., Larson, E., Fu, F., Bai, M., Patel, S., Landay, J.A., 2012. The Design and Evaluation of Prototype Eco-Feedback Displays for Fixture-Level Water Usage Data. In: Proceedings of the SIGCHI Conference on Human Factors in Computing Systems (CHI). ACM Press, New York, NY.

Greenberg, S., Buxton, B., 2008. Usability Evaluation Considered Harmful (Some of the Time). Proceedings of the SIGCHI Conference on Human Factors in Computing System (CHI 2008). ACM Press, New York, NY, pp. 111—120.

Harper, R.H.R., Lamming, M.G., Newman, W.M., 1992. Locating Systems at Work: Implications for the Development of Active Badge Applications. Interact. Comput. 4 (3), 343—363.

Hindus, D., Mainwaring, S., Leduc, N., Hagstr, A., Bayley, O., 2001. Casablanca: Designing Social Communication Devices for the Home. In: Proceedings of the SIGCHI Conference on Human Factors in Computing Systems (CHI 2001). ACM Press, New York, NY.

Intille, S., Larson, K., Tapia, E., Beaudin, J., Kaushik, P., Nawyn, J., Rockinson, R., 2006. Using a Live-In Laboratory for Ubiquitous Computing Research. In: Fishkin, K.P., Schiele, B., Nixon, P., Quigley, A. (Eds.), Pervasive Computing LNCS 3968. Springer, Heidelberg, pp. 349—365.

Judge, T.K., 2011. Patterns of Domestic Video Mediated Communication. Doctoral Dissertation. Department of Computer Science, Virginia Tech, Blacksburg, Virginia.

Judge, T.K., Neustaedter, C., 2010. Sharing Conversation and Sharing Life: Video Conferencing in the Home. In: Proceedings of the SIGCHI Conference on Human Factors in Computing Systems (CHI 2010). ACM Press, New York, NY.

Judge, T.K., Neustaedter, C., Kurtz, A., 2010. The Family Window: The Design and Evaluation of a Domestic Media Space. In: Proceedings of the SIGCHI Conference on Human Factors in Computing Systems (CHI 2010). ACM Press, New York, NY.

Judge, T.K., Neustaedter, C., Harrison, S., Blose, A., 2011. Family Portals: Connecting Families through a Multifamily Media Space. In: Proceedings of the CHI 2011. ACM Press, New York, NY.

Kidd, C., Orr, R., Abowd, G., Atkeson, C., Essa, I., MacIntyre, B., Mynatt, E., Starner, T., 1999. The Aware Home: A Living Laboratory for Ubiquitous Computing Research. In: Streitz, N.A., Hartkopf, V. (Eds.), CoBuild 1999 LNCS 1670. Springer, Heidelberg, pp. 191–198.

Kirk, D.S., Izadi, S., Sellen, A., Taylor, S., Banks, R., Hilliges, O., 2010. Opening up the Family Archive. In: Proceedings of the 2010 ACM conference on Computer supported cooperative work (CSCW 2010). ACM Press, New York, NY.

Korn, M., Bodker, S., 2012. Looking Ahead: How Field Trials Can Work in Iterative and Exploratory Design of Ubicomp Systems. In: Proceedings of the ACM Conference on Ubiquitous Computing. ACM Press, New York, NY.

Lindley, S., Harper, R., Sellen, A., 2010. Designing a Technological Playground: A Field Study of the Emergence of Play in Household Messaging. In: Proceedings of the 2010 SIGCHI conference on Human Factors in computing systems (CHI 2010). ACM Press, New York, NY.

Mynatt, E., Rowan, J., Craighill, S., Jacobs, A., 2001. Digital Family Portraits: Supporting Peace of Mind for Extended Family Members. In: Proceedings of the SIGCHI Conference on Human Factors in Computing Systems (CHI 2001). ACM Press, New York, NY.

Olson, J.S., Teasley, S., 1996. Groupware in the Wild: Lessons Learned from a Year of Virtual Collocation. In: Proceedings of the ACM conference on Computer supported cooperative work (CSCW 1996). ACM Press, New York, NY.

Neustaedter, C., Brush, A.J., 2006. 'LINC-ing' the Family: The Participatory Design of an Inkable Family Calendar. In: Proceedings of the SIGCHI Conference on Human Factors in Computing Systems (CHI 2006). ACM Press, New York NY.

Neustaedter, C., Brush, A.J., Greenberg, S., 2007. A Digital Family Calendar in the Home: Lessons from Field Trials of LINC. In: Proceedings of Graphics Interface 2007 (GI 2007). Canada, Montreal, Quebec.

Nielsen, J., 2004. Risks of Quantitative Studies. Nielsen Norman Group [online]. http://www.nngroup.com/articles/risks-of-quantitative-studies/.

Plaisant, C., Clamage, A., Hutchinson, H.B., Bederson, B.B., Druin, A., 2006. Shared Family Calendars: Promoting Symmetry and Accessibility. ACM Transactions on Computer-Human Interaction (TOCHI) 13 (3), 313–346.

Rogers, Y., Connelly, K., Tedesco, L., Hazlewood, W., Kurtz, A., Hall, R.E., Hursey, J., Toscos, T., 2007. Why It's Worth the Hassle: The Value of In-Situ Studies When Designing Ubicomp. In: Proceedings of the Conference on Ubiquitous Computing. Springer-Verlag, Berlin, Heidelberg.

Rowan, J., Mynatt, E.D., 2005. Digital Family Portrait Field Trial: Support for Aging in Place. In: Proceedings of the SIGCHI Conference on Human Factors in Computing Systems (CHI 2005). ACM Press, New York, NY.

Spradley, J., 1980. Participant Observation. Wadsworth Publishing Company, Belmont, CA.

Tolmie, P., Crabtree, A., 2008. Deploying Research Technology in the Home. In: Proceedings of the 2008 ACM conference on Computer supported cooperative work (CSCW 2008). ACM Press, New York, NY.

# Techniques for Studying Actual Use of Personal Communication Prototypes

## 11

John C. Tang, Sasa Junuzovic, Kori Inkpen, Gina Venolia
*Microsoft Research, Redmond, WA, USA*

## THE GROWING OPPORTUNITY OF REMOTE PERSONAL COMMUNICATION

With the increasing availability of technologies that support rich connections among people in the home and other social environments, we have been exploring technologies that enable remote people to share personal communication experiences. Consumer video chat technologies, such as Skype, Google+ Hangouts, and FaceTime, enable rich communication in social settings. Mobile clients for these tools on smartphones and tablets enable such sharing to occur in homes, public social spaces, outdoors, or wherever the activities occur. This convergence of trends has enabled us to explore developing prototypes that make possible remote personal communication in a wide variety of settings.

While there is a long tradition of studying video tools in work settings, studying personal communication differs in some fundamental ways. In this section, we contrast research on social communication with workplace collaboration, highlighting the methodological challenges that these differences present.

Personal communication usually involves specific people who share a close social relationship. Parents, kids, grandparents, spouses, long distance relationships, close friends, and so on all depend on connecting with specific people in their lives. While it is important for participants to be familiar with each other in studies of professional communications between geographically distributed teams (Espinosa et al. 2007), close ties between participants are mandatory for studies of personal communication. Testing prototypes in the lab with strangers working on simulated tasks together will not evoke all the effects of social connection that we try to support in our personal communication prototypes.

While personal communication tends to involve specific relationships and people, it occurs in a diverse range of locations and activities. Unlike workplace communication, which occurs in predictable locations such as offices or specially equipped conference rooms, social conversation can happen in various places (e.g., living room, kitchen, dining room, family room) within a home. Beyond the home, family events include birthday celebrations in restaurants, visiting museums or other places of interest, and kids' sports events outdoors. This much broader range of venues has implications not only for the technology, but also how it is studied.

Along with diverse settings, social communication can have a much wider range of activities than a typical workplace meeting. Ethnographic studies and surveys (Brubaker, Venolia, and Tang 2012) found a long list of shared activities remote people have tried over video chat, including watching movies together, cooking with Mom, diagnosing mechanical problems, and giving house tours. Furthermore, while workplace meetings are scheduled and occur during business hours, social communications can occur during a wider range of times (including early morning or late evening), and often with very flexible or unpredictable timing. Being able to study these diverse activities at the moments they arise adds to the challenge of researching personal communication.

Beyond the challenges of getting access to social communication mentioned so far, the personal nature of these interactions can make observing them difficult without unduly affecting the activity. While the effects of observation are always a research concern, they may have a more pronounced inhibiting effect on personal and social activities than on professional meetings. For example, a weekly team videoconference meeting is less likely to be affected by the presence of experimenters than the dynamics of a video chat between two young people in a romantic relationship. Finding a good balance between adequately capturing the activity for research analysis purposes and affording the participants the freedom and privacy that can be an integral part of the shared experience is a substantial methodological challenge.

We reflect on three recent research experiences in which we explored methodologies for studying prototypes to support personal communication. The experiences focused on embedding ourselves along with a prototype into an intact social group, deploying a prototype in the wild, and passively capturing user activities that occur in the wild. First, we describe how we recruited an intact social group of pre-teens through a researcher's own child. We deployed VideoPal, a tool for sharing video messages as threaded conversations, in this group to see how they would use it to share among close friends. Then we explain how we invited families and close friends to take the Experiences2Go prototype to environments outside the home to enable sharing family activities wherever they occurred. Following this, we show how, as part of testing the concept of remotely watching a video program together, we used a technique for recording participants' shared video-watching activity whenever and wherever it occurred for later analysis. For each case, we briefly describe the prototype and the goals we wanted to accomplish with it, explain the methodological choices we made in studying its realistic use, and reflect on what worked well and what challenges remain.

# VIDEOPAL: DEPLOYING A PROTOTYPE IN AN INTACT SOCIAL GROUP

VideoPal is a video-based asynchronous communication system that supports the easy exchange of video messages. Users can send, view, and reply to video messages that are organized according to conversational threads to keep related content grouped together. Messages can be directed to individuals or groups. The VideoPal system and the studies conducted with it are described in more detail by Inkpen et al. (2012).

## STUDY METHODOLOGY

Because we wanted to see how VideoPal supported sharing messages among social friends, we deployed a working prototype among an intact social group. We chose young kids because we expected that they would be more comfortable with video technologies and have a fresh perspective on how to use them in daily activities. Figure 11.1 shows snapshots from video messages sent during the study.

To have as much access to the group's interactions as possible, it was important to embed ourselves into the group. This required a strong trust relationship between us and the group. Therefore, we recruited a group of six pre-teen girls who were friends of a research team member's daughter. The group was recruited because they had strong friendships among themselves and frequently saw each other face to face. As a result, the deployment not only allowed us to capture an intact social group of friends, but also gave us access to observe the activities within an existing social context of trust between the kids and their parents.

For the duration of the study, the girls were given laptops pre-loaded with the VideoPal software and webcams. Each laptop had a connection to the Internet.

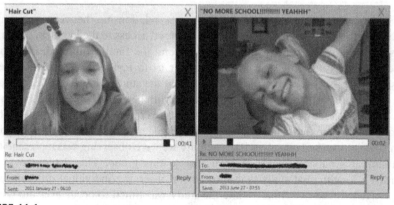

**FIGURE 11.1**

Example video messages sent during our study of VideoPal among kids.

At the time of this study, the group of girls did not communicate much outside of their face-to-face interactions, so we were curious to see if VideoPal messaging would augment those interactions. VideoPal was deployed into the girls' homes at the start of the school Christmas break, when they had extra time available to try it out.

The VideoPal software logged the girls' interactions with the system. Additionally, after using the system for more than a month, the girls participated in a debrief session in which they filled out a questionnaire and took part in a group interview to give us feedback on their use of the system. Researchers also had access to the content of the video messages. Being embedded in the group was helpful when we reviewed the messages because the researcher was aware of interesting topics and activities in which her own daughter was involved. The study enabled us to see enthusiastic uptake of VideoPal among the girls: in the first two weeks, 585 video messages were recorded and 2670 message views were logged.

## LESSONS AND CHALLENGES

Recruiting an intact social group was key in getting a sense of realistic use of Video-Pal. The strength of the girls' pre-existing social connections was a crucial factor in the generation of the hundreds of messages exchanged almost immediately. Their close relationships encouraged them to share messages not only about their shared interest in gymnastics, but also in personal details such as prized possessions in their rooms, gifts they got for Christmas, and what they ate for dinner.

> **LESSON**
>
> To get a sense of how a prototype for a personal communication tool is used among people with close ties, a useful approach is to recruit an intact social group for the study.

Furthermore, leveraging the existing trust relationship between the parent researcher, the kids, and their parents gave us broad access to the interactions during the study. The existing trust relationships among the families through their kids' shared activities not only opened the door for us to invite them to participate in the study, but also afforded informal chats about the study. The researcher's awareness of VideoPal use going on in her own home with her child helped focus the analysis and interpretation of the other data and shape the questions in the debriefing interview. In order for us to focus on the more generalizable activities, throughout the analysis, we asked ourselves if the activity we were observing was representative of a similar group of friends or particular to this group. This deployment also afforded a longitudinal study that allowed for observing individual differences in how usage evolved over time. While the study was timed to occur over the winter school break, use of VideoPal extended well beyond the debriefing interview that occurred after about a month.

> ### LESSON
>
> When studying the use of a personal communication prototype in an intact social group, it is important to have a trust relationship with the group and to be embedded in it.

While a pre-existing trust relationship is helpful for later analysis, it implies that participant recruitment was done through personal contacts, which raises the issue of compliance bias. The bias concern can be mitigated by having personal contact with as few participants as possible. For our study, we had just one connection where the researcher was directly aware of her child's activities. In addition, a personal connection to the participant may exclude some topics of conversation, especially if parents of teenagers are involved. It appears that this is less of an issue with groups of pre-teens, as there was plenty of natural conversation to observe in our study. Of course, not all researchers have personal contacts with the desired participant demographic. When this is the case, working through related social institutions could provide the necessary connections. For youth, that would include schools, sports teams, church youth groups, and other social or service clubs.

An important limitation of this study was that only one group was observed, so additional studies are needed to demonstrate generalizability. Doing a study in other groups would have helped identify aspects of the response that were more general and those that were more specific to a particular group. Nevertheless, we expect that other groups of kids with a strong shared interest would provide a similar context. It should be noted that all of the participants were girls who were between nine and ten years old. Communication patterns and technology use by youth in other age ranges, and of boys in particular, are likely to be different.

Equipping an entire social group with technology can be expensive, and once the study is over, retracting the deployed technology can be tricky, especially if the participants have taken to using it extensively. Having an exit plan and explaining it to the participants at the beginning of the study can help mitigate this issue.

## EXPERIENCES2GO: DEPLOYING A PROTOTYPE IN THE WILD

Experiences2Go (E2G) is a prototype designed to enable people to share experiences outside the home with remote friends and family. Many family events (e.g., kids' sports events, birthday celebrations, play activities) occur in a diverse range of locations, including schools, gymnasiums, and the outdoors. We designed E2G to be portable to enable it to go to all those locations and to have network connectivity everywhere. Inkpen et al. (2013) describe the E2G prototype and the study conducted with it.

The E2G prototype, shown in Figure 11.2, consisted of a tablet with an Internet connection and a camcorder connected to the tablet, all mounted on a tripod. The

**FIGURE 11.2**

Using the E2G prototype at a kids' swim practice session.

camcorder's telephoto lens enabled E2G to capture events at a distance, and that view was combined with a view of the local operator, which was captured using the tablet camera, so the remote person could see both views simultaneously. E2G's tripod mount allowed it to stand without being held, freeing the local operator to fully participate in the experience. E2G connected to the remote participant via a normal Skype call, which did not require any modification or installation effort on the remote end.

## STUDY METHODOLOGY

As with most situations involving social communication, people wanted to share the experience with a specific personal contact. Unfortunately, recruiting people on both sides of a close personal relationship is more difficult than recruiting individual participants. Thus, for this study, we used an approach in which we recruited one participant to take E2G to an activity of interest, and this participant in turn recruited a remote participant to share the experience. We provided suggestions, but it was up to the local participants to identify the events and the remote participants. We asked that all participants be comfortable using Skype for video chat, which was not too restrictive, given Skype's popularity. In the nine families we recruited, the remote participant was a spouse (seven), grandparent (one), or close friend (one).

We wanted the experience to reflect real life as much as possible, including the process of incorporating technology into the shared activity. Thus, we simply demonstrated how to use the devices and control the cameras, and made sure everything was working; otherwise, the participants did what they wanted and positioned E2G as they liked. The researchers unobtrusively watched the participants (typically from behind) and documented the study through photos and video recordings. They usually did not interact with the participants during the study session unless they needed to resolve technical problems.

After completing the study, we asked the local participants to complete a brief questionnaire, and then we conducted a short, semi-structured interview. The remote participant completed a similar questionnaire by email. We reviewed our interview and open-ended questionnaire response data for recurring themes and inductively compared specific instances of those themes across participants.

## LESSONS AND CHALLENGES

Our approach of letting participants choose the activity and communication partners yielded realistic use cases for us to observe. Local participants had an inherent interest in the activity and in their remote participants. Furthermore, their conversations alternated between the activity being observed and social chit chat, which was enabled by the strong social relationship the participants shared.

> **LESSON**
>
> When recruiting a close-tie relationship, an effective approach is to recruit one person and have that person recruit someone with whom he or she has close social ties to also participate in the study.

The realism enabled us to see scenarios that worked well, such as a spouse joining a sports event remotely from home and grandparents joining their grandkids from across the country. We also observed scenarios that were more complicated than expected, such as a spouse who could not talk much because of connecting while at work. This led us to identifying the bystanders at an event as important stakeholders in the shared experiences occurring in the wild. In a couple of cases, the remote person was able to use E2G to interact with local bystanders they knew at the event. In several other cases, local bystanders asked about E2G and the study, mostly out of curiosity.

The main challenge of taking the prototype to whatever activity the participants had chosen was that we as researchers had to be very flexible, and we had to make a significant time investment. For instance, we had to make ourselves available when the activity was happening, which was sometimes during business hours, often in the evenings, and, at times, during weekends. The researchers also had to be available for the duration of the activity to ensure that the prototype functioned properly, and allow extra time between sessions to account for traffic and to recharge the prototype and cameras used to document the session.

The prototype technology itself was another challenge. Although E2G was designed to work over 3G/4G, which should have provided networking connectivity virtually anywhere, network connectivity simply could not be achieved in one of the study locations. Furthermore, audio—both hearing the remote person and capturing intelligible audio for the remote person to hear—was often an issue in many of the environments. This problem prompted many local participants to wear a headset, which limited their mobility and made it less convenient for others to use E2G to interact with the remote person. Finally, the prototype was not waterproof, which would have been useful during the swimming activities observed or if there had been inclement weather at any of the outdoor activities.

> **LESSON**
>
> Allowing participants to choose their own activity and location for the shared experience yields realistic situations. However, compared to more controlled studies, it requires the prototypes to be robust and the researchers to have flexible schedules.

A final observation for this methodology was that data collection was trouble-some at times. While we were able to administer a survey and conduct an interview with the local participants, it was harder to get the remote participants to return a survey by email. One way to mitigate this issue is to give the remote participant the gratuity only after they have completed all study requirements. Unfortunately, we did not anticipate this problem, so we gave gratuities for both participants to the local participants and asked them to give one to the remote participants.

## TV2GETHER: CAPTURING ACTIVITY IN THE WILD

TV2Gether was a research project exploring how to enable geographically remote people to watch TV or other video programs together while they were connected through a Skype video call to share their reactions with each other (Macaranas et al. 2013). As part of the research, we wanted to understand how people were currently watching video programs together in their homes. This research interest led to the challenge of how to capture these sessions, which could happen at any time and among any participants.

We wanted to capture recordings in which we could see and hear the participants' reactions as they watched the video program together. Figure 11.3 shows a snapshot from one of the recordings where a funny thing had happened on the show the participants were watching. We can see them laughing together, even though they are geographically remote.

### STUDY METHODOLOGY

For the field study, we recruited pairs of people who knew each other but were in separate locations during the study. Many of the pairs were in romantic relationships (32%), were close friends (32%), or were immediate family members (29%), and 7% were acquaintances. Participants were familiar with using video chat applications (e.g., Skype, FaceTime, Google+ Hangouts), and 27 percent reported using a video chat application on a weekly basis.

Participants were free to schedule a time with their remote companions to watch a video program (e.g., broadcast TV, DVD, streaming Internet) together. As we did

**FIGURE 11.3**

Participants watching video together while connected through a Skype video call. This experience was captured by our auto-answer Skype account, which was added to the Skype group video call.

not control when they would watch video together, we designed a mechanism for capturing their shared sessions whenever they occurred. Fifteen minutes prior to watching the program, participants logged into Skype and initiated a video call with their remote companions. For an additional gratuity credit, participants had the option of escalating the call to a Skype group video call and adding our Skype account to the chat. All twenty-eight pairs of participants opted in to recording their shared video-watching experience. Participants were rewarded for their participation with credit that could be traded for company merchandise.

As the participants could choose to have the shared experience at any time, it was important that no action was needed from us when they added our account to the chat. Thus, we configured our account to auto-record the session using a third-party call-recording program, which enabled us to capture the session automatically, without any manual effort from the researchers. This reduced research effort and allowed this method to scale up to include larger numbers of participants. Note that as the auto-recording account does not have a camera generating a video stream, it does not appear in the group video call interface, and so it is not seen in Figure 11.3.

Once the group video call was established, participants tuned in or manually started the video program at the same time. While the program was running, participants were encouraged to act as they normally would while watching video programs together. We found that adding our account to the call did not seem to obstruct natural interactions between the participants. If anything, the automatic recording of their sessions were so transparent that, in several cases, they forgot about the recording and its privacy implications. After the video program was finished, participants disconnected the video call and completed an online survey.

The recorded video of their interaction enabled us to see any technical issues that arose, characterize the kinds of interaction they engaged in, and see where their attention was focused during the shared video watching. The surveys helped us understand more context of their activity, such as whether the video program and the Skype call were viewed on the same or different devices, and measure the sense of social presence using the Networked Minds Social Presence Scale (Biocca and Harris 2003).

## LESSONS AND CHALLENGES

The methodology used in the TV2Gether study enabled us to capture the shared video-watching experience whenever the participants wanted to engage in it. Unlike the E2G methodology, this approach freed up researcher time, as we no longer had to be available at the time of the study.

> **LESSON**
>
> Allowing users to choose the time and place of their shared activity and easily include a passive video recording of the activity enables a rich record of their naturally occurring activity to be captured with minimal researcher effort.

Because the researchers were not involved during the session, one concern was that the participants may run into technical problems they could not resolve. Thus, we provided step-by-step instructions on how to include our Skype account into the group video call. Since Skype's group video call is a premium, paid feature that one person must have, we added that service and the call recording software to our Skype account, so the participants did not incur any extra installation effort or expense to join in a recorded group video chat. This initial preparation helped us avoid having any of the participants experience technical difficulties with the Skype call.

Furthermore, the researchers being invisible during the participants' activities may have reduced participant inhibitions in what can be a very personal communication. Participants may be less aware that their activities are being observed for research purposes, which has privacy implications. Similar privacy concerns were raised when using a computer screen recording method, in which the researchers' recording activity was virtually invisible to the participants (Tang et al. 2006). We believe it is important to offer participants the option of excluding their recordings from the research data at any time if they realize they do not want the recordings to be studied. The participants did not request withholding any of the video recordings during this study.

While giving the participants flexibility around when and how they watched video together enabled us to capture realistic activity, it also introduced some variety that made comparing across all the sessions difficult. For example, some participants used different screens to watch the video (e.g., a TV) and to connect over Skype (e.g., laptop computer, tablet), whereas others used the same screen (e.g., laptop computer) for both. While we could detect and anticipate some differences in how they watched TV together that we could ask about in the surveys, we may be unaware of other differences, since we were not able to directly observe the activity.

## CONCLUSION AND DISCUSSION

While studying personal communication raises challenging issues around observing realistic behavior, given the personal relationships between participants, the private communications they share, and the diverse activities involved, our experiences illustrate approaches with which these issues can be addressed. Each approach goes beyond the traditional lab study to include the social contexts around how prototypes are used in the wild, which cannot be readily captured within a lab setting. While lab studies can be valuable for getting quick feedback before a prototype is mature enough to be deployed into the world, they are very limited in being able to recreate the social milieu that shapes the context of using personal communication tools.

Deploying prototypes into intact social groups in which researchers are personally embedded can offer personal access to the activities and interpretations of the group members' interactions, enabled by social trust. Participants who recruited their communication partners and chose their shared activities were able to enjoy the great flexibility of sharing experiences with others who had an inherent interest in the chosen activities. Enabling participants to include an auto-answer Skype account that automatically recorded the session in a group video call provided even more flexibility in capturing a rich record of the shared experience for later analysis without the researchers having to be involved.

Given the personal nature of social communication, it is important for researchers to be as unobtrusive as possible during study sessions while still being available to resolve technical issues that arise. Essentially, the participants should be free to have naturally occurring interactions within an established social context through personal communication technology. This freedom enables them to integrate and appropriate the technology for actual use in their everyday lives.

Of course, giving participants that much freedom also brings challenges. Audio, which is often an Achilles' heel of communication technology, can be a problem in settings where the researchers have no control of the factors that are important in capturing quality audio. Deploying prototypes into users' homes or in the wild implies that researchers must be available to resolve technical issues when they arise. This kind of technical support requires substantial investment of researchers' time and/or flexibility because they must be available to address problems. These kinds of deployments are typically limited in the number of people who can be observed or the length of time that such rich data can be collected. Refer to Chapter 9 to learn more about conducting single-home field deployments and Chapter 10 for multi-home field deployments. As with any rich, qualitative methodology, care must be taken to identify which observations are likely to generalize to other similar social groups and which might be specific to the few people who can be observed.

We share our experiences to illustrate how we have been able to address some issues in studying personal communication and help others continue to develop observational methodologies in this growing area of interest. While the methods we describe are especially useful in studying personal communication tools, they can be applied whenever specific people (e.g., experts at work) or diverse situations (e.g., mobile technologies) are involved. We believe these methods can be a valuable addition to a researcher's toolbox as communication technologies grow in the breadth and variety of situations in which they are used.

## ACKNOWLEDGMENTS

We first thank all of our anonymous participants who tried our prototypes and entrusted us with the data collected during the studies. The work presented in this chapter was drawn from work done in our research group that involved other contributors over the years. Honglu Du, Asta Roseway, Aaron Hoff, and Paul Johns contributed to the development, design, and study of VideoPal. Brett Taylor conducted the study of the Experiences2Go prototype. Anna Macaranas conducted the study of the TV2Gether prototype. We are particularly thankful to Tom Blank, Patrick Therien, Bruce Cleary, and Chris O'Dowd, who helped us with the physical design and assembly of the various prototypes.

## REFERENCES

Biocca, F., Harris, C., 2003. Networked Minds Social Presence Inventory (Scales only, Ver. 1.2). [online]. http://cogprints.org/6742/1/2002_netminds_scales.pdf (accessed 19.09.12.).

Brubaker, J.R., Venolia, G., Tang, J.C., 2012. Focusing on Shared Experiences: Moving beyond the Camera in Video Communication. Conf. Designing Interact. Syst. 2012, 96–105.

Espinosa, J.A., Slaughter, S.A., Kraut, R.E., Herbsleb, J.D., 2007. Familiarity, Complexity, and Team Performance in Geographically Distributed Software Development. Organ. Sci. 18 (4), 613–630.

Inkpen, K., Du, H., Roseway, A., Hoff, A., Johns, P., 2012. Video Kids: Augmenting Close Friendships with Asynchronous Video Conversations in VideoPal. In: Proceedings of the CHI Conference on Human Factors in Computing Systems (CHI 2012). ACM Press, New York, NY.

Inkpen, K., Taylor, B., Junuzovic, S., Tang, J.C., Venolia, G., 2013. Experiences2Go: Sharing Kids' Activities outside the Home with Remote Family Members. In: Proceedings of the 2013 conference on Computer supported cooperative work (CSCW 2013). ACM Press, New York, NY.

Macaranas, A., Venolia, G., Inkpen, K., Tang, J.C., 2013. Sharing Experiences over Video: Watching Video Programs together at a Distance. Interact 2013, 73–90.

Tang, J.C., Liu, S.B., Muller, M.J., Lin, J., Drews, C., 2006. Unobtrusive but Invasive: Using Screen Recording to Collect Field Data on Computer-Mediated Interaction. In: Proceedings of the 20th anniversary conference on Computer supported cooperative work (CSCW '06). ACM Press, New York, NY.

# Working with Community Groups to Inform the Design of Domestic Technologies

## 12

**Michael Massimi**
*Microsoft Research, Cambridge, UK*

## INTRODUCTION

This chapter provides descriptions and insights into how to design systems for the home by looking *outside* the home. In particular, the focus is on how bereavement support groups provided a great deal of detail and insight into how families grieve in their own ways, both in public and in the privacy of their homes.

As the other chapters in this book show, there are many ways to study how families develop routines and practices with respect to technology adoption, use, and abandonment. These vary widely in research questions, methods, epistemology, and assumptions about the makeup of the family or home in contemporary Western culture. On a large-scale, societal level, government institutes conduct censuses and organize surveys about family and home demographics such as those conducted by the Pew Research Center (Pew Research Center 2013).

These kinds of studies are relatively less common in Human-Computer Interaction (HCI), where the technology in question might involve an emerging technology that is not widely available. Domestic studies within HCI have generally used methods that involve fewer participants but provide richer data. These methods include interviews, which may be combined with a home visit (e.g., Hutchinson et al. 2003; Leonardi et al. 2009), in order to provide additional resources for participants to draw upon in the interview. (Refer to Chapter 3 to learn more about conducting home visits). Design-led approaches have also been successful through field trials and deployment studies (e.g., Brown et al. 2007) and can be evocative ways of eliciting stakeholder feedback when positioned as technology probes (Hutchinson et al. 2003). (Refer to Chapters 9 and 10 to learn more about conducting single- and multi-home field deployments). Indeed, when it comes to studying the home, HCI research has been particularly good at studying families *in situ* in order to provide rich, contextualized accounts of family life. The home, as a site for inquiry, has been important and instructive for technology design.

Without minimizing the importance of conducting research in the home as part of the development of domestic technologies, we must bear in mind that this way of understanding the home and its contents produces a *particular kind* of account. As researchers, we might make certain assumptions about the home or the family in order to conduct our research that aren't always completely true. For example, we might think of the home as a cultural imagining, left over from the 1960s, where the family and its living situation are found in a traditional American suburb: a nuclear family with two parents and children living together in their own home. In this vision, family members generally get along, and their activities are coordinated in a way that serves to reinforce familial bonds. Families mobilize technology toward this end, and novel technologies are introduced in order to further reinforce notions of togetherness, intimacy, and support.

As we know, however, families are not all so homogeneous and cooperative. (Refer to Chapter 13 to learn more about conflict in families). They have different priorities and goals, and individuals might disagree about how they would like to live their lives or relate to their family. No two relationships between specific people in a family are the same, and technologies are selectively used to reflect those differences. For example, the way a brother and sister use technology to constitute their relationship might be very different from the way either of them use it to communicate with their mother. Technologies might be involved to further one family member's goals ("It would be wonderful to be able to make sure my children are safe!") at the detriment of another ("My mom is spying on me!"). There are various kinds of families with their own religious and cultural contexts that shape what is considered to be acceptable "family-friendly" behavior.

HCI has not entirely missed this point. Recent work has brought to light that the home isn't always the site of productive happiness we think it to be. Le Dantec's work (2011) concerning mothers experiencing periodic homelessness, for example, draws attention to technology design in a context where the home is being lost, or where a family is being torn apart. Dimond et al. (2013) has similarly implicated the home in her work, where she examines how technologies that once bound people together—mobile phones, for example—can turn into technologies of monitoring and persecution when an intimate partner becomes violent or abusive.

Odom and Yarosh have both studied families that are divorced or separated, and how technology could be used to maintain a parent-child relationship without necessarily revealing too much about the parents' new living arrangements (Odom, Zimmerman, and Forlizzi 2010; Yarosh and Abowd 2009). These kinds of shifts in relationships need not even be situated in the home, per se. Sas and Whittaker (2013) discuss how technology is implicated in the context of a romantic breakup, including the need to delete or destroy digital assets in an effort to distance oneself from a partner. Other issues can be quite personal, such as addiction, but have ramifications for all those involved in the family; Yarosh's work on twelve-step fellowships demonstrates this aptly (Yarosh 2013).

In all of this, there is the observation that these "life disruptions" can cause domestic issues to "spill over" into the larger community. Massimi, Dimond, and Le Dantec (2012) compared and contrasted three life disruptions—the death of a loved one, intimate partner violence, and homelessness—and the ways that technology facilitated or complicated these transitions. Common to all of these was the way in which the personal sphere became, in some ways, public. Things that happened behind closed doors became observable by the community in some form, and technology played a role in how these observations were then made and managed. For example, a terminal illness can no longer be hidden when the sufferer passes away. Financial difficulties become observable when one cannot afford to live in one's home. The results of violence become visible when a partner escapes or is hurt.

When these familial issues break out of the privacy of the home, they can sometimes be addressed by local community support groups. These types of groups provide resources for people to cope with their changing situations by offering informational and emotional support. Examples of such organizations include homeless shelters, safe houses for people escaping intimate partner violence, addiction support groups, and bereavement support groups. Some, but not all, of these types of groups are affiliated with religious organizations that attempt to tend to spiritual matters, as well. These groups are generally non-profit, volunteer-run, and technology-poor, but provide what support they can for charitable reasons.

If these community support groups are considered as sites for the spillover of issues that originate within the domestic sphere, they can be additional resources with which to study the family and the home. By working with people who are providing and utilizing these community resources, we can find out what people are struggling with in their family lives. This provides a unique lens onto the home that complements the *in situ* approaches described earlier and helps to round out the understanding of family life.

In the remainder of this chapter, I describe my work with a community bereavement support group. While I never visited the homes of the participants, I learned a great deal about their families and home lives during a set of studies that were conducted primarily with people seeking support at a non-profit bereavement support center called Bereaved Families of Ontario (BFO) located in Toronto, Ontario, Canada. This occurred because the support they were looking for couldn't be found in their homes or in their families; they needed the perspective and counseling of someone *outside the home* to make sense of what was going on *inside*.

## ARRIVING AT A COMMUNITY APPROACH

I had previously conducted a web survey with bereaved individuals about how they used technology in the time following their loss (Massimi and Baecker 2010), and, early in the design process, I decided to focus on technologies for social support. Using a traditional user-centered design process (e.g., Preece, Rogers, and Sharp 2011), I read psychology and sociology texts on grief, bereavement, and mourning in order to better understand the various terminology and debates that were occurring in this space. During my reading, I formed an initial impression of grief and bereavement that guided my early design work. My reading suggested that bereaved people found a great deal of solace from discussing their grief with their friends and family members. In particular, the vulnerability that accompanies grief suggested that the times and places to talk about grief would be at home, where a person could find privacy and safety and be surrounded by loved ones. I arranged a handful of interviews with bereaved individuals who responded to advertisements on a web bulletin board. Based on those interviews and my reading, I began to sketch devices that would allow family members to communicate with one another and share in communal remembrance activities, eventually arriving at a sketch for an ambient display that could act as an in-home shrine or memorial (Figure 12.1). From my limited experience studying bereavement, this seemed to be a perfectly logical design approach, and I thought I was well on my way to building and deploying this system with a number of bereaved families.

At this point, I had the fortuitous opportunity to meet with a psychologist, Dr. Stephen Fleming, who had studied grief for decades. I had seen his writing and was surprised to find that he was working at York University, just up the road from University of Toronto, where I was completing my thesis. I emailed him and set up a preliminary meeting, at which I described my interest in technology to support the bereaved. He suggested that I take my sketches around to community organizations that specialized in social support for the bereaved in order to receive more early feedback about the concept. Armed with my sketches of a home shrine for social support, I decided to hold a series of focus groups with bereaved parents for feedback. Dr. Fleming facilitated introductions to two different community groups in Ontario, Canada, where I met with the groups' organizational leadership—bereaved people themselves—to describe my research interests. It became clear in our early conversations that the ways in which these people sought support was quite different from the ways that my initial thoughts suggested.

**FIGURE 12.1**

A prototype created in PowerPoint that was used as an example of an in-home "shrine." Intended as an ambient display, the imagined system would allow people in multiple households who were grieving the same loss to communicate in a private messaging system.

As my focus groups unfolded, I realized I had gotten many things wrong in my initial designs. The people at these focus groups told me that their grief brought them *out* of the home to an anonymous community center where they could talk frankly about their feelings. They explained that their relationships with their family members were complicated by the death, and that they did not want to burden or stress their loved ones with continued conversations about grief. For example, one woman who lost her son talked about how frustrated she was that her husband just didn't understand why she was still so upset so many years after the death. For this woman, talking to her husband, or even to other family members, was not an option and prompted her to turn to a support group at BFO. Other bereaved parents talked about how difficult it was for them to "put on a brave face" for their other children; while they were grieving the loss of one child, they still had others they were responsible for raising. Some parents expressed dismay at how unhelpful their friends were at this time. Though sympathetic, participants felt that their friends simply "didn't get it" because they hadn't lost a child themselves. These people wanted to know how other families managed their grief and sought advice about how to deal with their newfound circumstances.

In summary, my initial imagining of the home as a protective place, and of friends and family as continually-available sources of support, were off the mark. The homes of the bereaved people I spoke with were sometimes fractured and torn apart by the death, and these people were struggling to re-establish their family lives in the wake of the loss. I realized I had a lot more to learn, and I abandoned my original home-based shrine concept.

I established a partnership with the BFO and began to volunteer as an in-house technical adviser. In exchange, I was able to meet and speak with many bereaved people about their losses and what brought them to this organization. Working with a community organization was not my intention from the outset. However, it quickly became clear that the leadership and clients of BFO were rich sources of information about how the bereaved felt about technology in the domestic space.

## STUDY: BUILDING AND DEPLOYING A WEBSITE WITH BFO

BFO is a non-profit organization that provides free support groups to individuals who have experienced the loss of a loved one. I worked with BFO for three years, and, in addition to the focus groups described above, I had the opportunity to consult regularly with BFO leadership and clients. Because BFO was a community support organization, they noted that a website that did not require specialized hardware would be most appropriate for their client base. With that in mind, I set about building a website for social support that followed on from the values associated with BFO. These organizational tenets included the following:

1. **Like-loss membership.** Multiple groups run simultaneously and are organized based on the type of loss. Examples of recurring groups include parents who have lost an infant, parents who have lost a young or adult child, individuals who have lost a spouse or partner, and young adults (ages eighteen to thirty)

who have lost a parent or sibling. All members of a group, including the trained facilitator, must have experienced the same kind of loss. This value stems from the acknowledgment that those best suited to provide support must have experienced the loss themselves.

2. **Peer support.** The facilitators of the group are trained by BFO to ensure safety and respect among group members. Importantly, the facilitators are not professionals (e.g., psychologists, counselors, social workers). There is an emphasis placed on "not fixing": the facilitators are there only to help start and guide discussion, not to prescribe actions or treatment for dealing with grief. BFO includes only peers in groups in order to prevent a perceived power or authority imbalance among support group members; in particular, it was important to avoid situations where a professional might espouse a worldview that is overly prescriptive or narrow.

3. **One-on-one screenings.** Before attending a support group, each potential member must first complete a one-on-one interview with a BFO facilitator. During this session, the moderator judges whether the individual would be able to participate in a group effectively. The moderator's assessment depends on his or her own experiences in groups and time spent apprenticing with other moderators. The time between the death and the one-on-one interview varies from person to person, as does the time between the one-on-one and the beginning of the support group. This reflects BFO's understanding that we all grieve differently and on different timelines.

Based on these values, in combination with my own interviews and focus groups (Massimi and Baecker 2011), I built a prototype website called Besupp (short for "Bereavement Support") that allowed individuals to meet in online support groups. Details of Besupp and the full deployment study conducted have been reported in Massimi (2013). Summarily, Besupp contained features allowing participants to post chat messages to a shared wall; upload and share photos, videos, links, and stories; and keep a journal, if they so desired.

I conducted a deployment study in order to evaluate various aspects of Besupp. My contacts at BFO circulated a call for participants who would be interested in online social support, and this yielded nineteen bereaved individuals (coincidentally, all women) who had previously attended a support group at BFO. For purposes of the study, participants were placed into three separate groups based on the type of group meetings they attended at BFO:

- Young Adult (YA): people between ages eighteen and thirty who had suffered the loss of a parent or sibling
- Bereaved Parents (BP): parents who had suffered the loss of a child
- Spouses and Partners (SP): adults who had lost a spouse or romantic partner

These participants were asked to use Besupp for ten weeks, and each person participated in three interviews, one each at the beginning, middle, and end of this timeframe. This yielded approximately fifty-six hours of interviews, which

- How would you describe your experiences dealing with friends and family since your loss occurred?

- How did you come to your first support group?

- What do you hope to gain from being part of a support group? What would you like to discuss?

- Who do you currently talk to when you feel like you need support? Why?

**FIGURE 12.2**

Interview questions inviting potential discussion of family dynamics.

were transcribed and thematically analyzed (Massimi and Baecker 2011). In these interviews, participants were asked the questions shown in Figure 12.2, which led directly to responses concerning their family lives. Descriptions of their family situations also appeared in response to other questions throughout the interview.

I conducted a secondary analysis of the interview transcripts in order to identify quotes where participants talked about their families or homes. I then organized these quotes into themes based on their contents. These themes are presented below, and demonstrate how coming to a community support group reveals details about the participants' families and homes that may be relevant to technology design. Specifically, I set these out as a set of challenges for technologies in the home—situations that designers and researchers should consider when developing or deploying a system.

## CHALLENGES AND LESSONS

Based on the secondary analysis described above, I present a series of points that demonstrate how the challenging context of bereavement and, in particular, working in a community context, reveal critical design considerations when designing for families and the home. Participants are identified by their group abbreviation followed by their participant number.

### FAMILY MEMBERS NEED TIME AND SPACE APART

When a family is experiencing a challenging situation, there can be a need to disconnect from one another and reclaim space. As mentioned above, bereaved participants repeatedly described how they had trouble talking to their families about their grief or circumstances. Their turn toward a community group was often precipitated by this difficulty:

*It's good to be able to have an outlet that I wouldn't usually have and knowing that there are people who would respond, and it wasn't the response that I'd get from loved ones which is "stop complaining all the time." (YA2)*

This quote illustrates one of the chief reasons it was hard to talk to families gathered together in the home; they live together and are constantly exposed to one another's feelings. The amount of time that family members spend with one another is such that repeated expressions of grief can become burdensome. While most technologies seek to put family members in more constant or intimate contact, this study identifies a situation where that connectedness may be unwanted by some members of the family, which may make a member feel rejected or isolated. YA2, like many participants, found a more receptive audience during her weekly sessions at BFO.

> **LESSON**
>
> Constantly connecting families with technology may cause friction. Members of a family may need time apart from one another, and while technology is often thought of as a means for overcoming distance and time, constant family intimacy is not always a desirable state. Similarly, technology may make people feel that there is more support than there actually is in the home; just because a communication channel is available doesn't mean it is available for all conversations.

Participants also described the need for a separate space that was set apart from their usual domestic life. While Facebook, for example, had found its place in their home lives and routines, it was not considered to be a good place for expressions of grief or for seeking support. This was partially because it was not suitable for grief, both in terms of how it displayed information and who was able to see that information. For this reason, Besupp was built to be a closed system that was separate from other social media sites or accounts. In Besupp, participants were able to "be bereaved" for a while and then log out and get on with the rest of their lives.

> **LESSON**
>
> The type of data collected depends on who might be a recipient of the information shared. Facebook, one-on-one interviews, community groups, and so on are settings in which the types of things people say will vary considerably. Look to multiple sources of data and question what is, and isn't, being discussed.

As the above observations suggest, people experience grief in various ways. Differences in grieving styles among members of the home resulted in gaps in understanding. After her husband died, SP6 moved into a new home with a roommate. However, her roommate failed to grasp how someone could be experiencing grief so long after a death.

> *I feel compelled to discuss things and I know that there is an understanding there [at BFO] I don't get from anyone else. . . . [You've] got to have gone through it to understand it. My housemate doesn't understand how I am still going through this seven and a half years later. (SP6)*

Participants would often adjust their behavior or comments while at home in order to ensure the family order. By looking at this behavior through the lens of a bereavement support group, however, one person's emotions can be incongruent with household harmony. For example, various members of the household could be on different timeframes in reacting to their loss, or find particular aspects of the loss more difficult to deal with than others.

When a family member passes away, each person in that family experiences a different kind of loss. When a man dies, his death may simultaneously be the death of a husband, father, uncle, and son. Because losing one's father is a very different experience from losing one's husband, a given family member may not always be a preferred—or even available—conversation partner. Talking about the death may also complicate pre-existing relationships among family members. SP6 saw BFO's neutrality as a key reason to join:

> *It's like a third party, which is good. It's an objective view on something. Sometimes…it gets too subjective and can get really icky because people take sides or they have their own feelings. (SP6)*

Similarly, SP4 wanted to prevent her children from worrying about her, so she used the support group as a way to maintain her relationship with her children.

> *I think what I am most challenged with is helping my kids get through their challenges. . . . I was interested in sharing and hearing other people's stories about how it is for them and how I can help them. How do we parents help them? And how I can't always share this with them because I don't want to worry them, or tell them these things sometimes, but I still want to get them off my chest. (SP4)*

All of this makes a key distinction: *designing technologies for families doesn't always mean the technologies should be used by all family members*. In this case, creating a technology that can be used by a single person in order to discuss and make sense of his or her situation outside of a family setting may ultimately yield better outcomes than one that seeks to engage all members of the family in achieving this goal.

---

**LESSON**

Designers should expect technologies to be used differently by each member of the family, and should be aware that there may not be a singular "use case" for home technologies for the bereaved.

---

Indeed, technology might even bring to the surface particular conversations that are not wanted; for example, the presence of a technology in the home might say something about the individual who installed it there. In this sense, incorporating systems into existing platforms that allow plausible deniability might be a more useful way to approach the home. Rather than creating a specific appliance for bereavement support, one might create a mobile phone application or web page. Thus, other members of the household might simply think, "Mom is on the computer," rather than, "Mom needs support." In this sense, how to preserve the privacy of individuals in the home might be considered.

## PROTECTING THE FAMILY

The participants I spoke with told me about their interactions with strangers they met in a support group. While participants acknowledged a need to open up about themselves in the group, they were more protective of their family members and limited how much they shared about their family. In other words, they felt they did not have a moral right to reveal personal or sensitive information about other family members to the support group. This was especially the case with parents who were discussing their children's behaviors in the group setting.

> *I didn't want to share the specific details of it and because it was specific to my son I didn't want to label him or present him in a bad light. (SP4)*

When it came to sharing mementos about the deceased on the website, participants went to great lengths to present their family members in the most positive light possible. For example, they only showed photos of their family members in happy times. YA3 did not want to show any kind of photo to those outside of her family:

> *I thought that would diminish how special it is. To someone else they'd just look like photos of people. To me they're important pieces of memories. That they'd get out there . . . it'd diminish their importance. (YA3)*

Examining the support group setting shows how participants work to protect members of their family from criticism from outsiders and work to respect their family's history.

---

**LESSON**

Families want to avoid criticism from outsiders. When revealing the difficulties that may occur in the home to outsiders, it is critical to consider how family members might protect themselves from social stigma.

---

## FAMILY-TO-FAMILY INTERACTION

Although Bereaved Families of Ontario offers support groups for individuals, the word "families" appears in the organization's name. Why is this the case? An answer can be found in the interviews: while individual family members are the ones who attend support groups, their families benefit, as well. During the study, the concern and sympathy found at these sessions extended beyond the individual to the family. Participants described how their participation in these support groups was in order to help people navigate their own family matters and to bring back to their families the resources they needed in order to cope with their loss.

> *Talking about and sharing about helps you with your grieving process and helps others with the grieving process because it shows them they are not alone. That their feelings are similar. Many people think that their loss is so unique. For yourself it is unique, but there are many common characteristics in the whole thing. That's something that people who recently lost a child or a family member think that nobody has the same feelings but most of the feelings are common. (BP5)*

Participants in support groups undergo a process of interpreting their own situations and feelings in relationship to those around them. By comparing and contrasting these factors with others, bereaved individuals are able to identify potential paths forward for their own family and for others.

---

**LESSON**

Helping a single individual might have an effect that benefits the entire family. For example, if a technology were to help a mother cope with her loss, then the other members of her family may benefit from her increased availability, better mood, and so on. In this sense, "designing for families" might mean designing for a particular member of the family.

---

Being exposed to others' stories and making comparisons to one's own situation can sometimes offer concrete solutions moving forward. For example, the holiday season is often challenging for those who are struggling to remember the deceased while trying to participate in the festivities. At BFO, participants can learn about how others have navigated this situation and import the practices they like to their own families. BP1, who lost one son to cancer and the other to suicide, reported on how she adopted a candle-lighting tradition she learned about at BFO to help her in this situation.

> *I have to make sure people feel comfortable, and at Christmastime my mom wouldn't talk about them. I'd light candles at Christmastime to point out they were still with us, my mother got used to it. (BP1)*

This suggests that, while systems for sharing stories within families may be helpful for reminiscence and a sense of family identity, researchers might think about how to *design systems that expose one family's practices to help others learn how to cope*. In particular, families facing difficult transitions may benefit from learning about how others dealt with a similar situation. Whether it is a website or a more nuanced technology, exposing family practices to a wider audience results in an interesting design option for HCI. Technology can provide an opportunity for families to interact with one another in a supportive way; for example, a website might provide a place where families can share their ways of coping with others.

## SUMMARY AND DISCUSSION

Working with the bereaved can be a challenging context for many reasons: the family structure is changing, emotions are heightened, and the home is a different place than it usually is. This chapter has illustrated that, in order to observe the family in crisis, it is helpful to look to where the family members are obtaining outside support. Though I originally assumed that grief and bereavement would benefit from a home-based approach, the utility of a community-based approach that has extensions into the home via individual family members is tremendous.

This community-based approach may be especially helpful for researchers who want to develop or study home technologies associated with issues that are often considered taboo, disruptive, or exceptional. Just as there are taboos regarding sex, finances, abuse, religion, and so on, there is a strong taboo around death. Part of the success of a community-based approach is that people enter into the community organization as willing individuals and not as families. This strongly shapes the kinds of questions that can be safely asked and minimizes the repercussions that a family member might face as a result of his or her response. It is easy to imagine my participants changing their answers if they were asked these questions in front of their spouses or children. Furthermore, a community-based approach makes sense if the matter is simply one that cannot be adequately handled within a family or household; a rule of thumb is, if a situation requires governmental, legal, or charitable aid, then studying a community outside of the home might be a particularly insightful way to understand what is going on.

Although I worked with a non-profit community bereavement support organization, there is likely a great deal to learn about the home from other types of public locations. For example, school groups, medical centers, church groups, and so on may be informative places in which to learn about the variety of situations that arise in the home.

A community-based approach is not suited for all design situations. There are many matters that can be, and routinely are, handled successfully without a member of a family turning to outside assistance. In those cases, the methods should focus on the home environment itself and the ways that families routinely accomplish their tasks.

Note that studying a community context should not always preclude studying the home as well. The perspectives gained by conducting a home visit will, of course, yield different findings from a focus group at a community center. However, both of these perspectives can be valid and offer fresh or complementary perspectives on design.

When considering how to design technologies for families or for the home, several key points emerge that must be reinforced when examining a community perspective:

- Community centers show how individual members of the home behave and can provide a different perspective from interviewing them in the home or family context.

- Technologies that support the family may reasonably achieve their goals through individual use. If a system helps one member cope more effectively, the entire family or household could be considered better supported. This might be more appropriate than treating the family as a holistic, inseparable unit.
- Families and members of households have pre-existing relationships and are, in many ways, already very strongly connected. Technologies that bring families together or seek to connect households might inadvertently be presenting additional strain and exposure.

## CONCLUSION

In order to better understand family life, how the family is presented to outsiders must sometimes be investigated. One way of doing this is through community support groups, although there are other ways as well (e.g., governmental or health agencies). In this chapter, I presented some findings derived from talking to participants in bereavement support groups that shed light on how individuals conceive of their family's condition following the death of a loved one. The issues revealed in this approach differ from those characteristic of *in situ* approaches and could form the basis for a more holistic understanding of the family for technology design.

## ACKNOWLEDGMENTS

I would like to thank BFO, Ronald Baecker, Stephen Fleming, and the GRAND NCE, which supported this research.

## REFERENCES

Brown, B., Taylor, A.S., Izadi, S., Sellen, A., Kaye, J., Eardley, R., 2007. Locating Family Values: A Field Trial of the Whereabouts Clock. In: Proceedings of the 9th international conference on Ubiquitous computing (UbiComp 2007). Springer-Verlag, Berlin, Heidelberg.

Dimond, J., Dye, M., Larose, D., Bruckman, A., 2013. Hollaback!: The Role of Storytelling in a Social Movement Organization. In: Proceedings of the conference on Computer supported cooperative work (CSCW '13). ACM Press, New York, NY.

Hutchinson, H., et al., 2003. Technology Probes: Inspiring Design for and with Families. In: Proceedings of the SIGCHI Conference on Human Factors in Computing Systems (CHI 2003). ACM Press, New York, NY.

Le Dantec, C., Farrell, R.G., Christensen, J., Bailey, M., Ellis, J., Kellogg, W., Edwards, K., 2011. Publics in Practice: Ubiquitous Computing at a Shelter for Homeless Mothers. In: Proceedings of the SIGCHI Conference on Human Factors in Computing Systems (CHI '11). ACM Press, New York, NY.

Leonardi, C., Mennecozzi, C., Not, E., Pianesi, F., Zancanaro, M., Gennai, F., Cristoforetti, A., 2009. Knocking on Elders' Door: Investigating the Functional and Emotional Geography of Their Domestic Space. In: Proceedings of the SIGCHI Conference on Human Factors in Computing Systems (CHI '09). ACM Press, New York, NY.

Massimi, M., 2013. Exploring Remembrance and Social Support Behavior in an Online Bereavement Support Group. In: Proceedings of the conference on Computer supported cooperative work (CSCW 2013). ACM Press, New York, NY.

Massimi, M., Baecker, R., 2010. A Death in the Family: Opportunities for Designing Technologies for the Bereaved. In: Proceedings of the SIGCHI Conference on Human Factors in Computing Systems (CHI '10). ACM Press, New York, NY.

Massimi, M., Baecker, R., 2011. Dealing with Death in Design: Developing Systems for the Bereaved. In: Proceedings of the SIGCHI Conference on Human Factors in Computing Systems (CHI '11). ACM Press, New York, NY.

Massimi, M., Dimond, J.P., Le Dantec, C., 2012. Finding a New Normal: The Role of Technology in Life Disruptions. In: Proceedings of the ACM conference on Computer Supported Cooperative Work (CSCW '12). ACM Press, New York, NY.

Odom, W., Zimmerman, J., Forlizzi, J., 2010. Designing for Dynamic Family Structures: Divorced Families and Interactive Systems. In: Proceedings of the 8th ACM Conference on Designing Interactive Systems (DIS '10). ACM Press, New York, NY.

Pew Research Center. "Families." n.d. [online]. http://www.pewinternet.org/topics/Families.aspx?typeFilter=5 (Last accessed 01.03.13).

Preece, J., Rogers, Y., Sharp, H., 2011. Interaction Design: Beyond Human Computer Interaction. John Wiley & Sons, West Sussex, UK.

Sas, C., Whittaker, S., 2013. Design for Forgetting: Disposing of Digital Possessions after a Breakup. In: Proceedings of the 2013 Conference on Human factors in computing systems (CHI '13). ACM Press, New York, NY.

Yarosh, S., 2013. Shifting Dynamics or Breaking Sacred Traditions? The Role of Technology in Twelve-Step Fellowships. In: Proceedings of the SIGCHI Conference on Human Factors in Computing Systems (CHI '13). ACM Press, New York, NY.

Yarosh, S., Abowd, G.D., 2009. Supporting Parent−Child Communication in Divorced Families. International Journal of Human-Computer Studies (IJHCS) 67 (2), 192−203.

# Conflict in Families as an Ethical and Methodological Consideration

# 13

**Svetlana Yarosh**

*Computer Science & Engineering Department, University of Minnesota, Minneapolis, MN, USA*

## INTRODUCTION

Researchers in Human-Computer Interaction (HCI) and related fields have been designing systems for supporting family relationships since the late 1990s (e.g., Hindus et al. 2001). Most of these interventions for families have largely been concerned with stability, integration, and consensus; however, my work with separated families has forced me to acknowledge and respond to *family conflict*. Conflict in families focuses on the negotiation and renegotiation of relationships, expected behaviors, and value systems. All families experience conflict, and the occurrence of conflict does not reflect on the quality of the relationship; rather, the response to conflict is what determines the long-term quality of that family's interactions (Sillars, Canary, and Tafoya 2004). Thus, the lessons from my work apply not only to separated or divorced families, where conflict is obvious, but also to intact ones. Ethical and methodological considerations when dealing with family conflict and non-consensus go beyond compliance with Institutional Review Board (IRB) guidelines. These considerations are part of a process of learning from each other to plan and execute research that adheres to a set of values that is essential to collaborative work, such as trust, accountability, mutual respect, and fairness. I present an argument for considering family conflict in all investigations of families and share my hard-won experience for designing technology for separated families, planning and running studies, and analyzing the results.

## DEFINING CONFLICT

This chapter takes a broad perspective in defining conflict. Conflict represents types of family interactions that family members themselves find problematic or disconcerting (Sillars, Canary, and Tafoya 2004). A non-exhaustive list may include the following types of conflict:

- Divergent values in making decisions affecting other group members
- Disagreement in who should be included in the family group and in what ways

233

- Difficulty integrating the diverse goals and motivations of each member while making decisions affecting other group members
- Struggles in considering the divergent benefits and costs of specific decisions on each individual member of the group

In this chapter, I describe how these forms of conflict may manifest in families and affect how these families make decisions about technology and interact with researchers.

## SCENARIO FROM MY WORK: FAILING TO CONSIDER CONFLICT

To begin, I would like to share a scenario from my own research. Despite the fact that my work has always focused on family conflict, I failed to give it the proper consideration here. This resulted in a costly mistake, losing a potential participant family:

> I was getting ready to deploy a novel communication system in two divorced households in the Atlanta, Georgia area in the United States. One of these was meant to go in the house of the father and the other in the house of his son (who lives with his mom, about a ninety-minute drive away). I had already conducted initial interviews with both the parents and the child, distributed communication diaries to get a sense of their baseline-level of communication, gathered IRB-required consent and assent, and began the process of installing business-class Internet in both homes to support the bandwidth-hungry system I was about to install. I thought that all my ducks were in a row and I was excited to begin the first in-home deployment for the system that would form the bulk of my thesis work. However, as I was getting ready to reserve the truck to transport the system to the mother's home, I got a call from her: "Actually, we don't want to be in the study after all. Could you come by and pick up the communication diaries later this week?" I was disappointed and confused by her sudden change-of-heart. What happened? The mother explained: "Well, I live with my fiancé and when he found out about the study, he felt really uncomfortable with it. I'd love for [my son] to use this with his father, but it doesn't seem like a good option for us." My mistake was in only considering conflict between divorced parents and failing to consider possible disagreements about the system's perceived benefits and costs for other family members. Because I had failed to consider multiple sources of family conflict and relied exclusively on IRB-required procedures to cover my ethical bases, I had made a major mistake that cost me days of work and cost a family the opportunity to be in this study.

Though it may seem that this is a scenario that applies only in the unique case of divorced families, one goal of this chapter is to demonstrate that conflict is a consideration in all work done with families. I discuss common pitfalls and ways of avoiding them so other researchers can avoid repeating my costly mistakes.

> **LESSON**
>
> When recruiting high-conflict families, non-participants may have to be included in the consent procedures to account for dynamic family structures.

## EPISTEMOLOGICAL PERSPECTIVE

Two complementary paradigms are frequently employed to understand human relationships. One is known as the "sociology of regulation," which is concerned with understanding stability, integration, functional coordination, and consensus (Hirschheim and Klein 1989). This approach is common when considering the home and family as a unit with common goals, motivations, and needs. The other is the "sociology of radical change," which is more interested in change, conflict, disintegration, and coercion (Hirschheim and Klein 1989). I posit that diverging motivations and tensions that characterize family relationships have been largely overlooked in previous designs for families. I propose a more inclusive, alternative perspective by connecting with another epistemological framework.

Kling (1980) compared social analyses of computing in work organizations between 1950 and 1979 and found two distinct camps of study. The system rationalists emphasized the positive role of computing in improving the efficiency of organizations. On the other hand, the emerging camp of segmented institutionalists examined both the "legitimate" and the "illegitimate" consequences of computing by studying all stakeholders, including non-users. While the rationalists emphasize agreement on goals, the institutionalists assume stakeholders have overlapping and conflicting objectives and motivations. Many current designs for the family echo the system rationalist approach by focusing on improving family efficiency, assuming consensus on family objectives, including only users in the evaluation, and having an optimistic view of the impact of computing technology. While this is a reasonable lens for many family designs, a different perspective—segmented institutionalism—is offered at the intersection of the conflict and the subjective paradigms. I adapt the segmented institutionalism perspective to analyze computing in the family by focusing on: (1) achieving shared meaning rather than efficient function; (2) conflicting and overlapping goals rather than consensus; (3) including all stakeholders rather than only direct users; and (4) highlighting trade-offs rather than evidence of success. I have found that leveraging this perspective in designing family technologies provides a powerful guide for system analysis and highlights important ethical and methodological considerations.

Both epistemological approaches are valid ways of looking at the world and studying families, each highlighting different issues of interest, but I believe that most insightful research can incorporate aspects of both types of methodologies. I propose that the focus on conflict is a way of providing a frequently missing counterpoint in designing for families, and I discuss some lessons from incorporating this approach in my own work.

## CHAPTER OUTLINE

The main point of this chapter is that family conflict is a factor in all families and should be considered in how we design, implement, and present our research. I begin by presenting two studies from my own work, with a focus on the methods used: two sets of interview studies with parents and children and an in-home deployment of a novel system. Following this basic overview, I discuss four potential challenges relating to family conflict, how I have attempted to address these in my work, and what worked and what didn't work in my solutions. Finally, I conclude with five lessons for others who are conducting research with families.

## A TALE OF TWO STUDIES

In this section, I discuss examples of family conflict and non-consensus from my work, in which I aim to support communication between parents and children who live apart.

## INTERVIEWS WITH DIVORCED AND WORK-SEPARATED FAMILIES

I conducted two sets of interviews with parents and children in families who live apart: one set with those who are separated by divorce (Yarosh, Chew, and Abowd 2009) and another with those who are separated by work (Yarosh and Abowd 2011) such as military deployment and frequent business travel. My goal was to understand the lived experience of these families as they managed their separation, the challenges they faced, and the strategies they employed to overcome these challenges. In-depth interviews with parents and children (seven to fourteen years old) allowed me to collect rich narratives and stories from the participants' point of view.

### Study Methods and Strategies

In both studies, I recruited the families through word-of-mouth, ads on craigslist.org, and through local support organizations (e.g., military base parenting groups, divorce meet up groups). About half of the participants were recruited using these methods and the rest were referred through a secondary round of "snowball" recruiting (i.e., asking a participant to recommend other potential participants). I made an effort to conduct interviews in-person whenever possible because communication over video chat may present an additional barrier to younger children, but in both studies, one interview was conducted over video chat (for more on this approach, refer to Chapter 2 on conducting remote interviews with participants).

I asked parents to suggest the setting for the interview that would be most comfortable for them and their children (for more on interviewing children, refer to Chapter 4). Most families chose to be interviewed at home, though a few selected to come to my office or meet in a public community venue like a coffee shop. In general, I found that I could get significantly better data from younger participants if the interview was conducted in the home rather than in other settings. Being in the home reduced the power imbalance between the child and the researcher and frequently provided more privacy as the parent would usually return to their daily activities while the child was being interviewed (while in the coffee shop or office, they would remain seated at the same table). I return to the idea of separate versus side-by-side interviews later in this chapter.

There were two strategies that I found to be particularly successful in getting participants to open up and tell richer stories about their experiences. Most frequently, I used these strategies with children (who were more likely to be shy about relating their experience), but at times I also employed them with particularly terse or reticent parents. One strategy is to get the participant to show-and-tell. For example, "Show me where you usually are when you think about your dad?" or "Show me some apps that you use with your mom on your phone?" The second strategy was asking participants to think about potential future technology and draw or discuss things that would or wouldn't work for them (e.g., "What do you wish that kids would have in the future to help them stay in touch with their parents?"). Lastly, one question seemed to routinely succeed in getting both parents and children to open up about their experiences: "What advice would you give to other [parents/children] who have to live apart because of [work/divorce]?"

---

**LESSON**

Soliciting participants to give advice to others in the same context is a great way to get rich stories and insights. Two strategies that work well to elicit rich stories from children is asking them to show-and-tell about their current practices and asking them to draw potential future technologies.

---

Additional details about the questions asked and the analysis of the results can be found in the primary publications for these two studies (Yarosh, Chew, and Abowd 2009, Yarosh and Abowd 2011).

## *Insights on Family Conflict*

Though it is out of the scope of this chapter to discuss all of the findings from these two studies, I want to point out some of the lessons from this work about conflict in families. It is not surprising that managing tension and conflict was a big part of life for the divorced families interviewed. What was surprising was the level of awareness the children had of this tension compared to parents' estimates of their awareness. For example, seven out of the eight parents in the divorce interview study thought that their child was probably not aware of the competition over their time and affection between the parents. However, when asked about what was most difficult about staying close to both parents, children said things like:

> My mom has a way to make her voice sound like she doesn't care, but at the same time, you know that it's not true, and it really always hurts to hear that voice. And whenever I want to call my dad she always uses it saying, "Oh, so you're calling him?"

This points to the importance of interviewing both parents and children, as one side may not have the complete story. In this case, interviewing the child separately from the parent supported both in telling their side of the story without redacting to spare the feelings of the other party. Though it is not always possible to insist on interviewing separately, as parents may be wary of leaving the child alone with the researcher (especially with children younger than ten), I found it worthwhile to suggest this to the parent by framing it as an opportunity for the child to share his or her side of the story.

> **LESSON**
>
> Parents are not good proxies for children. Talking to and observing children directly is the best way to get at their lived experience.

What may be more surprising was that conflict was also a big part of the story with work-separated families. Most work-separated families rely heavily on the adult who is collocated with the child to manage and support communication with the remote parent. There is an assumption that this will go smoothly, but when this assumption breaks down, it affects the quality of contact with the child. For example, one mother complained:

> There were times when, if my husband and I weren't getting along . . . he was short in answer and so then I'm only able to email with [my daughter] and that was very upsetting.

In this case, contact between the child and mother was reduced to a poor medium because it was the only one that didn't require direct support from the father. The other source of non-consensus in these families was about what constitutes an appropriate amount of communication with the remote parent. The need to *increase* contact is a characteristic common of traveling parents, but less commonly seen in children. Spending more time communicating with the remote parent may, in fact, interfere with the strategies children use to cope with the separation, which frequently include focusing more on contact with collocated family members, rather than seeking remote contact (Yarosh and Abowd 2011). While only three children expressed displeasure with excessive contact from their traveling parent, a number of parents expressed frustration with short conversation and single-word replies, clearly pointing to some level of conflict in achieving agreement on appropriate practices. It is important for designers to consider the obligation to communicate that their system may impose on the child and what may happen if the parent's expectations for communication are not met. Again, this conflict could only become apparent by talking to multiple parties involved in the communication, rather than treating the family as a unit and talking to a parent as a proxy representative of this unit.

Consistent with the segmented institutionalism approach outlined in the introduction, talking to multiple members of the family (particularly if these interviews could be conducted separately) allowed me to highlight family members' conflicting and overlapping goals and perspectives, which were present both in divorced and intact families.

## THE SHARETABLE IN-HOME EVALUATION

Informed by the above interview studies, I sought to address some of the communicational challenges faced by parents and children in separated families (refer to (Yarosh and Abowd 2011; Yarosh, Chew, and Abowd 2009) for a detailed discussion of these challenges). To do so, I designed and built the ShareTable, a novel video-based communication system for the home. In this section, I describe the design of the ShareTable system, review our methods for evaluating it with two sets of divorced families, and discuss the insights on family conflict gleaned through this process.

### The ShareTable System Overview

The ShareTable is a synchronous communication technology aimed at addressing two communication challenges faced by parents and children in separated families. The system consists of two paired video chat communication appliances (see Figure 13.1). A ShareTable in the child's home is connected via broadband to a paired parent's table. Video chat provides a face-to-face view, while a camera-projector system superimposes a video stream of one table's surface on top of the other. The two video streams are aligned so that the parent and child can view and layer physical artifacts in this shared media space, enabling activities like doing homework and drawing together. In order to make it possible for the child to use the ShareTable without the help of a collocated adult, I leveraged a physical metaphor of interaction. The ShareTable video monitor is hidden behind a set of cabinet doors: opening these doors initiates a connection to the other home or answers an incoming call; closing these doors ends the connection. After an encouraging formative controlled-setting evaluation of the ShareTable system (Yarosh et al. 2009), I developed a robust functional prototype that could be tested with an in-home study.

### Study Methods and Strategies

I evaluated the ShareTable through a month-long in-home deployment in four divorced households (two sets of families) in the Atlanta, Georgia area of the United States (Yarosh et al. 2013).

The families participating in this study were selected through a professional recruitment firm, from a call for divorced families with young children who were

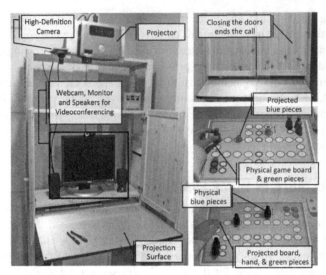

**FIGURE 13.1**

The ShareTable, consisting of video chat and a camera-projector system. Images from the two tabletops are overlaid, supporting shared activities with physical objects. Opening or closing the cabinet door controls the connection. For full details on how the system works, please refer to Yarosh et al. (2013).

interested in testing a new communication technology. Recruiting through a professional firm had a number of advantages: the families were not connected to the university or related research in any way, thus representing a less biased sample, and it allowed us to select for specific distances between the connected households (both needed to be in the greater Atlanta area, but at least a forty-minute drive apart). A month-long deployment allowed me to evaluate use over time and conduct a more in-depth investigation than would have been otherwise possible. The first family recruited for the study dropped out before the system was installed because the mother's new partner did not want a system with cameras connecting his home with that of the child's father (scenario described in the introduction). Learning from this experience, with subsequent families, I made sure that both sides of the families were interested in participating and gathered verbal consent from all other residents of each home, even if they were not slated to be direct users of our system. Using this strategy, I was able to recruit and retain four households to complete the in-home study. These households included children (ages three, seven, seven, and eleven), divorced parents, and new partners of those parents.

The main goal of this study was to understand the differences between the previous communication media used by the families and the ShareTable system. Consistent with the segmented institutionalism approach, I also wanted to make sure to gather data about both positive and negative effects of the deployment to focus on tradeoffs rather than simply highlight successes. To that end, I collected a number of baseline metrics. During the pre-deployment, I interviewed members of each family. To protect the privacy of each participant, interviews and questionnaires were conducted separately whenever possible. I spoke to any children over six years old who lived in the house, both of the parents, and any cohabitating current partners. The questions focused on strategies that each family used to stay in touch and the specific challenges of their arrangement. I asked each parent to fill out a Network of Relationships Inventory (NRI) (Furman and Buhrmester 2009) describing their relationships to their past partner, current partner, and the children participating in the study. I asked each child to fill out a shortened NRI inventory (presenting only one question from each scale of interest) describing their relationships with their parents and any stepparents. For each communication medium that the family used regularly, I asked both the parents and the children to fill out an appropriate version of the Affective Benefits and Costs of Communication Technologies (ABCCT) questionnaire (Yarosh, Markopoulos, and Abowd 2014). Finally, I provided each member of the family with a diary and asked them to log any remote contact between the parent and the child. Each family kept these preliminary diaries for at least fourteen days. During the deployment, the ShareTable was installed in each home and introduced using example scenarios. I also explained that the system would log use and locally record any ongoing calls. I asked participants to continue keeping communication diaries, and I continued weekly interviews with participants for the next twenty-eight days. At the end of the month-long deployment, each participant was asked to complete the NRI and ABCCT again. This approach allowed us to draw meaningful comparisons between pre- and during-deployment practices of the families who participated in the study.

Full details of analysis and findings can be found in the primary publication on this study (Yarosh et al. 2013). In the next section, I focus on insights relevant to the role of family conflict.

### Insights on Family Conflict

The ShareTable deployment highlighted three areas where family conflict, non-consensus, and conflicting interests were apparent: (1) in defining the family unit, (2) in deciding appropriate practices around the new technology, and (3) in understanding the specific trade-offs in using the system.

### Conflict Due to Reflexive Definitions of Family

The failure scenario described at the outset of this paper highlights one aspect of family conflict that recurred repeatedly throughout this work—the reflexive nature of defining "family." At the outset of the study, I was considering "family" from the perspective of the child, as including his mom, dad, and himself. However, the mother's definition of *her* family also included her new fiancé. My failure to consider that and obtain the consent of all the members of *her* family led to her withdrawing from the study. Once I was able to recruit additional families, I asked the question explicitly: "Who do you consider to be part of your family?" No two participants in the study (from the same family) listed the exact same set of family members! For example, in my second deployment, the direct users of the ShareTable consisted of an eleven-year-old brother, a seven-year-old sister, and their divorced mother and father. The brother defined his family as consisting of his sister, mom, and dad. The sister defined her family as consisting of her brother, her mom and dad, her stepfather, her dad's ex-girlfriend, and the girlfriend's daughter (her half-sister). The mother considered her family to consist of her son and daughter, her new husband, and her parents (the children's grandparents). The father considered only his son and two daughters to be his family. This issue is highlighted in divorced families but also holds true for intact families. For example, Judge et al. (2011) connected several households with always-on video chat, but found strong objections from some users when a connected household was not one that they considered to be close family (e.g., in-laws). In other words, the definition of family is "reflexive"—always referring back to the individual who is listing its members. When discussing family, it makes sense to discuss it from the perspective of a particular individual rather than as a "unit."

### Ongoing Negotiation of Appropriate Practices around Technology Use

The second class of issues highlighted by the ShareTable deployment was conflict over appropriate placement and use of the new technology. In the first family deployment, the big concern with the ShareTable was that remote contact might interrupt routines in the home, so all remote contact had to be preceded by a telephone call to the mother to make sure that it was a good time to call. By contrast, in the second family, the remote parent prioritized continued contact over the worry of interrupting the other home. While this did lead to more frequent use of the system, it also created conflict as routines were disrupted. In the first family, the father was often frustrated by the difficulty in arranging remote contact, while in the second family, the mother found it frustrating to have the children's routines interrupted by unexpected ShareTable calls—neither arrangement was ideal for both households. Another disagreement focused on the placement of the system. In the first family, the father was frustrated by the mother's decision to put the ShareTable in a rarely occupied room of the house, making spontaneous contact difficult. On the other hand, the mother was uncomfortable with the father's decision to place the table in a central, public area of the house because she felt that she was intruding on his home life. In the second family, the mother ended up regretting her decision to put the ShareTable in her son's room because it undermined her control over appropriate use of the system:

> If I had known that this would be the outcome of putting it in [my son]'s room . . . I would have probably put it in the living room so that I could have more control over when it gets used.

Negotiation over location and practices of use continued through the month of the system's deployment. The length of the deployment and the weekly interviews with each user (separate from other users) allowed me to witness the frustrations and struggles as each member of the family negotiated with others about the appropriate use of the system. Frequently, when talking about practices around communication technology, HCI researchers discuss practices as they *are*, failing to discuss the evolving, negotiated nature of use and the role of each party in forming and putting their rules into practice.

---

**LESSON**

Interview multiple times throughout a system deployment to capture the ongoing negotiation regarding its use between family members.

---

### Divergent Costs and Benefits for Each Family Member

Lastly, the ShareTable deployment highlighted that a system may provide benefits to some, but not all, members of the family. According to the segmented institutionalism perspective, it is important to acknowledge such tradeoffs explicitly in an evaluation of any system for multiple family members. In the ShareTable study, I asked each parent and child to complete a Network of Relationships Inventory before and after the deployment to understand the effect of the system on relationship quality. (The complete data can be found in Yarosh et al. 2013). The most striking changes were seen on the inventory of the son from the second family—he reported a more supportive relationship with his mother and a less antagonistic relationship with both his mother and father. Both the parents also reported a greater sense of intimacy in their relationships with both of their children. In contrast, the first family reported fewer changes on their NRI. The son reported a higher level of satisfaction in his relationship with his father, but no other positive changes. However, there was a marked negative change reported by the mother in her sense of reliable alliance with the father. Overall, the ShareTable may have contributed to some positive relationship outcomes for both families, but also some negatives ones for some members of the first family. Additionally, I used the ABCCT Questionnaire to understand the possible benefits and drawbacks that the ShareTable provided compared to previous technology used by each participant. While the ShareTable outperformed the previous technology (phone) on all four measures of benefits (emotional expressiveness, engagement, opportunity for social support, and a sense of presence-in-absence), it came at a cost of an increased threat to privacy. Understanding this tradeoff can inform decisions about the system's use; for example, it may not be appealing to a user who highly values privacy (e.g., the mother from the first family). Administering both of these instruments to each specific user helped highlight that some relationships and individuals benefited less from the system than others and potentially experienced additional costs.

---

**LESSON**

Use validated instruments such as relationship inventories to understand the impact of a researcher's intervention.

---

## CHALLENGES AND LESSONS

Based on my experiences in the studies described above, I discuss four common challenges that are influenced by family conflict and non-consensus and provide a few strategies from my own work for dealing with each of the following four issues: recruiting and retaining participants, operationalizing a definition of family, considering and investigating the processes for negotiating the use of technology, and measuring the impact of an intervention.

## RECRUITING AND RETAINING PARTICIPANTS

One consistent challenge in working with families lies in recruiting participants. Recruiting a family requires multiple members of the family to agree to participate, which may be a source of conflict. Frequently there is a high cost for an interested family member to get others in the home on board and arrange the logistics of participating in the study. This issue is amplified because the benefits of participation may be uncertain or temporary. In my work, I've taken several approaches to recruitment, each with its own trade-off.

The easiest and most freely available avenue for recruitment is word of mouth in one's own network. This includes posting a call to one's social networking site or local mailing list such as a university department list. This approach is most likely to recruit participants who are similar to the recruiter in terms of background and socio-economic status. This can be an advantage in early prototype deployments, in that the participants are likely to be tolerant of system errors, able to do basic troubleshooting, and be more familiar with the type of feedback that would be most useful to the researcher. On the other hand, this approach provides a biased sample and can prevent one from getting accurate measures of system use. For example, if the participants know the researcher and are his or her friends, they may be much more motivated to give "good" results). I have found that this approach is most appropriate for early prototype formative evaluations (e.g., Yarosh et al. 2009), but less so for summative evaluations (e.g., Yarosh et al. 2013).

I found that the best way of recruiting insightful, motivated participants was turning to context-specific forums or interest groups whenever possible. Examples of context-specific forums include subsets of larger services (such as Yahoo! groups) or dedicated sites. Interest group sites, such as meetup.com, provide a great alternative for recruiting local participants. Typically, it is easy to find meet-ups for specific sub-groups of families that one is interested in reaching. In both online forums and in-person interest groups, I found it valuable to spend time introducing myself and participating in the group as a member before soliciting participants.

One way of recruiting from the general community is to turn to local volunteer and classified sites such as craigslist.com. To be successful, this approach usually requires compensation for the participant's time. Though this is an easy forum through which to reach a wide audience, I have always had mixed results in terms of the quality of participants who reply to the call. For example, there is a much larger proportion of last-minute cancellations, no-shows, or replies that do not meet the selection criteria of the study. I typically use this as the last approach in recruiting participants, frequently adding additional selection criteria. For example, in the work-separated parenting interview study, I had a good sample of academics, military families, and business professionals, but I turned to craigslist to find interviewees from a lower income bracket. This kind of "stratified" sampling allowed me to get a more diverse group of participants.

Going through a professional recruitment firm is an excellent solution for times when the study requirements are very specific and there are no local groups that satisfy the criteria. This was the case for the ShareTable in-home deployment, where I was looking for families that met the following criteria: divorced, amicable in the sense that both parties would be willing to participate in the study without a court order, having at least one child between the ages of six and ten, both families living no more than a two hours' drive from the Atlanta area but no less than a forty-minute drive apart from each other, the non-residential parent currently seeing or contacting the child regularly, and both homes being in an area that can be equipped with high-speed broadband connection (a constraint that ruled out many rural regions of Georgia, USA). To satisfy all these constraints, I went through a professional recruitment firm, which has a large database of users and is able to check adherence to specific selection criteria. Though such firms are fairly expensive per user recruited, they are a great solution when one does not need a large number of users.

---

**LESSON**

Four approaches to recruiting include going through the researcher's own social network, turning to context-specific forums or meet-ups, casting a wide net through a community site such as craigslist, and, when all else fails, going through a professional recruitment firm.

---

Family members may disagree as to whether they want to participate in a study, which makes recruitment difficult; however, I hope the above suggestions for recruitment can support other researchers in reaching a wide base of potential participants, increasing the chance of finding families in which consent of all members can be obtained.

## OPERATIONAL DEFINITION OF FAMILY

It may be tempting to discuss a family as a unit of study, but in the examples from the ShareTable deployment, I point out that the definition of family is often reflexive and includes a different subset of members for each person asked. There is a danger in treating any one person as a proxy representative of the entire group. It may be helpful to the researcher to explicitly articulate which subsets of family members are included in the study and why, and it may be a good idea to get consent for the study from the relevant members, even if they are not going to be included as direct study participants. I find that the term "family" only makes sense in reference to a specific person, so "my family" is a subset of people, "my father's family" may be a different subset of people, but "the Yarosh family" is an amorphous and non-specific term that is more misleading than helpful in actually identifying a unit of interest.

Another potential solution is to discuss families in terms of living arrangements, rather than self-reported connections. For example, for the purpose of a particular study, I may be interested in talking only to people whose primary residence is in one house. However, this approach has the danger of excluding some common arrangements: the child in a divorced family who may spend some time living in two households but only lists one primary residence; the couple who has separate homes but frequently spends nights together in one home or the other, and the young adult who has gone off to live in a college dorm but still spends some weekends and all school breaks living in the parents' house. On the other hand, this definition may include a non-relevant person such as an unrelated person who rents a room at the house but rarely interacts with the other household members. Researchers should be aware of these as possible sources of confusion as participants define "members of a household," and explicitly address any possible misunderstandings.

Most importantly, I have found it helpful to acknowledge that my stereotypical idea of "family" reflects my own place in life and my biases. In any study, there are many potential benefits and only minor costs to asking all participants to describe and define their family as they see it.

---

**LESSON**

Do not assume what "family" means to individual participants; instead, ask them to define their own family as they see it.

---

## WHERE THE TECHNOLOGY GOES AND WHO MAKES RULES ABOUT ITS USE

The investigations described in this chapter point to multiple examples in which family members may disagree on appropriate practices around a particular technology. For example, in divorced families who used the ShareTable system, the parents frequently disagreed on where the system should be and how to coordinate appropriate times to contact the other home. While less explicit, there were also examples of similar conflict in non-divorced families. For example, in work-separated families I interviewed, children and parents frequently desired different amounts and types (spontaneous versus scheduled) of remote contact. Judge et al. (2011) found similar issues in their deployment of a multi-family media space—several members of each family resented the intrusion of a system that connected them to their in-laws with always-on video. These examples of conflicts bring up questions as to who is making decisions about the use of technology and who is excluded from this decision-making.

There are several potential approaches to take to manage this conflict, each with benefits and drawbacks. In some situations, it makes sense to explicitly select one member of the family and focus on those interests. For example, in terms of the design of the ShareTable system, I focused explicitly on the needs of the child (supporting easy, spontaneous communication and rich, activity-focused interaction) rather than the needs of the parents (supporting explicit scheduling, privacy, and multitasking). Unfortunately, this meant that the parents' needs were not always met. In the extreme case, taking this approach means that some study participants may refuse to use the system or even deliberately sabotage it if they feel it acts counter to their needs. When taking a stance that focuses on a single member of the family, I have found it helpful to explicitly discuss this stance with the other family members at the outset of the study. However, in other sensitive contexts, it may make sense to reach decisions through consensus. In my work, the decision of whether the divorced parents and their children would participate in the ShareTable study was made with consent from all the other family members residing in each household. Any of these members could have blocked the installation if they did not feel comfortable with the system. Unfortunately, this can lead to losing potential participants, but providing the opportunity for explicit discussion while trying to reach consensus gives a venue for potential conflicts to be brought up, discussed, and resolved. Overall, I find it easier to assume that there is or will be conflict over technology use and explicitly consider these issues in my protocol, rather than try to look the other way when it occurs.

Perhaps the most important lesson I've learned from my work is that participants are human beings who may have their biases but are almost always willing to negotiate and change their minds when given the opportunity to discuss their concerns and their points of view. In the ShareTable deployment, I found that the weekly interviews were key to giving the participants the opportunity to discuss ongoing issues and to help them brainstorm solutions, which can be difficult to do without seeming to "take sides." I am certainly not perfect at this, but I have found it helpful to ask the participants to explain their motivations, then ask them to consider the other individuals' motives, and finally, to reflect on what they would want if the positions were reversed. At times, sharing information from previous studies may help this process. For example, when talking to a parent who was disappointed because of short phone conversations with her child, I approached the parent as follows: "In my previous interviews, I found that children have a hard time connecting over the phone. If you were a child and your choice was talking to a disembodied voice or returning to play with your friends, how long would you want to keep talking to your remote parent?" This focus on the process of achieving shared meaning is key to segmented institutionalism and can often lead to a deeper, more insightful conversation with participants.

> **LESSON**
>
> Give participants from high-conflict families an opportunity to negotiate, come to an agreement, and change their minds.

There are no hard and fast rules for dealing with non-consensus and conflict over technology use. It is uncomfortable to become an unwilling witness to the private conflicts and negotiations of others' families. However, assuming that conflict does not exist, taking a single family member's point of view at face value as ground truth, or ignoring conflict when it does occur, may undermine the validity of the study and does not do justice to the complex and nuanced practices of families.

## MEASURING THE INDIVIDUAL AND RELATIONAL EFFECTS OF THE INTERVENTION

In order to expose and understand conflict, the segmented institutionalism approach encourages talking to multiple stakeholders, highlighting divergent objectives, and investigating tradeoffs rather than just evidence of success. In order to understand how each member of the family is affected by a technology, it is important to talk to each stakeholder about the effect of the technology on his or her individual goals and tradeoffs he or she faces. However, this may seem intractable: a family contains $n$ individuals and $n^2 - n$ relevant relationships between those individuals, each of which can be positively or negatively affected by an intervention on a number of different scales.

Understanding the individual experiences of each participant is already a complicated task, but adding relational effects substantially increases the number of variables that must be understood and measured. For example, in the first family who tried the ShareTable system, focusing on just the direct users of the system (father, mother, son) would mean measuring the system's effect on six different relationships (e.g., father's view of his relationship with the son, son's view of his relationship with his father, etc.). Adding relevant non-participants (stepmom, stepbrother, stepdad) would increase this number of relationships to thirty, quickly becoming intractable to measure or report. It is especially difficult to hold a child's attention for the length of time necessary to answer questions about the child's relationship with each other member of the family. In my work, I've used my stance as the designer and previous literature from family communication studies to inform which relationships I would measure explicitly in the course of a deployment. For example, my initial stance as a designer was that the ShareTable system was meant to help the child in the divorced family, so I only measured effects on the relationships most likely to affect the child according to previous literature: relationship with both parents (Amato 2000) and conflict between the parents (Smyth 2005). This approach is not perfect. For example, in retrospect, I also should have measured the relationship between siblings in one of the ShareTable deployments, but I realized it only after the deployment, so I could not collect baseline measures. However, focusing my data collection on factors identified as important in previous literature did provide a reasonable place to start.

> **LESSON**
>
> Focus data collection on factors identified as important in previous literature, but be open to both the positive and negative impacts of an intervention.

Trying to consider and measure individual and relational effects of an intervention may seem overwhelming, especially when the current standard of practice in the field rarely goes beyond discussing observed and reported *practices* during system deployment. However, there are big benefits to taking this step: a richer understanding of the possible unintended negative consequences of the system, empirical data showing who is or isn't helped by a particular intervention, and giving voice to participants whose experiences may otherwise not be discussed (e.g., children). Lastly, having data on each participant's experience may serve to guide design by helping the designer consider how to improve the experience of currently marginalized participants.

## LEARNINGS FOR FUTURE STUDIES

My own perspective on family conflict was largely informed by my work with divorced families; however, there are many lessons from this work that can benefit other types of family research. Many of these recommendations require nothing more than a shift of perspective and minor modifications of the study protocol, but they have the potential to provide significant benefits to investigations of technology for families.

### ARTICULATE THE RESEARCHER'S STANCE AS A DESIGNER

As a designer, I find it important to articulate who is the primary family member I am trying to help or what is the primary relationship I am trying to support with my design. For example, in the majority of the work described in this chapter, I have articulated my stance as "to help the child who lives apart from a parent." This helped constrain design decisions in an open solution space, providing a clear way of evaluating and selecting early design ideas. It also helped make methodological choices as to the most relevant metrics to measure when evaluating the impact of an intervention. (See the "Challenges" section of this chapter.) Lastly, it put me in the mindset that naturally treated the family as a group of individuals rather than a unit. It is frequently impractical to try help "the family" as a whole—as I have articulated in this chapter, "family" is an amorphous unit that loses meaning when viewed separate from a specific individual's perspective. Articulating that it is the *child* I'm trying to help by improving her relationships with *her* family helps me keep the reflexive definition of family in mind for the purpose of design and evaluation. Articulating a stance before starting the study helps me consider how I will handle conflict and non-consensus when it does arise.

---

**LESSON**

As a designer, decide up-front what the goals are for the system being built; in particular, decide who it will or will not help.

---

## OBTAIN CONSENT FROM AFFECTED NON-PARTICIPANTS

Though my intervention may be looking to help one or two specific participants as its primary goal, the deployment of my systems has frequently required me to consider the possible effects of the system on other users and non-participants. The first step in this process is to include all relevant parties—even if they will not be using the system or answering any questions—to participate in the process of deciding whether the intervention and study are reasonable for their situation. I failed to do so in one of my studies, leading to an expensive loss of a participant family. (See the anecdote in the introduction to the chapter.) Aside from withdrawing from the study, failing to gather consent and providing an opportunity for the family to explicitly negotiate possible conflicts over participation can lead to non-use of the system, or even intentional sabotage on the part of the marginalized party. For example, in Judge et al. (2011), some participants covered or turned the camera to circumvent the always-on video connection. Obtaining this consent and facilitating the negotiation takes additional coordination and may feel uncomfortable, but my personal experience has shown it to be less costly in the long run.

---

**LESSON**

Go beyond the policies of an ethics review board and obtain consent from affected non-participants in family studies.

---

## CONSIDER WHEN TO INTERVIEW PARTICIPANTS TOGETHER OR APART

I have found it helpful to combine sessions where family members answer my questions with those in which I get to talk to each participant one on one. Discussing a technology deployment with multiple participants at the same time provides the benefits of explicitly working out possible conflicts around technology use, letting participants help each other recall experiences and build on each other's stories, and helping shy or quiet participants (especially children) open up to the researcher. However, there are also a number of drawbacks of interviewing participants together: it reinforces existing power structures (e.g., a child may not be willing to discuss an experience that contradicts the parent's); it lets the more extroverted or well-spoken individuals take charge of the conversation, unintentionally marginalizing the other participants; it glosses over issues of non-consensus and conflict; and it encourages the construction of a common, consistent narrative among those in the room, rather than highlighting the different experiences of each individual. Combining the practices of interviewing together and interviewing apart in different parts of the study can be the best of both worlds. For example, in a situation where it is important to help the participant feel comfortable in expressing a divergent opinion (e.g., describing relationships), it may make sense to do separate interviews. However, for parts of the study where the researcher wants the family members to discuss something and come to a joint decision (e.g., deciding whether to participate in the study, do a design workshop, etc.), it may be better to bring the family together in the same room.

> **LESSON**
>
> Interviewing family members apart helps get divergent opinions and experiences; interviewing together helps family members come to a common agreement.

## MEASURE POSSIBLE NEGATIVE IMPACTS OF INTERVENTIONS ON EACH PARTICIPANT

Even a great technology with lots of benefits for the family members who use it will probably have potential drawbacks for each individual, as well as benefitting some family members more than others. Identifying these drawbacks and tradeoffs does not invalidate the design or intervention, but instead provides a more complete and balanced account of users' experience with the technology. It also serves to identify clear opportunities for design of future systems, which is quite useful to others in the research community. In my experience, it is most meaningful to contextualize these measurements by comparing and contrasting measures of use during intervention versus baseline/control, comparing the system's effect on variables of interest for each individual (e.g., relationship quality [Pierce 1991], costs and benefit of the tech [Yarosh, Markopoulos, and Abowd 2014], etc.). These measures complement traditional qualitative approaches to understanding family practices around novel technology, but also help better articulate what worked, what didn't work, to what extent, and for whom.

> **LESSON**
>
> Measure both the positive and negative effects of an intervention on stakeholders.

## BE MORE SPECIFIC THAN "FAMILY" AS A UNIT OF ANALYSIS

One of the main points of this chapter is that a "family" is not a meaningful unit of analysis. Families are composed of individuals, each with his or her own needs, motivations, and goals that frequently come in conflict with those of other family members. Which subset of these individuals is included in any given participants' view of his or her family is different for each person. I suggest discussing "family from X's perspective" to clarify possible confusion as to who is or isn't included. Units of analysis can be individuals, pairwise relationships between individuals, functional units of technology and people who use it, activities that incorporate people, tools, etc., but in all of these cases, it is important to clearly and unambiguously specify what is and what isn't included in the unit. A non-reflexive reference to "family" without a discussion of *"whose family"* and *"why those members and not others"* is frequently more misleading than helpful.

> **LESSON**
>
> Choose a unit of analysis that captures the perspective of the study participants, because different people think of their family "unit" in different ways.

## CONCLUSION

The purpose of this chapter is to share my strategies from years of working with both divorced and intact families. I share my hard-won experience in addressing some of the challenges that result from family conflict and provide five specific lessons that can be integrated into future studies to better understand, manage, and discuss family conflict with designing and deploying systems for the home. There are five points that I hope the reader can take away from this discussion:

1. Family conflict is present in all families, though it may be more obvious in some than others. The segmented institutionalism perspective considers conflict by focusing on: (1) the process of achieving shared meaning, (2) conflicting goals, rather than consensus, (3) all stakeholders, rather than only direct users, and (4) both costs and benefits of interventions.
2. Families are composed of individuals whose definitions of family may be divergent and asymmetric, so it is important to be explicit about who is or is not included in each context.
3. Families negotiate practices around technology use. It is important to understand who makes the final decisions and encourage discussion to achieve shared meaning.
4. A technology may provide different costs and benefits to each individual and relationship affected by it. Explicitly considering and measuring these as potential tradeoffs is important in adopting the technology.

**5.** Considering conflict in families can affect our design, the way we recruit participants and gather consent, and specifics of the methods we use, not just in investigating high-conflict families, but in all other home contexts as well.

These points are important for working not just with divorced families, but with all types of family arrangements. Through the understanding and application of these principles, our research community can better reflect and respond to family conflict in our investigations of the domestic space.

# REFERENCES

Amato, P.R., 2000. The Consequences of Divorce for Adults and Children. J. Marriage Fam. 62 (4), 1269–1287.

Furman, W., Buhrmester, D., 2009. The Network of Relationships Inventory: Behavioral Systems Version. Int. J. Behav. Dev. 33 (5), 470–478.

Hindus, D., Mainwaring, S.D., Leduc, N., Hagström, A.E., Bayley, O., 2001. Casablanca: Designing Social Communication Devices for the Home. In: Proceedings of the SIGCHI Conference on Human Factors in Computing Systems (CHI '01). ACM Press, New York, NY.

Hirschheim, R., Klein, H.K., 1989. Four Paradigms of Information Systems Development. Commun. ACM Press, 32 (10), 1199–1216.

Judge, T.K., Neustaedter, C., Harrison, S., Blose, A., 2011. Family Portals: Connecting Families through a Multifamily Media Space. In: Proceedings of the SIGCHI Conference on Human Factors in Computing Systems (CHI '11). ACM Press, New York, NY.

Kling, R., 1980. Social Analyses of Computing: Theoretical Orientations in Recent Empirical Research. ACM Comput. Surv. 12 (1), 61–110.

Pierce, G.R., 1991. Quality of Relationships Inventory: Assessing the Interpersonal Context of Social Support. Commun. Soc. Support, 246–266.

Sillars, A., Canary, D.J., Tafoya, M., 2004. Communication, Conflict, and the Quality of Family Relationships. In: Handbook of Family Communication. Lawrence Erlbaum Associates, Mahwah, NJ, pp. 413–446.

Smyth, B., 2005. Parent-Child Contact in Australia: Exploring Five Different Post-Separation Patterns of Parenting. Int. J. Law Policy Fam. 19 (April), 1–22.

Yarosh, S., Abowd, G.D., 2011. Mediated Parent-Child Contact in Work-Separated Families. In: Proceedings of the SIGCHI Conference on Human Factors in Computing Systems. (CHI '11). ACM Press, New York, NY.

Yarosh, S., Chew, Y.C., Abowd, G.D., 2009. Supporting Parent-Child Communication in Divorced Families. Int. J. Hum. Comput. Stud. 67 (2), 192–203.

Yarosh, S., Cuzzort, S., Müller, H., Abowd, G.D., 2009. Developing a Media Space for Remote Synchronous Parent-Child Interaction. In: Proceedings of the 8th International Conference on Interaction Design and Children (IDC '09). ACM Press, New York, NY.

Yarosh, S., Markopoulos, P., Abowd, G.D., 2014. Towards a Questionnaire for Measuring Affective Benefits and Costs of Communication Technologies. In: Proceedings of the ACM conference on Computer supported cooperative work & social computing (CSCW '14). ACM Press, New York, NY.

Yarosh, S., Tang, A., Mokashi, S., Abowd, G., 2013. 'Almost Touching:' Parent-Child Remote Communication Using the ShareTable System. In: Proceedings of the 2013 conference on Computer supported cooperative work (CSCW '13). ACM Press, New York, NY.

# Index

*Note*: Page numbers followed by "b", "f" and "t" indicate boxes, figures and tables respectively

Printed in the United States
By Bookmasters